# CAPTAIN
# JOHN SMITH

## CHARLES DUDLEY WARNER

# Captain John Smith

## Charles Dudley Warner

© 1st World Library, 2007
PO Box 2211
Fairfield, IA 52556
www.1stworldlibrary.com
First Edition

LCCN: 2007934096

Softcover ISBN: 978-1-4218-9631-1
Hardcover ISBN: 978-1-4218-9731-8
eBook ISBN: 978-1-4218-9531-4

Purchase *"Captain John Smith"*
as a traditional bound book at:
www.1stWorldLibrary.com/purchase.asp?ISBN=978-1-4218-9631-1

1st World Library is a literary, educational organization
dedicated to:

- Creating a free internet library of downloadable ebooks

- Hosting writing competitions and offering book publishing
scholarships.

Interested in more 1st World Library books? contact:
literacy@1stworldlibrary.com
Check us out at: www.1stworldlibrary.com

# 1<sup>st</sup> World Library Literary Society

## Giving Back to the World

"If you want to work on the core problem, it's early school literacy."

**- James Barksdale, former CEO of Netscape**

"No skill is more crucial to the future of a child, or to a democratic and prosperous society, than literacy."

**- Los Angeles Times**

"Literacy... means far more than learning how to read and write... The aim is to transmit... knowledge and promote social participation."

**- UNESCO**

"Literacy is not a luxury, it is a right and a responsibility. If our world is to meet the challenges of the twenty-first century we must harness the energy and creativity of all our citizens."

**- President Bill Clinton**

"Parents should be encouraged to read to their children, and teachers should be equipped with all available techniques for teaching literacy, so the varying needs and capacities of individual kids can be taken into account."

**- Hugh Mackay**

# PREFACE

When I consented to prepare this volume for a series, which should deal with the notables of American history with some familiarity and disregard of historic gravity, I did not anticipate the seriousness of the task. But investigation of the subject showed me that while Captain John Smith would lend himself easily enough to the purely facetious treatment, there were historic problems worthy of a different handling, and that if the life of Smith was to be written, an effort should be made to state the truth, and to disentangle the career of the adventurer from the fables and misrepresentations that have clustered about it.

The extant biographies of Smith, and the portions of the history of Virginia that relate to him, all follow his own narrative, and accept his estimate of himself, and are little more than paraphrases of his story as told by himself. But within the last twenty years some new contemporary evidence has come to light, and special scholars have expended much critical research upon different portions of his career. The result of this modern investigation has been to discredit much of the romance gathered about Smith and Pocahontas, and a good deal to reduce his heroic proportions. A vague report of—these scholarly studies has gone abroad, but no effort has been made to tell the real story of Smith as a connected whole in the light of the new researches.

This volume is an effort to put in popular form the truth about Smith's adventures, and to estimate his exploits and character. For this purpose I have depended almost entirely upon original contemporary material, illumined as it now is by the labors of special editors. I believe that I have read everything that is attributed to his pen, and have compared his own accounts with other contemporary narratives, and I think I have omitted the perusal of little that could throw any light upon his life or character. For the early part of his career—before he came to Virginia—there is absolutely no authority except Smith himself; but when he emerges from romance into history, he can be followed and checked by contemporary evidence. If he was always and uniformly untrustworthy it would be less perplexing to follow him, but his liability to tell the truth when vanity or prejudice does not interfere is annoying to the careful student.

As far as possible I have endeavored to let the actors in these pages tell their own story, and I have quoted freely from Capt. Smith himself, because it is as a writer that he is to be judged no less than as an actor. His development of the Pocahontas legend has been carefully traced, and all the known facts about that Indian—or Indese, as some of the old chroniclers call the female North Americans—have been consecutively set forth in separate chapters. The book is not a history of early Virginia, nor of the times of Smith, but merely a study of his life and writings. If my estimate of the character of Smith is not that which his biographers have entertained, and differs from his own candid opinion, I can only plead that contemporary evidence and a collation of his own stories show that he was mistaken. I am not aware that there has been before any systematic effort to collate his different accounts of his exploits. If he had ever undertaken the task, he might have disturbed that serene opinion of himself which marks him as a man who realized his own ideals.

Charles Dudley Warner

The works used in this study are, first, the writings of Smith, which are as follows:

"A True Relation," etc., London, 1608.

"A Map of Virginia, Description and Appendix," Oxford, 1612.

"A Description of New England," etc., London, 1616.

"New England's Trials," etc., London, 1620. Second edition, enlarged, 1622.

"The Generall Historie," etc., London, 1624. Reissued, with date of title-page altered, in 1626, 1627, and twice in 1632.

"An Accidence: or, The Pathway to Experience," etc., London, 1626.

"A Sea Grammar," etc., London, 1627. Also editions in 1653 and 1699.

"The True Travels," etc., London, 1630.

"Advertisements for the Unexperienced Planters of New England," etc., London, 1631.

Other authorities are:

"The Historie of Travaile into Virginia," etc., by William Strachey, Secretary of the colony 1609 to 1612. First printed for the Hakluyt Society, London, 1849.

"Newport's Relatyon," 1607. Am. Ant. Soc., Vol. 4.

"Wingfield's Discourse," etc., 1607. Am. Ant. Soc., Vol. 4.

"Purchas his Pilgrimage," London, 1613.

"Purchas his Pilgrimes," London, 1625-6.

"Ralph Hamor's True Discourse," etc., London, 1615.

"Relation of Virginia," by Henry Spelman, 1609. First printed by J. F. Hunnewell, London, 1872.

"History of the Virginia Company in London," by Edward D. Neill, Albany, 1869.

"William Stith's History of Virginia," 1753, has been consulted for the charters and letters-patent. The Pocahontas discussion has been followed in many magazine papers. I am greatly indebted to the scholarly labors of Charles Deane, LL.D., the accomplished editor of the "True Relation," and other Virginia monographs. I wish also to acknowledge the courtesy of the librarians of the Astor, the Lenox, the New York Historical, Yale, and Cornell libraries, and of Dr. J. Hammond Trumbull, the custodian of the Brinley collection, and the kindness of Mr. S. L. M. Barlow of New York, who is ever ready to give students access to his rich "Americana."

C. D. W. HARTFORD, June, 1881

# I

## BIRTH AND TRAINING

Fortunate is the hero who links his name romantically with that of a woman. A tender interest in his fame is assured. Still more fortunate is he if he is able to record his own achievements and give to them that form and color and importance which they assume in his own gallant consciousness. Captain John Smith, the first of an honored name, had this double good fortune.

We are indebted to him for the glowing picture of a knight-errant of the sixteenth century, moving with the port of a swash-buckler across the field of vision, wherever cities were to be taken and heads cracked in Europe, Asia, and Africa, and, in the language of one of his laureates—

"To see bright honor sparkled all in gore."

But we are specially his debtor for adventures on our own continent, narrated with naivete and vigor by a pen as direct and clear-cutting as the sword with which he shaved off the heads of the Turks, and for one of the few romances that illumine our early history.

Captain John Smith understood his good fortune in being the

recorder of his own deeds, and he preceded Lord Beacons-field (in "Endymion") in his appreciation of the value of the influence of women upon the career of a hero. In the dedication of his "General Historie" to Frances, Duchess of Richmond, he says:

"I have deeply hazarded myself in doing and suffering, and why should I sticke to hazard my reputation in recording? He that acteth two parts is the more borne withall if he come short, or fayle in one of them. Where shall we looke to finde a Julius Caesar whose atchievments shine as cleare in his owne Commentaries, as they did in the field? I confesse, my hand though able to wield a weapon among the Barbarous, yet well may tremble in handling a Pen among so many judicious; especially when I am so bold as to call so piercing and so glorious an Eye, as your Grace, to view these poore ragged lines. Yet my comfort is that heretofore honorable and vertuous Ladies, and comparable but amongst themselves, have offered me rescue and protection in my greatest dangers: even in forraine parts, I have felt reliefe from that sex. The beauteous Lady Tragabigzanda, when I was a slave to the Turks, did all she could to secure me. When I overcame the Bashaw of Nalbrits in Tartaria, the charitable Lady Callamata supplyed my necessities. In the utmost of my extremities, that blessed Pokahontas, the great King's daughter of Virginia, oft saved my life. When I escaped the cruelties of Pirats and most furious stormes, a long time alone in a small Boat at Sea, and driven ashore in France, the good Lady Chanoyes bountifully assisted me."

It is stated in his "True Travels" that John Smith was born in Willoughby, in Lincolnshire. The year of his birth is not given, but it was probably in 1579, as it appears by the portrait prefixed to that work that he was aged 37 years in 1616. We are able to add also that the rector of the Willoughby Rectory, Alford, finds in the register an entry of the baptism of John, son of George Smith, under date of Jan. 9, 1579. His biographers, following his account, represent him as of ancient lineage: "His father actually descended from the ancient Smiths of Crudley in Lancashire, his mother from the Rickands at great Heck in Yorkshire;" but the circumstances of his boyhood would indicate that like many other men who have made themselves a name, his origin was humble. If it had been otherwise he would scarcely have been bound as an apprentice, nor had so much difficulty in his advancement. But the boy was born with a merry disposition, and in his earliest years was impatient for adventure. The desire to rove was doubtless increased by the nature of his native shire, which offered every inducement to the lad of spirit to leave it.

Lincolnshire is the most uninteresting part of all England. It is frequently water-logged till late in the summer: invisible a part of the year, when it emerges it is mostly a dreary flat. Willoughby is a considerable village in this shire, situated about three miles and a half southeastward from Alford. It stands just on the edge of the chalk hills whose drives gently slope down to the German Ocean, and the scenery around offers an unvarying expanse of flats. All the villages in this part of Lincolnshire exhibit the same character. The name ends in by, the Danish word for hamlet or small village, and we can measure the progress of the Danish invasion of England by the number of towns which have the terminal by, distinguished from the Saxon thorpe, which generally ends the name of villages in Yorkshire. The population may be said to be Danish light-haired and blue-eyed. Such was John Smith. The sea was the natural element of his neighbors, and John when a boy must have heard many stories of the sea and enticing adventures told by the sturdy mariners who were recruited from the neighborhood of Willoughby, and whose oars had often cloven the Baltic Sea.

Willoughby boasts some antiquity. Its church is a spacious structure, with a nave, north and south aisles, and a chancel, and a tower at the west end. In the floor is a stone with a Latin inscription, in black letter, round the verge, to the memory of one Gilbert West, who died in 1404. The church is dedicated to St. Helen. In the village the Wesleyan Methodists also have a place of worship. According to the parliamentary returns of 1825, the parish including the hamlet of Sloothby contained 108 houses and 514 inhabitants. All the churches in Lincolnshire indicate the existence of a much larger population who were in the habit of attending service than exists at present. Many of these now empty are of size sufficient to accommodate the entire population of several villages. Such a one is Willoughby, which unites in its church the adjacent village of Sloothby.

The stories of the sailors and the contiguity of the salt water had more influence on the boy's mind than the free, schools of Alford and Louth which he attended, and when he was about thirteen he sold his books and satchel and intended to run away to sea: but the death of his father stayed him. Both his parents being now dead, he was left with, he says, competent means; but his guardians regarding his estate more than himself, gave him full liberty and no money, so that he was forced to stay at home.

At the age of fifteen he was bound apprentice to Mr. Thomas S. Tendall of Lynn. The articles, however, did not bind him very fast, for as his master refused to send him to sea, John took leave of his master and did not see him again for eight years. These details exhibit in the boy the headstrong independence of the man.

At length he found means to attach himself to a young son of the great soldier, Lord Willoughby, who was going into France. The narrative is not clear, but it appears that upon

Charles Dudley Warner

reaching Orleans, in a month or so the services of John were found to be of no value, and he was sent back to his friends, who on his return generously gave him ten shillings (out of his own estate) to be rid of him. He is next heard of enjoying his liberty at Paris and making the acquaintance of a Scotchman named David Hume, who used his purse—ten shillings went a long ways in those days—and in return gave him letters of commendation to prefer him to King James. But the boy had a disinclination to go where he was sent. Reaching Rouen, and being nearly out of money, he dropped down the river to Havre de Grace, and began to learn to be a soldier.

Smith says not a word of the great war of the Leaguers and Henry IV., nor on which side he fought, nor is it probable that he cared. But he was doubtless on the side of Henry, as Havre was at this time in possession of that soldier. Our adventurer not only makes no reference to the great religious war, nor to the League, nor to Henry, but he does not tell who held Paris when he visited it. Apparently state affairs did not interest him. His reference to a "peace" helps us to fix the date of his first adventure in France. Henry published the Edict of Nantes at Paris, April 13, 1598, and on the 2d of May following, concluded the treaty of France with Philip II. at Vervins, which closed the Spanish pretensions in France. The Duc de Mercoeur (of whom we shall hear later as Smith's "Duke of Mercury" in Hungary), Duke of Lorraine, was allied with the Guises in the League, and had the design of holding Bretagne under Spanish protection. However, fortune was against him and he submitted to Henry in February, 1598, with no good grace. Looking about for an opportunity to distinguish himself, he offered his services to the Emperor Rudolph to fight the Turks, and it is said led an army of his French followers, numbering 15,000, in 1601, to Hungary, to raise the siege of Coniza, which was beleaguered by Ibrahim Pasha with 60,000 men.

Chance of fighting and pay failing in France by reason of the peace, he enrolled himself under the banner of one of the roving and fighting captains of the time, who sold their swords in the best market, and went over into the Low Countries, where he hacked and hewed away at his fellow-men, all in the way of business, for three or four years. At the end of that time he bethought himself that he had not delivered his letters to Scotland. He embarked at Aucusan for Leith, and seems to have been shipwrecked, and detained by illness in the "holy isle" in Northumberland, near Barwick. On his recovery he delivered his letters, and received kind treatment from the Scots; but as he had no money, which was needed to make his way as a courtier, he returned to Willoughby.

The family of Smith is so "ancient" that the historians of the county of Lincoln do not allude to it, and only devote a brief paragraph to the great John himself. Willoughby must have been a dull place to him after his adventures, but he says he was glutted with company, and retired into a woody pasture, surrounded by forests, a good ways from any town, and there built himself a pavilion of boughs—less substantial than the cabin of Thoreau at Walden Pond—and there he heroically slept in his clothes, studied Machiavelli's "Art of War," read "Marcus Aurelius," and exercised on his horse with lance and ring. This solitary conduct got him the name of a hermit, whose food was thought to be more of venison than anything else, but in fact his men kept him supplied with provisions. When John had indulged in this ostentatious seclusion for a time, he allowed himself to be drawn out of it by the charming discourse of a noble Italian named Theodore Palaloga, who just then was Rider to Henry, Earl of Lincoln, and went to stay with him at Tattershall. This was an ancient town, with a castle, which belonged to the Earls of Lincoln, and was situated on the River Bane, only fourteen miles from Boston, a name that at once establishes a connection between

Smith's native county and our own country, for it is nearly as certain that St. Botolph founded a monastery at Boston, Lincoln, in the year 654, as it is that he founded a club afterwards in Boston, Massachusetts.

Whatever were the pleasures of Tattershall, they could not long content the restless Smith, who soon set out again for the Netherlands in search of adventures.

The life of Smith, as it is related by himself, reads like that of a belligerent tramp, but it was not uncommon in his day, nor is it in ours, whenever America produces soldiers of fortune who are ready, for a compensation, to take up the quarrels of Egyptians or Chinese, or go wherever there is fighting and booty. Smith could now handle arms and ride a horse, and longed to go against the Turks, whose anti-Christian contests filled his soul with lamentations; and besides he was tired of seeing Christians slaughter each other. Like most heroes, he had a vivid imagination that made him credulous, and in the Netherlands he fell into the toils of three French gallants, one of whom pretended to be a great lord, attended by his gentlemen, who persuaded him to accompany them to the "Duchess of Mercury," whose lord was then a general of Rodolphus of Hungary, whose favor they could command. Embarking with these arrant cheats, the vessel reached the coast of Picardy, where his comrades contrived to take ashore their own baggage and Smith's trunk, containing his money and goodly apparel, leaving him on board. When the captain, who was in the plot, was enabled to land Smith the next day, the noble lords had disappeared with the luggage, and Smith, who had only a single piece of gold in his pocket, was obliged to sell his cloak to pay his passage.

Thus stripped, he roamed about Normandy in a forlorn condition, occasionally entertained by honorable persons who had heard of his misfortunes, and seeking always means of continuing his travels, wandering from port to port on the chance of embarking on a man-of-war. Once he was found in a forest near dead with grief and cold, and rescued by a rich farmer; shortly afterwards, in a grove in Brittany, he chanced upon one of the gallants who had robbed him, and the two out swords and fell to cutting. Smith had the satisfaction of wounding the rascal, and the inhabitants of a ruined tower near by, who witnessed the combat, were quite satisfied with the event.

Our hero then sought out the Earl of Ployer, who had been brought up in England during the French wars, by whom he was refurnished better than ever. After this streak of luck, he roamed about France, viewing the castles and strongholds, and at length embarked at Marseilles on a ship for Italy. Rough weather coming on, the vessel anchored under the lee of the little isle St. Mary, off Nice, in Savoy.

The passengers on board, among whom were many pilgrims bound for Rome, regarded Smith as a Jonah, cursed him for a Huguenot, swore that his nation were all pirates, railed against Queen Elizabeth, and declared that they never should have fair weather so long as he was on board. To end the dispute, they threw him into the sea. But God got him ashore on the little island, whose only inhabitants were goats and a few kine. The next day a couple of trading vessels anchored near, and he was taken off and so kindly used that he decided to cast in his fortune with them. Smith's discourse of his adventures so entertained the master of one of the vessels, who is described as "this noble Britaine, his neighbor, Captaine la Roche, of Saint Malo," that the much-tossed wanderer was accepted as a friend. They sailed to the Gulf of Turin, to Alessandria, where they discharged freight, then up to Scanderoon, and coasting for some time among the Grecian islands, evidently in search of more freight, they at length came round to Cephalonia, and lay to for some days

Charles Dudley Warner

betwixt the isle of Corfu and the Cape of Otranto. Here it presently appeared what sort of freight the noble Britaine, Captain la Roche, was looking for.

An argosy of Venice hove in sight, and Captaine la Roche desired to speak to her. The reply was so "untoward" that a man was slain, whereupon the Britaine gave the argosy a broadside, and then his stem, and then other broadsides. A lively fight ensued, in which the Britaine lost fifteen men, and the argosy twenty, and then surrendered to save herself from sinking. The noble Britaine and John Smith then proceeded to rifle her. He says that "the Silkes, Velvets, Cloth of Gold, and Tissue, Pyasters, Chiqueenes, and Suitanies, which is gold and silver, they unloaded in four-and-twenty hours was wonderful, whereof having sufficient, and tired with toils, they cast her off with her company, with as much good merchandise as would have freighted another Britaine, that was but two hundred Tunnes, she four or five hundred." Smith's share of this booty was modest. When the ship returned he was set ashore at "the Road of Antibo in Piamon," "with five hundred chiqueenes [sequins] and a little box God sent him worth neere as much more." He always devoutly acknowledged his dependence upon divine Providence, and took willingly what God sent him.

## II

## FIGHTING IN HUNGARY

Smith being thus "refurnished," made the tour of Italy, satisfied himself with the rarities of Rome, where he saw Pope Clement the Eighth and many cardinals creep up the holy stairs, and with the fair city of Naples and the kingdom's nobility; and passing through the north he came into Styria, to the Court of Archduke Ferdinand; and, introduced by an Englishman and an Irish Jesuit to the notice of Baron Kisell, general of artillery, he obtained employment, and went to Vienna with Colonel Voldo, Earl of Meldritch, with whose regiment he was to serve.

He was now on the threshold of his long-desired campaign against the Turks. The arrival on the scene of this young man, who was scarcely out of his teens, was a shadow of disaster to the Turks. They had been carrying all before them. Rudolph II., Emperor of Germany, was a weak and irresolute character, and no match for the enterprising Sultan, Mahomet III., who was then conducting the invasion of Europe. The Emperor's brother, the Archduke Mathias, who was to succeed him, and Ferdinand, Duke of Styria, also to become Emperor of Germany, were much abler men, and maintained a good front against the Moslems in Lower Hungary, but the Turks all the time steadily advanced. They

Charles Dudley Warner

had long occupied Buda (Pesth), and had been in possession of the stronghold of Alba Regalis for some sixty years. Before Smith's advent they had captured the important city of Caniza, and just as he reached the ground they had besieged the town of Olumpagh, with two thousand men. But the addition to the armies of Germany, France, Styria, and Hungary of John Smith, "this English gentleman," as he styles himself, put a new face on the war, and proved the ruin of the Turkish cause. The Bashaw of Buda was soon to feel the effect of this re-enforcement.

Caniza is a town in Lower Hungary, north of the River Drave, and just west of the Platen Sea, or Lake Balatin, as it is also called. Due north of Caniza a few miles, on a bend of the little River Raab (which empties into the Danube), and south of the town of Kerment, lay Smith's town of Olumpagh, which we are able to identify on a map of the period as Olimacum or Oberlymback. In this strong town the Turks had shut up the garrison under command of Governor Ebersbraught so closely that it was without intelligence or hope of succor.

In this strait, the ingenious John Smith, who was present in the reconnoitering army in the regiment of the Earl of Meldritch, came to the aid of Baron Kisell, the general of artillery, with a plan of communication with the besieged garrison. Fortunately Smith had made the acquaintance of Lord Ebersbraught at Gratza, in Styria, and had (he says) communicated to him a system of signaling a message by the use of torches. Smith seems to have elaborated this method of signals, and providentially explained it to Lord Ebersbraught, as if he had a presentiment of the latter's use of it. He divided the alphabet into two parts, from A to L and from M to Z. Letters were indicated and words spelled by the means of torches: "The first part, from A to L, is signified by showing and holding one linke so oft as there is letters from

A to that letter you name; the other part, from M to Z, is mentioned by two lights in like manner. The end of a word is signifien by showing of three lights."

General Kisell, inflamed by this strange invention, which Smith made plain to him, furnished him guides, who conducted him to a high mountain, seven miles distant from the town, where he flashed his torches and got a reply from the governor. Smith signaled that they would charge on the east of the town in the night, and at the alarum Ebersbraught was to sally forth. General Kisell doubted that he should be able to relieve the town by this means, as he had only ten thousand men; but Smith, whose fertile brain was now in full action, and who seems to have assumed charge of the campaign, hit upon a stratagem for the diversion and confusion of the Turks.

On the side of the town opposite the proposed point of attack lay the plain of Hysnaburg (Eisnaburg on Ortelius's map). Smith fastened two or three charred pieces of match to divers small lines of an hundred fathoms in length, armed with powder. Each line was tied to a stake at each end. After dusk these lines were set up on the plain, and being fired at the instant the alarm was given, they seemed to the Turks like so many rows of musketeers. While the Turks therefore prepared to repel a great army from that side, Kisell attacked with his ten thousand men, Ebersbraught sallied out and fell upon the Turks in the trenches, all the enemy on that side were slain or drowned, or put to flight. And while the Turks were busy routing Smith's sham musketeers, the Christians threw a couple of thousand troops into the town. Whereupon the Turks broke up the siege and retired to Caniza. For this exploit General Kisell received great honor at Kerment, and Smith was rewarded with the rank of captain, and the command of two hundred and fifty horsemen. From this time our hero must figure as Captain John Smith. The rank is not high, but he has made the title great, just as he has made the name of John Smith unique.

After this there were rumors of peace for these tormented countries; but the Turks, who did not yet appreciate the nature of this force, called John Smith, that had come into the world against them, did not intend peace, but went on levying soldiers and launching them into Hungary. To oppose these fresh invasions, Rudolph II., aided by the Christian princes, organized three armies: one led by the Archduke Mathias and his lieutenant, Duke Mercury, to defend Low Hungary; the second led by Ferdinand, the Archduke of Styria, and the Duke of Mantua, his lieutenant, to regain Caniza; the third by Gonzago, Governor of High Hungary, to join with Georgio Busca, to make an absolute conquest of Transylvania.

In pursuance of this plan, Duke Mercury, with an army of thirty thousand, whereof nearly ten thousand were French, besieged Stowell-Weisenberg, otherwise called Alba Regalis, a place so strong by art and nature that it was thought impregnable.

This stronghold, situated on the northeast of the Platen Sea, was, like Caniza and Oberlympack, one of the Turkish advanced posts, by means of which they pushed forward their operations from Buda on the Danube.

This noble friend of Smith, the Duke of Mercury, whom Haylyn styles Duke Mercurio, seems to have puzzled the biographers of Smith. In fact, the name of "Mercury" has given a mythological air to Smith's narration and aided to transfer it to the region of romance. He was, however, as we have seen, identical with a historical character of some importance, for the services he rendered to the Church of Rome, and a commander of some considerable skill. He is no other than Philip de Lorraine, Duc de Mercceur.'

[So far as I know, Dr. Edward Eggleston was the first to identify him. There is a sketch of him in the "Biographie Universelle," and a life with an account of his exploits in Hungary, entitled: Histoire de Duc Mercoeur, par Bruseles de Montplain Champs, Cologne, 1689-97]

At the siege of Alba Regalis, the Turks gained several successes by night sallies, and, as usual, it was not till Smith came to the front with one of his ingenious devices that the fortune of war changed. The Earl Meldritch, in whose regiment Smith served, having heard from some Christians who escaped from the town at what place there were the greatest assemblies and throngs of people in the city, caused Captain Smith to put in practice his "fiery dragons." These instruments of destruction are carefully described: "Having prepared fortie or fiftie round-bellied earthen pots, and filled them with hand Gunpowder, then covered them with Pitch, mingled with Brimstone and Turpentine, and quartering as many Musket-bullets, that hung together but only at the center of the division, stucke them round in the mixture about the pots, and covered them againe with the same mixture, over that a strong sear-cloth, then over all a goode thicknesse of Towze-match, well tempered with oyle of Linseed, Campheer, and powder of Brimstone, these he fitly placed in slings, graduated so neere as they could to the places of these assemblies."

These missiles of Smith's invention were flung at midnight, when the alarum was given, and "it was a perfect sight to see the short flaming course of their flight in the air, but presently after their fall, the lamentable noise of the miserable slaughtered Turkes was most wonderful to heare."

While Smith was amusing the Turks in this manner, the Earl

Rosworme planned an attack on the opposite suburb, which was defended by a muddy lake, supposed to be impassable. Furnishing his men with bundles of sedge, which they threw before them as they advanced in the dark night, the lake was made passable, the suburb surprised, and the captured guns of the Turks were turned upon them in the city to which they had retreated. The army of the Bashaw was cut to pieces and he himself captured.

The Earl of Meldritch, having occupied the town, repaired the walls and the ruins of this famous city that had been in the possession of the Turks for some threescore years.

It is not our purpose to attempt to trace the meteoric course of Captain Smith in all his campaigns against the Turks, only to indicate the large part he took in these famous wars for the possession of Eastern Europe. The siege of Alba Regalis must have been about the year 1601—Smith never troubles himself with any dates—and while it was undecided, Mahomet III.—this was the prompt Sultan who made his position secure by putting to death nineteen of his brothers upon his accession—raised sixty thousand troops for its relief or its recovery. The Duc de Mercoeur went out to meet this army, and encountered it in the plains of Girke. In the first skirmishes the Earl Meldritch was very nearly cut off, although he made "his valour shine more bright than his armour, which seemed then painted with Turkish blood." Smith himself was sore wounded and had his horse slain under him. The campaign, at first favorable to the Turks, was inconclusive, and towards winter the Bashaw retired to Buda. The Duc de Mercoeur then divided his army. The Earl of Rosworme was sent to assist the Archduke Ferdinand, who was besieging Caniza; the Earl of Meldritch, with six thousand men, was sent to assist Georgio Busca against the Transylvanians; and the Duc de Mercoeur set out for France to raise new forces. On his way he received great honor at

Vienna, and staying overnight at Nuremberg, he was royally entertained by the Archdukes Mathias and Maximilian. The next morning after the feast—how it chanced is not known— he was found dead His brother-inlaw died two days afterwards, and the hearts of both, with much sorrow, were carried into France.

We now come to the most important event in the life of Smith before he became an adventurer in Virginia, an event which shows Smith's readiness to put in practice the chivalry which had in the old chronicles influenced his boyish imagination; and we approach it with the satisfaction of knowing that it loses nothing in Smith's narration.

It must be mentioned that Transylvania, which the Earl of Meldritch, accompanied by Captain Smith, set out to relieve, had long been in a disturbed condition, owing to internal dissensions, of which the Turks took advantage. Transylvania, in fact, was a Turkish dependence, and it gives us an idea of the far reach of the Moslem influence in Europe, that Stephen VI., vaivode of Transylvania, was, on the commendation of Sultan Armurath III., chosen King of Poland.

To go a little further back than the period of Smith's arrival, John II. of Transylvania was a champion of the Turk, and an enemy of Ferdinand and his successors. His successor, Stephen VI., surnamed Battori, or Bathor, was made vaivode by the Turks, and afterwards, as we have said, King of Poland. He was succeeded in 1575 by his brother Christopher Battori, who was the first to drop the title of vaivode and assume that of Prince of Transylvania. The son of Christopher, Sigismund Battori, shook off the Turkish bondage, defeated many of their armies, slew some of their pashas, and gained the title of the Scanderbeg of the times in which he lived. Not able to hold out, however, against so potent an adversary, he resigned his estate to the Emperor

Rudolph II., and received in exchange the dukedoms of Oppelon and Ratibor in Silesia, with an annual pension of fifty thousand joachims. The pension not being well paid, Sigismund made another resignation of his principality to his cousin Andrew Battori, who had the ill luck to be slain within the year by the vaivode of Valentia. Thereupon Rudolph, Emperor and King of Hungary, was acknowledged Prince of Transylvania. But the Transylvania soldiers did not take kindly to a foreign prince, and behaved so unsoldierly that Sigismund was called back. But he was unable to settle himself in his dominions, and the second time he left his country in the power of Rudolph and retired to Prague, where, in 1615, he died unlamented.

It was during this last effort of Sigismund to regain his position that the Earl of Meldritch, accompanied by Smith, went to Transylvania, with the intention of assisting Georgio Busca, who was the commander of the Emperor's party. But finding Prince Sigismund in possession of the most territory and of the hearts of the people, the earl thought it best to assist the prince against the Turk, rather than Busca against the prince. Especially was he inclined to that side by the offer of free liberty of booty for his worn and unpaid troops, of what they could get possession of from the Turks.

This last consideration no doubt persuaded the troops that Sigismund had "so honest a cause." The earl was born in Transylvania, and the Turks were then in possession of his father's country. In this distracted state of the land, the frontiers had garrisons among the mountains, some of which held for the emperor, some for the prince, and some for the Turk. The earl asked leave of the prince to make an attempt to regain his paternal estate. The prince, glad of such an ally, made him camp-master of his army, and gave him leave to plunder the Turks. Accordingly the earl began to make incursions of the frontiers into what Smith calls the Land of

Zarkam—among rocky mountains, where were some Turks, some Tartars, but most Brandittoes, Renegadoes, and such like, which he forced into the Plains of Regall, where was a city of men and fortifications, strong in itself, and so environed with mountains that it had been impregnable in all these wars.

It must be confessed that the historians and the map-makers did not always attach the importance that Smith did to the battles in which he was conspicuous, and we do not find the Land of Zarkam or the city of Regall in the contemporary chronicles or atlases. But the region is sufficiently identified. On the River Maruch, or Morusus, was the town of Alba Julia, or Weisenberg, the residence of the vaivode or Prince of Transylvania. South of this capital was the town Millenberg, and southwest of this was a very strong fortress, commanding a narrow pass leading into Transylvania out of Hungary, probably where the River Maruct: broke through the mountains. We infer that it was this pass that the earl captured by a stratagem, and carrying his army through it, began the siege of Regall in the plain. "The earth no sooner put on her green habit," says our knight-errant, "than the earl overspread her with his troops." Regall occupied a strong fortress on a promontory and the Christians encamped on the plain before it.

In the conduct of this campaign, we pass at once into the age of chivalry, about which Smith had read so much. We cannot but recognize that this is his opportunity. His idle boyhood had been soaked in old romances, and he had set out in his youth to do what equally dreamy but less venturesome devourers of old chronicles were content to read about. Everything arranged itself as Smith would have had it. When the Christian army arrived, the Turks sallied out and gave it a lively welcome, which cost each side about fifteen hundred men. Meldritch had but eight thousand soldiers, but he was re-enforced by the arrival of nine thousand more, with six-and-twenty pieces of ordnance, under Lord Zachel Moyses, the general of the army, who took command of the whole.

After the first skirmish the Turks remained within their fortress, the guns of which commanded the plain, and the Christians spent a month in intrenching themselves and mounting their guns.

The Turks, who taught Europe the art of civilized war, behaved all this time in a courtly and chivalric manner, exchanging with the besiegers wordy compliments until such time as the latter were ready to begin. The Turks derided the slow progress of the works, inquired if their ordnance was in pawn, twitted them with growing fat for want of exercise, and expressed the fear that the Christians should depart without making an assault.

In order to make the time pass pleasantly, and exactly in accordance with the tales of chivalry which Smith had read, the Turkish Bashaw in the fortress sent out his challenge: "That to delight the ladies, who did long to see some courtlike pastime, the Lord Tubashaw did defy any captaine that had the command of a company, who durst combat with him for his head."

This handsome offer to swap heads was accepted; lots were cast for the honor of meeting the lord, and, fortunately for us, the choice fell upon an ardent fighter of twenty-three years, named Captain John Smith. Nothing was wanting to give dignity to the spectacle. Truce was made; the ramparts of this fortress-city in the mountains (which we cannot find on the map) were "all beset with faire Dames and men in Armes"; the Christians were drawn up in battle array; and upon the theatre thus prepared the Turkish Bashaw, armed and mounted, entered with a flourish of hautboys; on his shoulders were fixed a pair of great wings, compacted of eagles' feathers within a ridge of silver richly garnished with gold and precious stones; before him was a janissary bearing his lance, and a janissary walked at each side leading his steed.

This gorgeous being Smith did not keep long waiting. Riding into the field with a flourish of trumpets, and only a simple page to bear his lance, Smith favored the Bashaw with a courteous salute, took position, charged at the signal, and before the Bashaw could say "Jack Robinson," thrust his lance through the sight of his beaver, face, head and all, threw him dead to the ground, alighted, unbraced his helmet, and cut off his head. The whole affair was over so suddenly that as a pastime for ladies it must have been disappointing. The Turks came out and took the headless trunk, and Smith, according to the terms of the challenge, appropriated the head and presented it to General Moyses.

This ceremonious but still hasty procedure excited the rage of one Grualgo, the friend of the Bashaw, who sent a particular challenge to Smith to regain his friend's head or lose his own, together with his horse and armor. Our hero varied the combat this time. The two combatants shivered lances and then took to pistols; Smith received a mark upon the "placard," but so wounded the Turk in his left arm that he was unable to rule his horse. Smith then unhorsed him, cut off his head, took possession of head, horse, and armor, but returned the rich apparel and the body to his friends in the most gentlemanly manner.

Captain Smith was perhaps too serious a knight to see the humor of these encounters, but he does not lack humor in describing them, and he adopted easily the witty courtesies of the code he was illustrating. After he had gathered two heads, and the siege still dragged, he became in turn the challenger, in phrase as courteously and grimly facetious as was permissible, thus:

"To delude time, Smith, with so many incontradictible perswading reasons, obtained leave that the Ladies might know he was not so much enamored of their servants' heads, but if any Turke of their ranke would come to the place of combat to redeem them, should have also his, upon like conditions, if he could winne it."

This considerate invitation was accepted by a person whom Smith, with his usual contempt for names, calls "Bonny Mulgro." It seems difficult to immortalize such an appellation, and it is a pity that we have not the real one of the third Turk whom Smith honored by killing. But Bonny Mulgro, as we must call the worthiest foe that Smith's prowess encountered, appeared upon the field. Smith understands working up a narration, and makes this combat long and doubtful. The challenged party, who had the choice of weapons, had marked the destructiveness of his opponent's lance, and elected, therefore, to fight with pistols and battle-axes. The pistols proved harmless, and then the battle-axes came in play, whose piercing bills made sometime the one, sometime the other, to have scarce sense to keep their saddles. Smith received such a blow that he lost his battle-axe, whereat the Turks on the ramparts set up a great shout. "The Turk prosecuted his advantage to the utmost of his power; yet the other, what by the readiness of his horse, and his judgment and dexterity in such a business, beyond all men's expectations, by God's assistance, not only avoided the Turke's violence, but having drawn his Faulchion, pierced the Turke so under the Culets throrow backe and body, that although he alighted from his horse, he stood not long ere he lost his head, as the rest had done."

There is nothing better than this in all the tales of chivalry, and John Smith's depreciation of his inability to equal Caesar in describing his own exploits, in his dedicatory letter to the Duchess of Richmond, must be taken as an excess of modesty. We are prepared to hear that these beheadings gave such encouragement to the whole army that six thousand soldiers, with three led horses, each preceded by a soldier bearing a Turk's head on a lance, turned out as a guard to Smith and conducted him to the pavilion of the general, to whom he presented his trophies. General Moyses (occasionally Smith calls him Moses) took him in his arms and embraced him with much respect, and gave him a fair horse, richly furnished, a scimeter, and a belt worth three hundred ducats. And his colonel advanced him to the position of sergeant-major of his regiment. If any detail was wanting to round out and reward this knightly performance in strict accord with the old romances, it was supplied by the subsequent handsome conduct of Prince Sigismund.

When the Christians had mounted their guns and made a couple of breaches in the walls of Regall, General Moyses ordered an attack one dark night "by the light that proceeded from the murdering muskets and peace-making cannon." The enemy were thus awaited, "whilst their slothful governor lay in a castle on top of a high mountain, and like a valiant prince asketh what's the matter, when horrour and death stood amazed at each other, to see who should prevail to make him victorious." These descriptions show that Smith could handle the pen as well as the battleaxe, and distinguish him from the more vulgar fighters of his time. The assault succeeded, but at great cost of life. The Turks sent a flag of truce and desired a "composition," but the earl, remembering the death of his father, continued to batter the town and when he took it put all the men in arms to the sword, and then set their heads upon stakes along the walls, the Turks having ornamented the walls with Christian heads when they captured the fortress. Although the town afforded much pillage, the loss of so many troops so mixed the sour with the sweet that General Moyses could only allay his grief by sacking three other towns, Veratis, Solmos, and Kapronka. Taking from these a couple of thousand prisoners, mostly women and children, Earl Moyses marched north to Weisenberg (Alba Julia), and camped near the palace of Prince Sigismund.

When Sigismund Battori came out to view his army he was made acquainted with the signal services of Smith at "Olumpagh, Stowell-Weisenberg, and Regall," and rewarded him by conferring upon him, according to the law of—arms, a shield of arms with "three Turks' heads." This was granted by a letter-patent, in Latin, which is dated at "Lipswick, in Misenland, December 9, 1603" It recites that Smith was taken captive by the Turks in Wallachia November 18, 1602; that he escaped and rejoined his fellow-soldiers. This patent, therefore, was not given at Alba Julia, nor until Prince Sigismund had finally left his country, and when the Emperor was, in fact, the Prince of Transylvania. Sigismund styles himself, by the grace of God, Duke of Transylvania, etc. Appended to this patent, as published in Smith's "True Travels," is a certificate by William Segar, knight of the garter and principal king of arms of England, that he had seen this patent and had recorded a copy of it in the office of the Herald of Armes. This certificate is dated August 19, 1625, the year after the publication of the General Historie.

Smith says that Prince Sigismund also gave him his picture in gold, and granted him an annual pension of three hundred ducats. This promise of a pension was perhaps the most unsubstantial portion of his reward, for Sigismund himself became a pensioner shortly after the events last narrated.

The last mention of Sigismund by Smith is after his escape from captivity in Tartaria, when this mirror of virtues had abdicated. Smith visited him at "Lipswicke in Misenland," and the Prince "gave him his Passe, intimating the service he had done, and the honors he had received, with fifteen hundred ducats of gold to repair his losses." The "Passe" was doubtless the "Patent" before introduced, and we hear no word of the annual pension.

Affairs in Transylvania did not mend even after the capture of Regall, and of the three Turks' heads, and the destruction of so many villages. This fruitful and strong country was the prey of faction, and became little better than a desert under the ravages of the contending armies. The Emperor Rudolph at last determined to conquer the country for himself, and sent Busca again with a large army. Sigismund finding himself poorly supported, treated again with the Emperor and agreed to retire to Silicia on a pension. But the Earl Moyses, seeing no prospect of regaining his patrimony, and determining not to be under subjection to the Germans, led his troops against Busca, was defeated, and fled to join the Turks. Upon this desertion the Prince delivered up all he had to Busca and retired to Prague. Smith himself continued with the imperial party, in the regiment of Earl Meldritch. About this time the Sultan sent one Jeremy to be vaivode of Wallachia, whose tyranny caused the people to rise against him, and he fled into Moldavia. Busca proclaimed Lord Rodoll vaivode in his stead. But Jeremy assembled an army of forty thousand Turks, Tartars, and Moldavians, and retired into Wallachia. Smith took active part in Rodoll's campaign to recover Wallachia, and narrates the savage war that ensued. When the armies were encamped near each other at Raza and Argish, Rodoll cut off the heads of parties he captured going to the Turkish camp, and threw them into the enemy's trenches. Jeremy retorted by skinning alive the Christian parties he captured, hung their skins upon poles, and their carcasses and heads on stakes by them. In the first battle Rodoll was successful and established himself in Wallachia, but Jeremy rallied and began ravaging the country. Earl Meldritch was sent against him, but the Turks' force was much superior, and the Christians were caught in a trap. In order to reach Rodoll, who was at Rottenton, Meldritch with his small army was obliged to cut his way through the solid body of the enemy. A device of Smith's assisted him. He covered two or three hundred trunks—probably small branches of trees—with wild-fire. These fixed upon the heads of lances and set on fire when the troops charged in the night, so terrified the horses of the Turks that they fled in dismay. Meldritch was for a moment victorious, but when within three leagues of Rottenton he was overpowered by forty thousand Turks, and the last desperate fight followed, in which nearly all the friends of the Prince were slain, and Smith himself was left for dead on the field.

On this bloody field over thirty thousand lay headless, armless, legless, all cut and mangled, who gave knowledge to the world how dear the Turk paid for his conquest of Transylvania and Wallachia—a conquest that might have been averted if the three Christian armies had been joined against the "cruel devouring Turk." Among the slain were many Englishmen, adventurers like the valiant Captain whom Smith names, men who "left there their bodies in testimony of their minds." And there, "Smith among the slaughtered dead bodies, and many a gasping soule with toils and wounds lay groaning among the rest, till being found by the Pillagers he was able to live, and perceiving by his armor and habit, his ransome might be better than his death, they led him prisoner with many others." The captives were taken to Axopolis and all sold as slaves. Smith was bought by Bashaw Bogall, who forwarded him by way of Adrianople to Constantinople, to be a slave to his mistress. So chained by the necks in gangs of twenty they marched to the city of Constantine, where Smith was delivered over to the mistress of the Bashaw, the young Charatza Tragabigzanda.

# III

## CAPTIVITY AND WANDERING

Our hero never stirs without encountering a romantic adventure. Noble ladies nearly always take pity on good-looking captains, and Smith was far from ill-favored. The charming Charatza delighted to talk with her slave, for she could speak Italian, and would feign herself too sick to go to the bath, or to accompany the other women when they went to weep over the graves, as their custom is once a week, in order to stay at home to hear from Smith how it was that Bogall took him prisoner, as the Bashaw had written her, and whether Smith was a Bohemian lord conquered by the Bashaw's own hand, whose ransom could adorn her with the glory of her lover's conquests. Great must have been her disgust with Bogall when she heard that he had not captured this handsome prisoner, but had bought him in the slave-market at Axopolis. Her compassion for her slave increased, and the hero thought he saw in her eyes a tender interest. But she had no use for such a slave, and fearing her mother would sell him, she sent him to her brother, the Tymor Bashaw of Nalbrits in the country of Cambria, a province of Tartaria (wherever that may be). If all had gone on as Smith believed the kind lady intended, he might have been a great Bashaw and a mighty man in the Ottoman Empire, and we might never have heard of Pocahontas. In sending him to her

Charles Dudley Warner

brother, it was her intention, for she told him so, that he should only sojourn in Nalbrits long enough to learn the language, and what it was to be a Turk, till time made her master of herself. Smith himself does not dissent from this plan to metamorphose him into a Turk and the husband of the beautiful Charatza Tragabigzanda. He had no doubt that he was commended to the kindest treatment by her brother; but Tymor "diverted all this to the worst of cruelty." Within an hour of his arrival, he was stripped naked, his head and face shaved as smooth as his hand, a ring of iron, with a long stake bowed like a sickle, riveted to his neck, and he was scantily clad in goat's skin. There were many other slaves, but Smith being the last, was treated like a dog, and made the slave of slaves.

The geographer is not able to follow Captain Smith to Nalbrits. Perhaps Smith himself would have been puzzled to make a map of his own career after he left Varna and passed the Black Sea and came through the straits of Niger into the Sea Disbacca, by some called the Lake Moetis, and then sailed some days up the River Bruapo to Cambria, and two days more to Nalbrits, where the Tyrnor resided.

Smith wrote his travels in London nearly thirty years after, and it is difficult to say how much is the result of his own observation and how much he appropriated from preceding romances. The Cambrians may have been the Cossacks, but his description of their habits and also those of the "Crym-Tartars" belongs to the marvels of Mandeville and other wide-eyed travelers. Smith fared very badly with the Tymor. The Tymor and his friends ate pillaw; they esteemed "samboyses" and "musselbits" "great dainties, and yet," exclaims Smith, "but round pies, full of all sorts of flesh they can get, chopped with variety of herbs." Their best drink was "coffa" and sherbet, which is only honey and water. The common victual of the others was the entrails of horses and "ulgries" (goats?) cut up and boiled in a caldron with "cuskus," a preparation made from grain. This was served in great bowls set in the ground, and when the other prisoners had raked it thoroughly with their foul fists the remainder was given to the Christians. The same dish of entrails used to be served not many years ago in Upper Egypt as a royal dish to entertain a distinguished guest.

It might entertain but it would too long detain us to repeat Smith's information, probably all secondhand, about this barbarous region. We must confine ourselves to the fortunes of our hero. All his hope of deliverance from thraldom was in the love of Tragabigzanda, whom he firmly believed was ignorant of his bad usage. But she made no sign. Providence at length opened a way for his escape. He was employed in thrashing in a field more than a league from the Tymor's home. The Bashaw used to come to visit his slave there, and beat, spurn, and revile him. One day Smith, unable to control himself under these insults, rushed upon the Tymor, and beat out his brains with a thrashing bat—"for they had no flails," he explains—put on the dead man's clothes, hid the body in the straw, filled a knapsack with corn, mounted his horse and rode away into the unknown desert, where he wandered many days before he found a way out. If we may believe Smith this wilderness was more civilized in one respect than some parts of our own land, for on all the crossings of the roads were guide-boards. After traveling sixteen days on the road that leads to Muscova, Smith reached a Muscovite garrison on the River Don. The governor knocked off the iron from his neck and used him so kindly that he thought himself now risen from the dead. With his usual good fortune there was a lady to take interest in him—"the good Lady Callamata largely supplied all his wants."

After Smith had his purse filled by Sigismund he made a thorough tour of Europe, and passed into Spain, where being

satisfied, as he says, with Europe and Asia, and understanding that there were wars in Barbary, this restless
adventurer passed on into Morocco with several comrades on
a French man-of-war. His observations on and tales about
North Africa are so evidently taken from the books of other
travelers that they add little to our knowledge of his career.
For some reason he found no fighting going on worth his
while. But good fortune attended his return. He sailed in a
man-of-war with Captain Merham. They made a few
unimportant captures, and at length fell in with two Spanish
men-of-war, which gave Smith the sort of entertainment he
most coveted. A sort of running fight, sometimes at close
quarters, and with many boardings and repulses, lasted for a
couple of days and nights, when having battered each other
thoroughly and lost many men, the pirates of both nations
separated and went cruising, no doubt, for more profitable
game. Our wanderer returned to his native land, seasoned
and disciplined for the part he was to play in the New World.
As Smith had traveled all over Europe and sojourned in
Morocco, besides sailing the high seas, since he visited
Prince Sigismund in December, 1603, it was probably in the
year 1605 that he reached England. He had arrived at the
manly age of twenty-six years, and was ready to play a man's
part in the wonderful drama of discovery and adventure upon
which the Britons were then engaged.

# IV

## FIRST ATTEMPTS IN VIRGINIA

John Smith has not chosen to tell us anything of his life during the interim—perhaps not more than a year and a half—between his return from Morocco and his setting sail for Virginia. Nor do his contemporaries throw any light upon this period of his life.

One would like to know whether he went down to Willoughby and had a reckoning with his guardians; whether he found any relations or friends of his boyhood; whether any portion of his estate remained of that "competent means" which he says he inherited, but which does not seem to have been available in his career. From the time when he set out for France in his fifteenth year, with the exception of a short sojourn in Willoughby seven or eight years after, he lived by his wits and by the strong hand. His purse was now and then replenished by a lucky windfall, which enabled him to extend his travels and seek more adventures. This is the impression that his own story makes upon the reader in a narrative that is characterized by the boastfulness and exaggeration of the times, and not fuller of the marvelous than most others of that period.

The London to which Smith returned was the London of

Shakespeare. We should be thankful for one glimpse of him in this interesting town. Did he frequent the theatre? Did he perhaps see Shakespeare himself at the Globe? Did he loaf in the coffee-houses, and spin the fine thread of his adventures to the idlers and gallants who resorted to them? If he dropped in at any theatre of an afternoon he was quite likely to hear some allusion to Virginia, for the plays of the hour were full of chaff, not always of the choicest, about the attractions of the Virgin-land, whose gold was as plentiful as copper in England; where the prisoners were fettered in gold, and the dripping-pans were made of it; and where—an unheard-of thing—you might become an alderman without having been a scavenger.

Was Smith an indulger in that new medicine for all ills, tobacco? Alas! we know nothing of his habits or his company. He was a man of piety according to his lights, and it is probable that he may have had the then rising prejudice against theatres. After his return from Virginia he and his exploits were the subject of many a stage play and spectacle, but whether his vanity was more flattered by this mark of notoriety than his piety was offended we do not know. There is certainly no sort of evidence that he engaged in the common dissipation of the town, nor gave himself up to those pleasures which a man rescued from the hardships of captivity in Tartaria might be expected to seek. Mr. Stith says that it was the testimony of his fellow soldiers and adventurers that "they never knew a soldier, before him, so free from those military vices of wine, tobacco, debts, dice, and oathes."

But of one thing we may be certain: he was seeking adventure according to his nature, and eager for any heroic employment; and it goes without saying that he entered into the great excitement of the day—adventure in America. Elizabeth was dead. James had just come to the throne, and

Raleigh, to whom Elizabeth had granted an extensive patent of Virginia, was in the Tower. The attempts to make any permanent lodgment in the countries of Virginia had failed. But at the date of Smith's advent Captain Bartholomew Gosnold had returned from a voyage undertaken in 1602 under the patronage of the Earl of Southampton, and announced that he had discovered a direct passage westward to the new continent, all the former voyagers having gone by the way of the West Indies. The effect of this announcement in London, accompanied as it was with Gosnold's report of the fruitfulness of the coast of New England which he explored, was something like that made upon New York by the discovery of gold in California in 1849. The route by the West Indies, with its incidents of disease and delay, was now replaced by the direct course opened by Gosnold, and the London Exchange, which has always been quick to scent any profit in trade, shared the excitement of the distinguished soldiers and sailors who were ready to embrace any chance of adventure that offered.

It is said that Captain Gosnold spent several years in vain, after his return, in soliciting his friends and acquaintances to join him in settling this fertile land he had explored; and that at length he prevailed upon Captain John Smith, Mr. Edward Maria Wingfield, the Rev. Mr. Robert Hunt, and others, to join him. This is the first appearance of the name of Captain John Smith in connection with Virginia. Probably his life in London had been as idle as unprofitable, and his purse needed replenishing. Here was a way open to the most honorable, exciting, and profitable employment. That its mere profit would have attracted him we do not believe; but its danger, uncertainty, and chance of distinction would irresistibly appeal to him. The distinct object of the projectors was to establish a colony in Virginia. This proved too great an undertaking for private persons. After many vain projects the scheme was commended to several of the nobility, gentry, and merchants, who came into it heartily, and the memorable expedition of 1606 was organized.

The patent under which this colonization was undertaken was obtained from King James by the solicitation of Richard Hakluyt and others. Smith's name does not appear in it, nor does that of Gosnold nor of Captain Newport. Richard Hakluyt, then clerk prebendary of Westminster, had from the first taken great interest in the project. He was chaplain of the English colony in Paris when Sir Francis Drake was fitting out his expedition to America, and was eager to further it. By his diligent study he became the best English geographer of his time; he was the historiographer of the East India Company, and the best informed man in England concerning the races, climates, and productions of all parts of the globe. It was at Hakluyt's suggestion that two vessels were sent out from Plymouth in 1603 to verify Gosnold's report of his new short route. A further verification of the feasibility of this route was made by Captain George Weymouth, who was sent out in 1605 by the Earl of Southampton.

The letters-patent of King James, dated April 10, 1606, licensed the planting of two colonies in the territories of America commonly called Virginia. The corporators named in the first colony were Sir Thos. Gates, Sir George Somers, knights, and Richard Hakluyt and Edward Maria Wingfield, adventurers, of the city of London. They were permitted to settle anywhere in territory between the 34th and 41st degrees of latitude.

The corporators named in the second colony were Thomas Hankam, Raleigh Gilbert, William Parker, and George Popham, representing Bristol, Exeter, and Plymouth, and the west counties, who were authorized to make a settlement anywhere between the 38th and 48th degrees of latitude.

The—letters commended and generously accepted this noble work of colonization, "which may, by the Providence of Almighty God, hereafter tend to the glory of his Divine Majesty, in propagating of Christian religion to such people as yet live in darkness and miserable ignorance of all true knowledge and worship of God, and may in time bring the infidels and savages living in those parts to human civility and to a settled and quiet government." The conversion of the Indians was as prominent an object in all these early adventures, English or Spanish, as the relief of the Christians has been in all the Russian campaigns against the Turks in our day.

Before following the fortunes of this Virginia colony of 1606, to which John Smith was attached, it is necessary to glance briefly at the previous attempt to make settlements in this portion of America.

Although the English had a claim upon America, based upon the discovery of Newfoundland and of the coast of the continent from the 38th to the 68th north parallel by Sebastian Cabot in 1497, they took no further advantage of it than to send out a few fishing vessels, until Sir Humphrey Gilbert, a noted and skillful seaman, took out letters-patent for discovery, bearing date the 11th of January, 1578. Gilbert was the half-brother of Sir Walter Raleigh and thirteen years his senior. The brothers were associated in the enterprise of 1579, which had for its main object the possession of Newfoundland. It is commonly said, and in this the biographical dictionaries follow one another, that Raleigh accompanied his brother on this voyage of 1579 and went with him to Newfoundland. The fact is that Gilbert did not reach Newfoundland on that voyage, and it is open to doubt if Raleigh started with him. In April, 1579, when Gilbert took active steps under the charter of 1578, diplomatic difficulties arose, growing out of Elizabeth's policy with the

Spaniards, and when Gilbert's ships were ready to sail he was stopped by an order from the council. Little is known of this unsuccessful attempt of Gilbert's. He did, after many delays, put to sea, and one of his contemporaries, John Hooker, the antiquarian, says that Raleigh was one of the assured friends that accompanied him. But he was shortly after driven back, probably from an encounter with the Spaniards, and returned with the loss of a tall ship.

Raleigh had no sooner made good his footing at the court of Elizabeth than he joined Sir Humphrey in a new adventure. But the Queen peremptorily retained Raleigh at court, to prevent his incurring the risks of any "dangerous sea-fights." To prevent Gilbert from embarking on this new voyage seems to have been the device of the council rather than the Queen, for she assured Gilbert of her good wishes, and desired him, on his departure, to give his picture to Raleigh for her, and she contributed to the large sums raised to meet expenses "an anchor guarded by a lady," which the sailor was to wear at his breast. Raleigh risked L 2,000 in the venture, and equipped a ship which bore his name, but which had ill luck. An infectious fever broke out among the crew, and the "Ark Raleigh" returned to Plymouth. Sir Humphrey wrote to his brother admiral, Sir George Peckham, indignantly of this desertion, the reason for which he did not know, and then proceeded on his voyage with his four remaining ships. This was on the 11th of January, 1583. The expedition was so far successful that Gilbert took formal possession of Newfoundland for the Queen. But a fatality attended his further explorations: the gallant admiral went down at sea in a storm off our coast, with his crew, heroic and full of Christian faith to the last, uttering, it is reported, this courageous consolation to his comrades at the last moment: "Be of good heart, my friends. We are as near to heaven by sea as by land."

In September, 1583, a surviving ship brought news of the disaster to Falmouth. Raleigh was not discouraged. Within six months of this loss he had on foot another enterprise. His brother's patent had expired. On the 25th of March, 1584, he obtained from Elizabeth a new charter with larger powers, incorporating himself, Adrian Gilbert, brother of Sir Humphrey, and John Davys, under the title of "The College of the Fellowship for the Discovery of the Northwest Passage." But Raleigh's object was colonization. Within a few days after his charter was issued he despatched two captains, Philip Amadas and Arthur Barlow, who in July of that year took possession of the island of Roanoke.

The name of Sir Walter Raleigh is intimately associated with Carolina and Virginia, and it is the popular impression that he personally assisted in the discovery of the one and the settlement of the other. But there is no more foundation for the belief that he ever visited the territory of Virginia, of which he was styled governor, than that he accompanied Sir Humphrey Gilbert to Newfoundland. An allusion by William Strachey, in his "Historie of Travaile into Virginia," hastily read, may have misled some writers. He speaks of an expedition southward, "to some parts of Chawonock and the Mangoangs, to search them there left by Sir Walter Raleigh." But his further sketch of the various prior expeditions shows that he meant to speak of settlers left by Sir Ralph Lane and other agents of Raleigh in colonization. Sir Walter Raleigh never saw any portion of the coast of the United States.

In 1592 he planned an attack upon the Spanish possessions of Panama, but his plans were frustrated. His only personal expedition to the New World was that to Guana in 1595.

The expedition of Captain Amadas and Captain Barlow is described by Captain Smith in his compilation called the "General Historie," and by Mr. Strachey. They set sail April

27, 1584, from the Thames. On the 2d of July they fell with the coast of Florida in shoal water, "where they felt a most delicate sweet smell," but saw no land. Presently land appeared, which they took to be the continent, and coasted along to the northward a hundred and thirty miles before finding a harbor. Entering the first opening, they landed on what proved to be the Island of Roanoke. The landing-place was sandy and low, but so productive of grapes or vines overrunning everything, that the very surge of the sea sometimes overflowed them. The tallest and reddest cedars in the world grew there, with pines, cypresses, and other trees, and in the woods plenty of deer, conies, and fowls in incredible abundance.

After a few days the natives came off in boats to visit them, proper people and civil in their behavior, bringing with them the King's brother, Granganameo (Quangimino, says Strachey). The name of the King was Winginia, and of the country Wingandacoa. The name of this King might have suggested that of Virginia as the title of the new possession, but for the superior claim of the Virgin Queen. Granganameo was a friendly savage who liked to trade. The first thing he took a fancy was a pewter dish, and he made a hole through it and hung it about his neck for a breastplate. The liberal Christians sold it to him for the low price of twenty deerskins, worth twenty crowns, and they also let him have a copper kettle for fifty skins. They drove a lively traffic with the savages for much of such "truck," and the chief came on board and ate and drank merrily with the strangers. His wife and children, short of stature but well-formed and bashful, also paid them a visit. She wore a long coat of leather, with a piece of leather about her loins, around her forehead a band of white coral, and from her ears bracelets of pearls of the bigness of great peas hung down to her middle. The other women wore pendants of copper, as did the children, five or six in an ear. The boats of these savages were hollowed trunks of trees. Nothing could exceed the kindness and trustfulness the Indians exhibited towards their visitors. They kept them supplied with game and fruits, and when a party made an expedition inland to the residence of Granganameo, his wife (her husband being absent) came running to the river to welcome them; took them to her house and set them before a great fire; took off their clothes and washed them; removed the stockings of some and washed their feet in warm water; set plenty of victual, venison and fish and fruits, before them, and took pains to see all things well ordered for their comfort. "More love they could not express to entertain us." It is noted that these savages drank wine while the grape lasted. The visitors returned all this kindness with suspicion.

They insisted upon retiring to their boats at night instead of lodging in the house, and the good woman, much grieved at their jealousy, sent down to them their half-cooked supper, pots and all, and mats to cover them from the rain in the night, and caused several of her men and thirty women to sit all night on the shore over against them. "A more kind, loving people cannot be," say the voyagers.

In September the expedition returned to England, taking specimens of the wealth of the country, and some of the pearls as big as peas, and two natives, Wanchese and Manteo. The "lord proprietary" obtained the Queen's permission to name the new lands "Virginia," in her honor, and he had a new seal of his arms cut, with the legend, Propria insignia Walteri Ralegh, militis, Domini et Gubernatoris Virginia.

The enticing reports brought back of the fertility of this land, and the amiability of its pearl-decked inhabitants, determined Raleigh at once to establish a colony there, in the hope of the ultimate salvation of the "poor seduced infidell" who wore the pearls. A fleet of seven vessels, with one hundred householders, and many things necessary to begin a new state, departed from Plymouth in April, 1585. Sir Richard Grenville had command of the expedition, and Mr. Ralph Lane was made governor of the colony, with Philip Amadas for his deputy. Among the distinguished men who accompanied them were Thomas Hariot, the mathematician, and Thomas Cavendish, the naval discoverer. The expedition encountered as many fatalities as those that befell Sir Humphrey Gilbert; and Sir Richard was destined also to an early and memorable death. But the new colony suffered more from its own imprudence and want of harmony than from natural causes.

In August, Grenville left Ralph Lane in charge of the colony and returned to England, capturing a Spanish ship on the way. The colonists pushed discoveries in various directions, but soon found themselves involved in quarrels with the Indians, whose conduct was less friendly than formerly, a change partly due to the greed of the whites. In June, when Lane was in fear of a conspiracy which he had discovered against the life of the colony, and it was short of supplies, Sir Francis Drake appeared off Roanoke, returning homeward with his fleet from the sacking of St. Domingo, Carthagena, and St. Augustine. Lane, without waiting for succor from England, persuaded Drake to take him and all the colony back home. Meantime Raleigh, knowing that the colony would probably need aid, was preparing a fleet of three well appointed ships to accompany Sir Richard Grenville, and an "advice ship," plentifully freighted, to send in advance to give intelligence of his coming. Great was Grenville's chagrin, when he reached Hatorask, to find that the advice boat had arrived, and finding no colony, had departed again for England. However, he established fifteen men ("fifty," says the "General Historie") on the island, provisioned for two years, and then returned home.

[Sir Richard Grenville in 1591 was vice-admiral of a fleet, under command of Lord Thomas Howard, at the Azores, sent against a Spanish Plate-fleet. Six English vessels were suddenly opposed by a Spanish convoy of 53 ships of war. Left behind his comrades, in embarking from an island, opposed by five galleons, he maintained a terrible fight for fifteen hours, his vessel all cut to pieces, and his men nearly all slain. He died uttering aloud these words: "Here dies Sir Richard Grenville, with a joyful and quiet mind, for that I have ended my life as a true soldier ought to do, fighting for his country, queen, religion, and honor."]

Mr. Ralph Lane's colony was splendidly fitted out, much better furnished than the one that Newport, Wingfield, and Gosnold conducted to the River James in 1607; but it needed a man at the head of it. If the governor had possessed Smith's pluck, he would have held on till the arrival of Grenville.

Lane did not distinguish himself in the conduct of this governorship, but he nevertheless gained immortality. For he is credited with first bringing into England that valuable medicinal weeds called tobacco, which Sir Walter Raleigh made fashionable, not in its capacity to drive "rheums" out of the body, but as a soother, when burned in the bowl of a pipe and drawn through the stem in smoke, of the melancholy spirit.

The honor of introducing tobacco at this date is so large that it has been shared by three persons—Sir Francis Drake, who brought Mr. Lane home; Mr. Lane, who carried the precious result of his sojourn in America; and Sir Walter Raleigh, who commended it to the use of the ladies of Queen Elizabeth's court.

But this was by no means its first appearance in Europe. It was already known in Spain, in France, and in Italy, and no doubt had begun to make its way in the Orient. In the early part of the century the Spaniards had discovered its virtues. It is stated by John Neander, in his "Tobaco Logia," published in Leyden in 1626, that Tobaco took its name from a province in Yucatan, conquered by Fernando Cortez in 1519. The name Nicotiana he derives from D. Johanne Nicotino Nemansensi, of the council of Francis II., who first introduced the plant into France. At the date of this volume (1626) tobacco was in general use all over Europe and in the East. Pictures are given of the Persian water pipes, and descriptions of the mode of preparing it for use. There are reports and traditions of a very ancient use of tobacco in Persia and in China, as well as in India, but we are convinced that the substance supposed to be tobacco, and to be referred to as such by many writers, and described as "intoxicating," was really India hemp, or some plant very different from the tobacco of the New World. At any rate there is evidence that in the Turkish Empire as late as 1616 tobacco was still somewhat a novelty, and the smoking of it was regarded as vile, and a habit only of the low. The late Hekekian Bey, foreign minister of old Mahomet Ali, possessed an ancient Turkish MS which related an occurrence at Smyrna about the year 1610, namely, the punishment of some sailors for the use of tobacco, which showed that it was a novelty and accounted a low vice at that time. The testimony of the trustworthy George Sandys, an English traveler into Turkey, Egypt, and Syria in 1610 (afterwards, 1621, treasurer of the colony in Virginia), is to the same effect as given in his "Relation," published in London in 1621. In his minute description of the people and manners of Constantinople, after speaking of opium, which makes the Turks "giddy-headed" and "turbulent dreamers," he says: "But perhaps for the self-same cause they delight in Tobacco: which they take through reedes that have joyned with them great heads of wood to containe it, I doubt not but lately taught them as brought them by the English; and were it not sometimes lookt into (for Morat Bassa [Murad III.?] not long since commanded a pipe to be thrust through the nose of a Turke, and to be led in derision through the Citie), no question but it would prove a principal commodity. Nevertheless they will take it in corners; and are so ignorant therein, that that which in England is not saleable, doth passe here among them for most excellent."

Mr. Stith ("History of Virginia," 1746) gives Raleigh credit for the introduction of the pipe into good society, but he cautiously says, "We are not informed whether the queen made use of it herself: but it is certain she gave great countenance to it as a vegetable of singular strength and power, which might therefore prove of benefit to mankind, and advantage to the nation." Mr. Thomas Hariot, in his observations on the colony at Roanoke, says that the natives esteemed their tobacco, of which plenty was found, their "chief physicke."

It should be noted, as against the claim of Lane, that Stowe in his "Annales" (1615) says: "Tobacco was first brought and made known in England by Sir John Hawkins, about the year 1565, but not used by Englishmen in many years after, though at this time commonly used by most men and many women." In a side-note to the edition of 1631 we read: "Sir Walter Raleigh was the first that brought tobacco in use, when all men wondered what it meant." It was first commended for its medicinal virtues. Harrison's "Chronologie," under date of 1573, says: "In these daies the taking in of the smoke of the Indian herbe called 'Tabaco' by an instrument formed like a little ladell, whereby it passeth from the mouth into the hed and stomach, is gretlie taken-up and used in England, against Rewmes and some other diseases ingendred in the longes and inward partes, and not without effect." But Barnaby Rich, in "The Honestie of this Age," 1614, disagrees with Harrison about its benefit: "They say it is good for a cold, for a pose, for rewmes, for aches, for dropsies, and for all manner of diseases proceeding of moyst humours; but I cannot see but that those that do take it fastest are as much (or more) subject to all these infirmities (yea, and to the poxe itself) as those that have nothing at all to do with it." He learns that 7,000 shops in London live by the trade of tobacco-selling, and calculates that there is paid for it L 399,375 a year, "all spent in smoake." Every base groom must have his pipe with his pot of ale; it "is vendible in every taverne, inne, and ale-house; and as for apothecaries shops, grosers shops, chandlers shops, they are (almost) never without company that, from morning till night, are still taking of tobacco." Numbers of houses and shops had no other trade to live by. The wrath of King James was probably never cooled against tobacco, but the expression of it was somewhat tempered when he perceived what a source of revenue it became.

The savages of North America gave early evidence of the possession of imaginative minds, of rare power of invention, and of an amiable desire to make satisfactory replies to the inquiries of their visitors. They generally told their questioners what they wanted to know, if they could ascertain what sort of information would please them. If they had known the taste of the sixteenth century for the marvelous they could not have responded more fitly to suit it. They filled Mr. Lane and Mr. Hariot full of tales of a wonderful copper mine on the River Maratock (Roanoke), where the metal was dipped out of the stream in great bowls. The colonists had great hopes of this river, which Mr. Hariot thought flowed out of the Gulf of Mexico, or very near the South Sea. The Indians also conveyed to the mind of this sagacious observer the notion that they had a very respectably developed religion; that they believed in one chief god who existed from all eternity, and who made many gods of less degree; that for mankind a woman was first created, who by one of the gods brought forth children; that they believed in the immortality of the soul, and that for good works a soul will be conveyed to bliss in the tabernacles of the gods, and for bad deeds to pokogusso, a great pit in the furthest part of the world, where the sun sets, and where they burn continually. The Indians knew this because two men lately dead had revived and come back to tell them of the other world. These stories, and many others of like kind, the Indians told of themselves, and they further pleased Mr. Hariot by kissing his Bible and rubbing it all over their bodies, notwithstanding he told them there was no virtue in the material book itself, only in its doctrines. We must do Mr. Hariot the justice to say, however, that he had some little suspicion of the "subtiltie" of the weroances (chiefs) and the priests.

Raleigh was not easily discouraged; he was determined to plant his colony, and to send relief to the handful of men that Grenville had left on Roanoke Island. In May, 1587, he sent out three ships and a hundred and fifty householders, under command of Mr. John White, who was appointed Governor of the colony, with twelve assistants as a Council, who were incorporated under the name of "The Governor and Assistants of the City of Ralegh in Virginia," with instructions to change their settlement to Chesapeake Bay. The expedition found there no one of the colony (whether it was fifty or fifteen the writers disagree), nothing but the bones of one man where the plantation had been; the houses were unhurt, but overgrown with weeds, and the fort was defaced. Captain Stafford, with twenty men, went to Croatan to seek the lost colonists. He heard that the fifty had been set upon by three hundred Indians, and, after a sharp skirmish and the loss of one man, had taken boats and gone to a small island near Hatorask, and afterwards had departed no one knew whither.

Mr. White sent a band to take revenge upon the Indians who

were suspected of their murder through treachery, which was guided by Mateo, the friendly Indian, who had returned with the expedition from England. By a mistake they attacked a friendly tribe. In August of this year Mateo was Christianized, and baptized under the title of Lord of Roanoke and Dassomonpeake, as a reward for his fidelity. The same month Elinor, the daughter of the Govemor, the wife of Ananias Dare, gave birth to a daughter, the first white child born in this part of the continent, who was named Virginia.

Before long a dispute arose between the Governor and his Council as to the proper person to return to England for supplies. White himself was finally prevailed upon to go, and he departed, leaving about a hundred settlers on one of the islands of Hatorask to form a plantation.

The Spanish invasion and the Armada distracted the attention of Europe about this time, and the hope of plunder from Spanish vessels was more attractive than the colonization of America. It was not until 1590 that Raleigh was able to despatch vessels to the relief of the Hatorask colony, and then it was too late. White did, indeed, start out from Biddeford in April, 1588, with two vessels, but the temptation to chase prizes was too strong for him, and he went on a cruise of his own, and left the colony to its destruction.

In March, 1589-90, Mr. White was again sent out, with three ships, from Plymouth, and reached the coast in August. Sailing by Croatan they went to Hatorask, where they descried a smoke in the place they had left the colony in 1587. Going ashore next day, they found no man, nor sign that any had been there lately. Preparing to go to Roanoke next day, a boat was upset and Captain Spicer and six of the crew were drowned. This accident so discouraged the sailors that they could hardly be persuaded to enter on the search for the colony. At last two boats, with nineteen men, set out for Hatorask, and landed at that part of Roanoke where the colony had been left. When White left the colony three years before, the men had talked of going fifty miles into the mainland, and had agreed to leave some sign of their departure. The searchers found not a man of the colony; their houses were taken down, and a strong palisade had been built. All about were relics of goods that had been buried and dug up again and scattered, and on a post was carved the name "CROATAN." This signal, which was accompanied by no sign of distress, gave White hope that he should find his comrades at Croatan. But one mischance or another happening, his provisions being short, the expedition decided to run down to the West Indies and "refresh" (chiefly with a little Spanish plunder), and return in the spring and seek their countrymen; but instead they sailed for England and never went to Croatan. The men of the abandoned colonies were never again heard of. Years after, in 1602, Raleigh bought a bark and sent it, under the charge of Samuel Mace, a mariner who had been twice to Virginia, to go in search of the survivors of White's colony. Mace spent a month lounging about the Hatorask coast and trading with the natives, but did not land on Croatan, or at any place where the lost colony might be expected to be found; but having taken on board some sassafras, which at that time brought a good price in England, and some other barks which were supposed to be valuable, he basely shirked the errand on which he was hired to go, and took himself and his spicy woods home.

The "Lost Colony" of White is one of the romances of the New World. Governor White no doubt had the feelings of a parent, but he did not allow them to interfere with his more public duties to go in search of Spanish prizes. If the lost colony had gone to Croatan, it was probable that Ananias Dare and his wife, the Governor's daughter, and the little Virginia Dare, were with them. But White, as we have seen, had such confidence in Providence that he left his dear relatives to its care, and made no attempt to visit Croatan.

Stith says that Raleigh sent five several times to search for the lost, but the searchers returned with only idle reports and frivolous allegations. Tradition, however, has been busy with the fate of these deserted colonists. One of the unsupported conjectures is that the colonists amalgamated with the tribe of Hatteras Indians, and Indian tradition and the physical characteristics of the tribe are said to confirm this idea. But the sporadic birth of children with white skins (albinos) among black or copper-colored races that have had no intercourse with white people, and the occurrence of light hair and blue eyes among the native races of America and of New Guinea, are facts so well attested that no theory of amalgamation can be sustained by such rare physical manifestations. According to Captain John Smith, who wrote of Captain Newport's explorations in 1608, there were no tidings of the waifs, for, says Smith, Newport returned "without a lump of gold, a certainty of the South Sea, or one of the lost company sent out by Sir Walter Raleigh."

In his voyage of discovery up the Chickahominy, Smith seem; to have inquired about this lost colony of King Paspahegh, for he says, "what he knew of the dominions he spared not to acquaint me with, as of certaine men cloathed at a place called Ocanahonan, cloathcd like me."

[Among these Hatteras Indians Captain Amadas, in 1584, saw children with chestnut-colored hair.]

We come somewhat nearer to this matter in the "Historie of Travaile into Virginia Britannia," published from the manuscript by thc Hakluyt Socicty in 1849, in which it is intimated that seven of these deserted colonists were afterwards rescued. Strachey is a first-rate authority for what he saw. He arrived in Virginia in 1610 and remained there two years, as secretary of the colony, and was a man of importance. His "Historie" was probably written between 1612 and 1616. In the first portion of it, which is descriptive of the territory of Virginia, is this important passage: "At Peccarecamek and Ochanahoen, by the relation of Machumps, the people have houses built with stone walls, and one story above another, so taught them by those English who escaped the slaughter of Roanoke. At what time this our colony, under the conduct of Captain Newport, landed within the Chesapeake Bay, where the people breed up tame turkies about their houses, and take apes in the mountains, and where, at Ritanoe, the Weroance Eyanaco, preserved seven of the English alive—four men, two boys, and one young maid (who escaped [that is from Roanoke] and fled up the river of Chanoke), to beat his copper, of which he hath certain mines at the said Ritanoe, as also at Pamawauk are said to be store of salt stones."

This, it will be observed, is on the testimony of Machumps. This pleasing story is not mentioned in Captain Newport's "Discoveries" (May, 1607). Machumps, who was the brother of Winganuske, one of the many wives of Powhatan, had been in England. He was evidently a lively Indian. Strachey had heard him repeat the "Indian grace," a sort of incantation before meat, at the table of Sir Thomas Dale. If he did not differ from his red brothers he had a powerful imagination, and was ready to please the whites with any sort of a marvelous tale. Newport himself does not appear to have seen any of the "apes taken in the mountains." If this story is to be accepted as true we have to think of Virginia Dare as growing up to be a woman of twenty years, perhaps as other white maidens have been, Indianized and the wife of a native. But the story rests only upon a romancing Indian. It is possible that Strachey knew more of the matter than he relates, for in his history he speaks again of those betrayed

Charles Dudley Warner

people, "of whose end you shall hereafter read in this decade." But the possessed information is lost, for it is not found in the remainder of this "decade" of his writing, which is imperfect. Another reference in Strachey is more obscure than the first. He is speaking of the merciful intention of King James towards the Virginia savages, and that he does not intend to root out the natives as the Spaniards did in Hispaniola, but by degrees to change their barbarous nature, and inform them of the true God and the way to Salvation, and that his Majesty will even spare Powhatan himself. But, he says, it is the intention to make "the common people likewise to understand, how that his Majesty has been acquainted that the men, women, and children of the first plantation of Roanoke were by practice of Powhatan (he himself persuaded thereunto by his priests) miserably slaughtered, without any offense given him either by the first planted (who twenty and odd years had peaceably lived intermixed with those savages, and were out of his territory) or by those who are now come to inhabit some parts of his distant lands," etc.

Strachey of course means the second plantation and not the first, which, according to the weight of authority, consisted of only fifteen men and no women.

In George Percy's Discourse concerning Captain Newport's exploration of the River James in 1607 (printed in Purchas's "Pilgrims") is this sentence: "At Port Cotage, in our voyage up the river, we saw a savage boy, about the age of ten years, which had a head of hair of a perfect yellow, and reasonably white skin, which is a miracle amongst all savages." Mr. Neill, in his "History of the Virginia Company," says that this boy "was no doubt the offspring of the colonists left at Roanoke by White, of whom four men, two boys, and one young maid had been preserved from slaughter by an Indian Chief." Under the circumstances, "no doubt" is a very strong expression for a historian to use.

This belief in the sometime survival of the Roanoke colonists, and their amalgamation with the Indians, lingered long in colonial gossip. Lawson, in his History, published in London in 1718, mentions a tradition among the Hatteras Indians, "that several of their ancestors were white people and could talk from a book; the truth of which is confirmed by gray eyes being among these Indians and no others."

But the myth of Virginia Dare stands no chance beside that of Pocahontas.

# V

## FIRST PLANTING OF THE COLONY

The way was now prepared for the advent of Captain John Smith in Virginia. It is true that we cannot give him his own title of its discoverer, but the plantation had been practically abandoned, all the colonies had ended in disaster, all the governors and captains had lacked the gift of perseverance or had been early drawn into other adventures, wholly disposed, in the language of Captain John White, "to seek after purchase and spoils," and but for the energy and persistence of Captain Smith the expedition of 1606 might have had no better fate. It needed a man of tenacious will to hold a colony together in one spot long enough to give it root. Captain Smith was that man, and if we find him glorying in his exploits, and repeating upon single big Indians the personal prowess that distinguished him in Transylvania and in the mythical Nalbrits, we have only to transfer our sympathy from the Turks to the Sasquesahanocks if the sense of his heroism becomes oppressive.

Upon the return of Samuel Mace, mariner, who was sent out in 1602 to search for White's lost colony, all Raleigh's interest in the Virginia colony had, by his attainder, escheated to the crown. But he never gave up his faith in Virginia: neither the failure of nine several expeditions nor twelve years imprisonment shook it. On the eve of his fall he had written, "I shall yet live to see it an English nation:" and he lived to see his prediction come true.

The first or Virginian colony, chartered with the Plymouth colony in April, 1606, was at last organized by the appointment of Sir Thomas Smith, the 'Chief of Raleigh's assignees, a wealthy London merchant, who had been ambassador to Persia, and was then, or shortly after, governor of the East India Company, treasurer and president of the meetings of the council in London; and by the assignment of the transportation of the colony to Captain Christopher Newport, a mariner of experience in voyages to the West Indies and in plundering the Spaniards, who had the power to appoint different captains and mariners, and the sole charge of the voyage. No local councilors were named for Virginia, but to Captain Newport, Captain Bartholomew Gosnold, and Captain John Ratcliffe were delivered sealed instructions, to be opened within twenty-four hours after their arrival in Virginia, wherein would be found the names of the persons designated for the Council.

This colony, which was accompanied by the prayers and hopes of London, left the Thames December 19, 1606, in three vessels—the Susan Constant, one hundred tons, Captain Newport, with seventy-one persons; the God-Speed, forty tons, Captain Gosnold, with fifty-two persons; and a pinnace of twenty tons, the Discovery, Captain Ratcliffe, with twenty persons. The Mercure Francais, Paris, 1619, says some of the passengers were women and children, but there is no other mention of women. Of the persons embarked, one hundred and five were planters, the rest crews. Among the planters were Edward Maria Wingfield, Captain John Smith, Captain John Martin, Captain Gabriel Archer, Captain George Kendall, Mr. Robert Hunt, preacher, and Mr. George Percie, brother of the Earl of

Northumberland, subsequently governor for a brief period, and one of the writers from whom Purchas compiled. Most of the planters were shipped as gentlemen, but there were four carpenters, twelve laborers, a blacksmith, a sailor, a barber, a bricklayer, a mason, a tailor, a drummer, and a chirurgeon.

The composition of the colony shows a serious purpose of settlement, since the trades were mostly represented, but there were too many gentlemen to make it a working colony. And, indeed, the gentlemen, like the promoters of the enterprise in London, were probably more solicitous of discovering a passage to the South Sea, as the way to increase riches, than of making a state. They were instructed to explore every navigable river they might find, and to follow the main branches, which would probably lead them in one direction to the East Indies or South Sea, and in the other to the Northwest Passage. And they were forcibly reminded that the way to prosper was to be of one mind, for their own and their country's good.

This last advice did not last the expedition out of sight of land. They sailed from Blackwell, December 19, 1606, but were kept six weeks on the coast of England by contrary winds. A crew of saints cabined in those little caravels and tossed about on that coast for six weeks would scarcely keep in good humor. Besides, the position of the captains and leaders was not yet defined. Factious quarrels broke out immediately, and the expedition would likely have broken up but for the wise conduct and pious exhortations of Mr. Robert Hunt, the preacher. This faithful man was so ill and weak that it was thought he could not recover, yet notwithstanding the stormy weather, the factions on board, and although his home was almost in sight, only twelve miles across the Downs, he refused to quit the ship. He was unmoved, says Smith, either by the weather or by "the scandalous imputations (of some few little better than atheists, of the greatest rank amongst us)." With "the water of his patience" and "his godly exhortations" he quenched the flames of envy and dissension.

They took the old route by the West Indies. George Percy notes that on the 12th of February they saw a blazing star, and presently a storm. They watered at the Canaries, traded with savages at San Domingo, and spent three weeks refreshing themselves among the islands. The quarrels revived before they reached the Canaries, and there Captain Smith was seized and put in close confinement for thirteen weeks.

We get little light from contemporary writers on this quarrel. Smith does not mention the arrest in his "True Relation," but in his "General Historie," writing of the time when they had been six weeks in Virginia, he says: "Now Captain Smith who all this time from their departure from the Canaries was restrained as a prisoner upon the scandalous suggestion of some of the chiefs (envying his repute) who fancied he intended to usurp the government, murder the Council, and make himself King, that his confedcrates were dispersed in all three ships, and that divers of his confederates that revealed it, would affirm it, for this he was committed a prisoner; thirteen weeks he remained thus suspected, and by that time they should return they pretended out of their commiserations, to refer him to the Council in England to receive a check, rather than by particulating his designs make him so odious to the world, as to touch his life, or utterly overthrow his reputation. But he so much scorned their charity and publically defied the uttermost of their cruelty, he wisely prevented their policies, though he could not suppress their envies, yet so well he demeaned himself in this business, as all the company did see his innocency, and his adversaries' malice, and those suborned to accuse him accused his accusers of subornation; many untruths were alleged against him; but being apparently disproved, begot a general hatred in the hearts of the company against such unjust Commanders, that the President was adjudged to give him L 200, so that all he had was seized upon, in part of satisfaction, which Smith presently returned to the store for the general use of the colony."—

Neither in Newport's "Relatyon" nor in Mr. Wingfield's "Discourse" is the arrest mentioned, nor does Strachey speak of it.

About 1629, Smith, in writing a description of the Isle of Mevis (Nevis) in his "Travels and Adventures," says: "In this little [isle] of Mevis, more than twenty years agone, I have remained a good time together, to wod and water—and refresh my men." It is characteristic of Smith's vivid imagination, in regard to his own exploits, that he should speak of an expedition in which he had no command, and was even a prisoner, in this style: "I remained," and "my men." He goes on: "Such factions here we had as commonly attend such voyages, and a pair of gallows was made, but Captaine Smith, for whom they were intended, could not be persuaded to use them; but not any one of the inventors but their lives by justice fell into his power, to determine of at his pleasure, whom with much mercy he favored, that most basely and unjustly would have betrayed him." And it is true that Smith, although a great romancer, was often magnanimous, as vain men are apt to be.

King James's elaborate lack of good sense had sent the expedition to sea with the names of the Council sealed up in a box, not to be opened till it reached its destination. Consequently there was no recognized authority. Smith was a young man of about twenty-eight, vain and no doubt somewhat "bumptious," and it is easy to believe that

Wingfield and the others who felt his superior force and realized his experience, honestly suspected him of designs against the expedition. He was the ablest man on board, and no doubt was aware of it. That he was not only a born commander of men, but had the interest of the colony at heart, time was to show.

The voyagers disported themselves among the luxuries of the West Indies. At Guadaloupe they found a bath so hot that they boiled their pork in it as well as over the fire. At the Island of Monaca they took from the bushes with their hands near two hogsheads full of birds in three or four hours. These, it is useless to say, were probably not the "barnacle geese" which the nautical travelers used to find, and picture growing upon bushes and dropping from the eggs, when they were ripe, full-fledged into the water. The beasts were fearless of men. Wild birds and natives had to learn the whites before they feared them.

"In Mevis, Mona, and the Virgin Isles," says the "General Historie," "we spent some time, where with a lothsome beast like a crocodile, called a gwayn [guana], tortoises, pellicans, parrots, and fishes, we feasted daily."

Thence they made sail-in search of Virginia, but the mariners lost their reckoning for three days and made no land; the crews were discomfited, and Captain Ratcliffe, of the pinnace, wanted to up helm and return to England. But a violent storm, which obliged them "to hull all night," drove them to the port desired. On the 26th of April they saw a bit of land none of them had ever seen before. This, the first land they descried, they named Cape Henry, in honor of the Prince of Wales; as the opposite cape was called Cape Charles, for the Duke of York, afterwards Charles I. Within these capes they found one of the most pleasant places in the world, majestic navigable rivers, beautiful mountains, hills, and plains, and a fruitful and delightsome land.

Mr. George Percy was ravished at the sight of the fair meadows and goodly tall trees. As much to his taste were the large and delicate oysters, which the natives roasted, and in which were found many pearls. The ground was covered with fine and beautiful strawberries, four times bigger than those in England.

Masters Wingfield, Newport, and Gosnold., with thirty men, went ashore on Cape Henry, where they were suddenly set upon by savages, who came creeping upon all-fours over the hills, like bears, with their bows in their hands; Captain Archer was hurt in both hands, and a sailor dangerously wounded in two places on his body. It was a bad omen.

The night of their arrival they anchored at Point Comfort, now Fortress Monroe; the box was opened and the orders read, which constituted Edward Maria Wingfield, Bartholomew Gosnold, John Smith, Christopher Newport, John Ratcliffe, John Martin, and George Kendall the Council, with power to choose a President for a year. Until the 13th of May they were slowly exploring the River Powhatan, now the James, seeking a place for the settlement. They selected a peninsula on the north side of the river, forty miles from its mouth, where there was good anchorage, and which could be readily fortified. This settlement was Jamestown. The Council was then sworn in, and Mr. Wingfield selected President. Smith being under arrest was not sworn in of the Council, and an oration was made setting forth the reason for his exclusion.

When they had pitched upon a site for the fort, every man set to work, some to build the fort, others to pitch the tents, fell trees and make clapboards to reload the ships, others to make gardens and nets. The fort was in the form of a triangle with a half-moon at each corner, intended to mount four or five guns.

President Wingfield appears to have taken soldierly precautions, but Smith was not at all pleased with him from the first. He says "the President's overweening jealousy would admit of no exercise at arms, or fortifications but the boughs of trees cast together in the form of a half-moon by the extraordinary pains and diligence of Captain Kendall." He also says there was contention between Captain Wingfield and Captain Gosnold about the site of the city.

The landing was made at Jamestown on the 14th of May, according to Percy. Previous to that considerable explorations were made. On the 18th of April they launched a shallop, which they built the day before, and "discovered up the bay." They discovered a river on the south side running into the mainland, on the banks of which were good stores of mussels and oysters, goodly trees, flowers of all colors, and strawberries. Returning to their ships and finding the water shallow, they rowed over to a point of land, where they found from six to twelve fathoms of water, which put them in good comfort, therefore they named that part of the land Cape Comfort. On the 29th they set up a cross on Chesapeake Bay, on Cape Henry, and the next day coasted to the Indian town of Kecoughton, now Hampton, where they were kindly entertained. When they first came to land the savages made a doleful noise, laying their paws to the ground and scratching the earth with their nails. This ceremony, which was taken to be a kind of idolatry, ended, mats were brought from the houses, whereon the guests were seated, and given to eat bread made of maize, and tobacco to smoke. The savages also entertained them with dancing and singing and antic tricks and grimaces. They were naked except a covering of skins about the loins, and many were painted in black and red, with artificial knots of lovely colors, beautiful and pleasing to the eye. The 4th of May they were entertained by the chief of Paspika, who favored them with a long oration, making a foul noise and vehement in action, the purport of which they did not catch. The savages were full of hospitality. The next day the weroance, or chief, of Rapahanna sent a messenger to invite them to his seat. His majesty received them in as modest a proud fashion as if he had been a prince of a civil government. His body was painted in crimson and his face in blue, and he wore a chain of beads about his neck and in his ears bracelets of pearls and a bird's claw. The 8th of May they went up the river to the country Apomatica, where the natives received them in hostile array, the chief, with bow and arrows in one hand, and a pipe of tobacco in the other, offering them war or peace.

These savages were as stout and able as any heathen or Christians in the world. Mr. Percy said they bore their years well. He saw among the Pamunkeys a savage reported to be 160, years old, whose eyes were sunk in his head, his teeth gone his hair all gray, and quite a big beard, white as snow; he was a lusty savage, and could travel as fast as anybody.

The Indians soon began to be troublesome in their visits to the plantations, skulking about all night, hanging around the fort by day, bringing sometimes presents of deer, but given to theft of small articles, and showing jealousy of the occupation. They murmured, says Percy, at our planting in their country. But worse than the disposition of the savages was the petty quarreling in the colony itself.

In obedience to the orders to explore for the South Sea, on the 22d of May, Newport, Percy, Smith, Archer, and twenty others were sent in the shallop to explore the Powhatan, or James River.

Passing by divers small habitations, and through a land abounding in trees, flowers, and small fruits, a river full of fish, and of sturgeon such as the world beside has none, they came on the 24th, having passed the town of Powhatan, to the head of the river, the Falls, where they set up the cross and proclaimed King James of England.

Smith says in his "General Historie" they reached Powhatan on the 26th. But Captain Newport's "Relatyon" agrees with Percy's, and with, Smith's "True Relation." Captain Newport, says Percy, permitted no one to visit Powhatan except himself.

Captain Newport's narration of the exploration of the James is interesting, being the first account we have of this historic river. At the junction of the Appomattox and the James, at a place he calls Wynauk, the natives welcomed them with rejoicing and entertained them with dances. The Kingdom of Wynauk was full of pearl-mussels. The king of this tribe was at war with the King of Paspahegh. Sixteen miles above this point, at an inlet, perhaps Turkey Point, they were met by eight savages in a canoe, one of whom was intelligent enough to lay out the whole course of the river, from Chesapeake Bay to its source, with a pen and paper which they showed him how to use. These Indians kept them company for some time, meeting them here and there with presents of strawberries, mulberries, bread, and fish, for which they received pins, needles, and beads. They spent one night at Poore Cottage (the Port Cotage of Percy, where he saw the white boy), probably now Haxall. Five miles above they went ashore near the now famous Dutch Gap, where King Arahatic gave them a roasted deer, and caused his women to bake cakes for them. This king gave Newport his crown, which was of deer's hair dyed red. He was a subject of the great King Powhatan. While they sat making merry with the savages, feasting and taking tobacco and seeing the dances, Powhatan himself appeared and was received with great show of honor, all rising from their seats except King Arahatic, and shouting loudly. To Powhatan ample presents were made of penny-knives, shears, and toys, and he invited them to visit him at one of his seats called Powhatan, which was within a mile of the Falls, where now stands the city of Richmond. All along the shore the inhabitants stood in clusters, offering food to the strangers. The habitation of Powhatan was situated on a high hill by the water side, with a meadow at its foot where was grown wheat, beans, tobacco, peas, pompions, flax, and hemp.

Powhatan served the whites with the best he had, and best of all with a friendly welcome and with interesting discourse of the country. They made a league of friendship. The next day he gave them six men as guides to the falls above, and they left with him one man as a hostage.

On Sunday, the 24th of May, having returned to Powhatan's seat, they made a feast for him of pork, cooked with peas, and the Captain and King ate familiarly together; "he eat very freshly of our meats, dranck of our beere, aquavite, and sack." Under the influence of this sack and aquavite the King was very communicative about the interior of the country, and promised to guide them to the mines of iron and copper; but the wary chief seems to have thought better of it when he got sober, and put them off with the difficulties and dangers of the way.

On one of the islets below the Falls, Captain Newport set up a cross with the inscription "Jacobus, Rex, 1607," and his own name beneath, and James was proclaimed King with a great shout. Powhatan was displeased with their importunity to go further up the river, and departed with all the Indians, except the friendly Navirans, who had accompanied them from Arahatic. Navirans greatly admired the cross, but

Newport hit upon an explanation of its meaning that should dispel the suspicions of Powhatan. He told him that the two arms of the cross signified King Powhatan and himself, the fastening of it in the middle was their united league, and the shout was the reverence he did to Powhatan. This explanation being made to Powhatan greatly contented him, and he came on board and gave them the kindest farewell when they dropped down the river. At Arahatic they found the King had provided victuals for them, but, says Newport, "the King told us that he was very sick and not able to sit up long with us." The inability of the noble red man to sit up was no doubt due to too much Christian sack and aquavite, for on "Monday he came to the water side, and we went ashore with him again. He told us that our hot drinks, he thought, caused him grief, but that he was well again, and we were very welcome."

It seems, therefore, that to Captain Newport, who was a good sailor in his day, and has left his name in Virginia in Newport News, must be given the distinction of first planting the cross in Virginia, with a lie, and watering it, with aquavite.

They dropped down the river to a place called Mulberry Shade, where the King killed a deer and prepared for them another feast, at which they had rolls and cakes made of wheat. "This the women make and are very cleanly about it. We had parched meal, excellent good, sodd [cooked] beans, which eat as sweet as filbert kernels, in a manner, straw-berries; and mulberries were shaken off the tree, dropping on our heads as we sat. He made ready a land turtle, which we ate; and showed that he was heartily rejoiced in our company." Such was the amiable disposition of the natives before they discovered the purpose of the whites to dispossess them of their territory. That night they stayed at a place called "Kynd Woman's Care," where the people offered them abundant victual and craved nothing in return.

Next day they went ashore at a place Newport calls Queen Apumatuc's Bower. This Queen, who owed allegiance to Powhatan, had much land under cultivation, and dwelt in state on a pretty hill. This ancient representative of woman's rights in Virginia did honor to her sex. She came to meet the strangers in a show as majestical as that of Powhatan himself: "She had an usher before her, who brought her to the matt prepared under a faire mulberry-tree; where she sat down by herself, with a stayed countenance. She would permitt none to stand or sitt neare her. She is a fatt, lustie, manly woman. She had much copper about her neck, a coronet of copper upon her hed. She had long, black haire, which hanged loose down her back to her myddle; which only part was covered with a deare's skyn, and ells all naked. She had her women attending her, adorned much like herself (except they wanted the copper). Here we had our accustomed eates, tobacco, and welcome. Our Captaine presented her with guyfts liberally, whereupon shee cheered somewhat her countenance, and requested him to shoote off a piece; whereat (we noted) she showed not near the like feare as Arahatic, though he be a goodly man."

The company was received with the same hospitality by King Pamunkey, whose land was believed to be rich in copper and pearls. The copper was so flexible that Captain Newport bent a piece of it the thickness of his finger as if it had been lead. The natives were unwilling to part with it. The King had about his neck a string of pearls as big as peas, which would have been worth three or four hundred pounds, if the pearls had been taken from the mussels as they should have been.

Arriving on their route at Weanock, some twenty miles above the fort, they were minded to visit Paspahegh and another chief Jamestown lay in the territory of Paspahegh—but suspicious signs among the natives made them apprehend trouble at the fort, and they hastened thither to find their suspicions verified. The day before, May 26th, the colony had been attacked by two hundred Indians (four hundred, Smith says), who were only beaten off when they had nearly entered the fort, by the use of the artillery. The Indians made a valiant fight for an hour; eleven white men were wounded, of whom one died afterwards, and a boy was killed on the pinnace. This loss was concealed from the Indians, who for some time seem to have believed that the whites could not be hurt. Four of the Council were hurt in this fight, and President Wingfield, who showed himself a valiant gentleman, had a shot through his beard. They killed eleven of the Indians, but their comrades lugged them away on their backs and buried them in the woods with a great noise. For several days alarms and attacks continued, and four or five men were cruelly wounded, and one gentleman, Mr. Eustace Cloville, died from the effects of five arrows in his body.

Upon this hostility, says Smith, the President was contented the fort should be palisaded, and the ordnance mounted, and the men armed and exercised. The fortification went on, but the attacks continued, and it was unsafe for any to venture beyond the fort.

Dissatisfaction arose evidently with President Wingfield's management. Captain Newport says: "There being among the gentlemen and all the company a murmur and grudge against certain proceedings and inconvenient courses [Newport] put up a petition to the Council for reformation." The Council heeded this petition, and urged to amity by Captain Newport, the company vowed faithful love to each other and obedience to the superiors. On the 10th of June, Captain Smith was sworn of the Council. In his "General

Historie," not published till 1624, he says: "Many were the mischiefs that daily sprung from their ignorant (yet ambitious) spirits; but the good doctrine and exhortation of our preacher Mr. Hunt, reconciled them and caused Captain Smith to be admitted to the Council." The next day they all partook of the holy communion.

In order to understand this quarrel, which was not by any means appeased by this truce, and to determine Captain Smith's responsibility for it, it is necessary to examine all the witnesses. Smith is unrestrained in his expression of his contempt for Wingfield. But in the diary of Wingfield we find no accusation against Smith at this date. Wingfield says that Captain Newport before he departed asked him how he thought himself settled in the government, and that he replied "that no disturbance could endanger him or the colony, but it must be wrought either by Captain Gosnold or Mr. Archer, for the one was strong with friends and followers and could if he would; and the other was troubled with an ambitious spirit and would if he could."

The writer of Newport's "Relatyon" describes the Virginia savages as a very strong and lusty race, and swift warriors. "Their skin is tawny; not so borne, but with dyeing and painting themselves, in which they delight greatly." That the Indians were born white was, as we shall see hereafter, a common belief among the first settlers in Virginia and New England. Percy notes a distinction between maids and married women: "The maids shave close the fore part and sides of their heads, and leave it long behind, where it is tied up and hangs down to the hips. The married women wear their hair all of a length, but tied behind as that of maids is. And the women scratch on their bodies and limbs, with a sharp iron, pictures of fowls, fish, and beasts, and rub into the 'drawings' lively colors which dry into the flesh and are permanent." The "Relatyon" says the people are witty and ingenious and allows them many good qualities, but makes this exception: "The people steal anything comes near them; yea, are so practiced in this art, that looking in our face, they would with their foot, between their toes, convey a chisel, knife, percer, or any indifferent light thing, which having once conveyed, they hold it an injury to take the same from them. They are naturally given to treachery; howbeit we could not find it in our travel up the river, but rather a most kind and loving people."

# VI

## QUARRELS AND HARDSHIPS

On Sunday, June 21st, they took the communion lovingly together. That evening Captain Newport gave a farewell supper on board his vessel. The 22d he sailed in the Susan Constant for England, carrying specimens of the woods and minerals, and made the short passage of five weeks. Dudley Carleton, in a letter to John Chamberlain dated Aug. 18, 1607, writes "that Captain Newport has arrived without gold or silver, and that the adventurers, cumbered by the presence of the natives, have fortified themselves at a place called Jamestown." The colony left numbered one hundred and four.

The good harmony of the colony did not last. There were other reasons why the settlement was unprosperous. The supply of wholesome provisions was inadequate. The situation of the town near the Chickahominy swamps was not conducive to health, and although Powhatan had sent to make peace with them, and they also made a league of amity with the chiefs Paspahegh and Tapahanagh, they evidently had little freedom of movement beyond sight of their guns. Percy says they were very bare and scant of victuals, and in wars and dangers with the savages.

Smith says in his "True Relation," which was written on the spot, and is much less embittered than his "General Historie," that they were in good health and content when Newport departed, but this did not long continue, for President Wingfield and Captain Gosnold, with the most of the Council, were so discontented with each other that nothing was done with discretion, and no business transacted with wisdom. This he charges upon the "hard-dealing of the President," the rest of the Council being diversely affected through his audacious command. "Captain Martin, though honest, was weak and sick; Smith was in disgrace through the malice of others; and God sent famine and sickness, so that the living were scarce able to bury the dead. Our want of sufficient good food, and continual watching, four or five each night, at three bulwarks, being the chief cause; only of sturgeon we had great store, whereon we would so greedily surfeit, as it cost many their lives; the sack, Aquavite, and other preservations of our health being kept in the President's hands, for his own diet and his few associates."

In his "General Historie," written many years later, Smith enlarges this indictment with some touches of humor characteristic of him. He says:

"Being thus left to our fortunes, it fortuned that within ten days scarce ten amongst us could either go, or well stand, such extreme weakness and sicknes oppressed us. And thereat none need marvaile if they consider the cause and reason, which was this: whilst the ships stayed, our allowance was somewhat bettered, by a daily proportion of Bisket, which the sailors would pilfer to sell, give, or exchange with us for money, Saxefras, furres, or love. But when they departed, there remained neither taverne, beere-house, nor place of reliefe, but the common Kettell. Had we beene as free from all sinnes as gluttony, and drunkennesse, we might have been canonized for Saints. But our President would never have been admitted, for ingrissing to his private, Oatmeale, Sacke, Oyle, Aquavitz, Beef, Egges, or what not, but the Kettell: that indeed he allowed equally to be distributed, and that was half a pint of wheat, and as much barley boyled with water for a man a day, and this being fryed some twenty-six weeks in the ship's hold, contained as many wormes as graines; so that we might truly call it rather so much bran than corrne, our drinke was water, our lodgings Castles in the ayre; with this lodging and dyet, our extreme toile in bearing and planting Pallisadoes, so strained and bruised us, and our continual labour in the extremitie of the heat had so weakened us, as were cause sufficient to have made us miserable in our native countrey, or any other place in the world."

Affairs grew worse. The sufferings of this colony in the summer equaled that of the Pilgrims at Plymouth in the winter and spring. Before September forty-one were buried, says Wingfield; fifty, says Smith in one statement, and forty-six in another; Percy gives a list of twenty-four who died in August and September. Late in August Wingfield said, "Sickness had not now left us seven able men in our town." "As yet," writes Smith in September, "we had no houses to cover us, our tents were rotten, and our cabins worse than nought."

Percy gives a doleful picture of the wretchedness of the colony: "Our men were destroyed with cruel sickness, as swellings, fluxes, burning-fevers, and by wars, and some departed suddenly, but for the most part they died of mere famine.... We watched every three nights, lying on the cold bare ground what weather soever came, worked all the next day, which brought our men to be most feeble wretches, our food was but a small can of barley, sod in water to five men a day, our drink but cold water taken out of the river, which was at the flood very salt, at a low tide full of shrimp and filth, which was the destruction of many of our men. Thus we lived for the space of five months in this miserable distress, but having five able men to man our bulwarks upon any occasion. If it had not pleased God to put a terror in the savage hearts, we had all perished by those wild and cruel Pagans, being in that weak state as we were: our men night and day groaning in every corner of the fort, most pitiful to hear. If there were any conscience in men, it would make their hearts to bleed to hear the pitiful murmurings and outcries of our sick men, without relief, every night and day, for the space of six weeks: some departing out of the world; many times three or four in a night; in the morning their bodies trailed out of their cabins, like dogs, to be buried. In this sort did I see the mortality of divers of our people."

A severe loss to the colony was the death on the 22d of August of Captain Bartholomew Gosnold, one of the Council, a brave and adventurous mariner, and, says Wingfield, a "worthy and religious gentleman." He was honorably buried, "having all the ordnance in the fort shot off with many volleys of small shot." If the Indians had known that those volleys signified the mortality of their comrades, the colony would no doubt have been cut off entirely. It is a melancholy picture, this disheartened and half-famished band of men quarreling among themselves; the occupation of the half-dozen able men was nursing the sick and digging graves. We anticipate here by saying, on the authority of a contemporary manuscript in the State Paper office, that when Captain Newport arrived with the first supply in January, 1608, "he found the colony consisting of no more than forty persons; of those, ten only able men."

After the death of Gosnold, Captain Kendall was deposed from the Council and put in prison for sowing discord between the President and Council, says Wingfield; for heinous matters which were proved against him, says Percy;

for "divers reasons," says Smith, who sympathized with his dislike of Wingfield. The colony was in very low estate at this time, and was only saved from famine by the providential good-will of the Indians, who brought them corn half ripe, and presently meat and fruit in abundance.

On the 7th of September the chief Paspahegh gave a token of peace by returning a white boy who had run away from camp, and other runaways were returned by other chiefs, who reported that they had been well used in their absence. By these returns Mr. Wingfield was convinced that the Indians were not cannibals, as Smith believed.

On the 10th of September Mr. Wingfield was deposed from the presidency and the Council, and Captain John Ratcliffe was elected President. Concerning the deposition there has been much dispute; but the accounts of it by Captain Smith and his friends, so long accepted as the truth, must be modified by Mr. Wingfield's "Discourse of Virginia," more recently come to light, which is, in a sense, a defense of his conduct.

In his "True Relation" Captain Smith is content to say that "Captain Wingfield, having ordered the affairs in such sort that he was hated of them all, in which respect he was with one accord deposed from the presidency."

In the "General Historie" the charges against him, which we have already quoted, are extended, and a new one is added, that is, a purpose of deserting the colony in the pinnace: "the rest seeing the President's projects to escape these miseries in our pinnace by flight (who all this time had neither felt want nor sickness), so moved our dead spirits we deposed him."

In the scarcity of food and the deplorable sickness and death, it was inevitable that extreme dissatisfaction should be felt with the responsible head. Wingfield was accused of keeping the best of the supplies to himself. The commonalty may have believed this. Smith himself must have known that the supplies were limited, but have been willing to take advantage of this charge to depose the President, who was clearly in many ways incompetent for his trying position. It appears by Mr. Wingfield's statement that the supply left with the colony was very scant, a store that would only last thirteen weeks and a half, and prudence in the distribution of it, in the uncertainty of Newport's return, was a necessity. Whether Wingfield used the delicacies himself is a question which cannot be settled. In his defense, in all we read of him, except that written by Smith and his friends, he seems to be a temperate and just man, little qualified to control the bold spirits about him.

As early as July, "in his sickness time, the President did easily fortell his own deposing from his command," so much did he differ from the Council in the management of the colony. Under date of September 7th he says that the Council demanded a larger allowance for themselves and for some of the sick, their favorites, which he declined to give without their warrants as councilors. Captain Martin of the Council was till then ignorant that only store for thirteen and a half weeks was in the hands of the Cape Merchant, or treasurer, who was at that time Mr. Thomas Studley. Upon a representation to the Council of the lowness of the stores, and the length of time that must elapse before the harvest of grain, they declined to enlarge the allowance, and even ordered that every meal of fish or flesh should excuse the allowance of porridge. Mr. Wingfield goes on to say: "Nor was the common store of oyle, vinegar, sack, and aquavite all spent, saving two gallons of each: the sack reserved for the Communion table, the rest for such extremities as might fall upon us, which the President had only made known to Captain Gosnold; of which course he liked well. The vessels wear, therefore, boonged upp. When Mr. Gosnold was dead, the President did acquaint the rest of the Council with the said remnant; but, Lord, how they then longed for to supp up that little remnant: for they had now emptied all their own bottles, and all other that they could smell out."

Shortly after this the Council again importuned the President for some better allowance for themselves and for the sick. He protested his impartiality, showed them that if the portions were distributed according to their request the colony would soon starve; he still offered to deliver what they pleased on their warrants, but would not himself take the responsibility of distributing all the stores, and when he divined the reason of their impatience he besought them to bestow the presidency among themselves, and he would be content to obey as a private. Meantime the Indians were bringing in supplies of corn and meat, the men were so improved in health that thirty were able to work, and provision for three weeks' bread was laid up.

Nevertheless, says Mr. Wingfield, the Council had fully plotted to depose him. Of the original seven there remained, besides Mr. Wingfield, only three in the Council. Newport was in England, Gosnold was dead, and Kendall deposed. Mr. Wingfield charged that the three—Ratcliffe, Smith, and Martin—forsook the instructions of his Majesty, and set up a Triumvirate. At any rate, Wingfield was forcibly deposed from the Council on the 10th of September. If the object had been merely to depose him, there was an easier way, for Wingfield was ready to resign. But it appears, by subsequent proceedings, that they wished to fasten upon him the charge of embezzlement, the responsibility of the sufferings of the colony, and to mulct him in fines. He was arrested, and confined on the pinnace. Mr. Ratcliffe was made President.

On the 11th of September Mr. Wingfield was brought before

the Council sitting as a court, and heard the charges against him. They were, as Mr. Wingfield says, mostly frivolous trifles. According to his report they were these:

First, Mister President [Radcliffe] said that I had denied him a penny whitle, a chicken, a spoonful of beer, and served him with foul corn; and with that pulled some grain out of a bag, showing it to the company.

Then starts up Mr. Smith and said that I had told him plainly how he lied; and that I said, though we were equal here, yet if we were in England, he [I] would think scorn his man should be my companion.

Mr. Martin followed with: "He reported that I do slack the service in the colony, and do nothing but tend my pot, spit, and oven; but he hath starved my son, and denied him a spoonful of beer. I have friends in England shall be revenged on him, if ever he come in London."

Voluminous charges were read against Mr. Wingfield by Mr. Archer, who had been made by the Council, Recorder of Virginia, the author, according to Wingfield, of three several mutinies, as "always hatching of some mutiny in my time."

Mr. Percy sent him word in his prison that witnesses were hired to testify against him by bribes of cakes and by threats. If Mr. Percy, who was a volunteer in this expedition, and a man of high character, did send this information, it shows that he sympathized with him, and this is an important piece of testimony to his good character.

Wingfield saw no way of escape from the malice of his accusers, whose purpose he suspected was to fine him fivefold for all the supplies whose disposition he could not account for in writing: but he was finally allowed to appeal

Charles Dudley Warner

to the King for mercy, and recommitted to the pinnace. In regard to the charge of embezzlement, Mr. Wingfield admitted that it was impossible to render a full account: he had no bill of items from the Cape Merchant when he received the stores, he had used the stores for trade and gifts with the Indians; Captain Newport had done the same in his expedition, without giving any memorandum. Yet he averred that he never expended the value of these penny whittles [small pocket-knives] to his private use.

There was a mutinous and riotous spirit on shore, and the Council professed to think Wingfield's life was in danger. He says: "In all these disorders was Mr. Archer a ringleader." Meantime the Indians continued to bring in supplies, and the Council traded up and down the river for corn, and for this energy Mr. Wingfield gives credit to "Mr. Smith especially," "which relieved the colony well." To the report that was brought him that he was charged with starving the colony, he replies with some natural heat and a little show of petulance, that may be taken as an evidence of weakness, as well as of sincerity, and exhibiting the undignified nature of all this squabbling:

"I did alwaises give every man his allowance faithfully, both of corne, oyle, aquivite, etc., as was by the counsell proportioned: neyther was it bettered after my tyme, untill, towards th' end of March, a bisket was allowed to every working man for his breakfast, by means of the provision brought us by Captn. Newport: as will appeare hereafter. It is further said, I did much banquit and ryot. I never had but one squirrel roasted; whereof I gave part to Mr. Ratcliffe then sick: yet was that squirrel given me. I did never heate a flesh pott but when the comon pott was so used likewise. Yet how often Mr. President's and the Counsellors' spitts have night and daye bene endaungered to break their backes-so, laden with swanns, geese, ducks, etc.! how many times their flesh potts have swelled, many hungrie eies did behold, to their great longing: and what great theeves and theeving thear hath been in the comon stoare since my tyme, I doubt not but is already made knowne to his Majesty's Councell for Virginia."

Poor Wingfield was not left at ease in his confinement. On the 17th he was brought ashore to answer the charge of Jehu [John?] Robinson that he had with Robinson and others intended to run away with the pinnace to Newfoundland; and the charge by Mr. Smith that he had accused Smith of intending mutiny. To the first accuser the jury awarded one hundred pounds, and to the other two hundred pounds damages, for slander. "Seeing their law so speedy and cheap," Mr. Wingfield thought he would try to recover a copper kettle he had lent Mr. Crofts, worth half its weight in gold. But Crofts swore that Wingfield had given it to him, and he lost his kettle: "I told Mr. President I had not known the like law, and prayed they would be more sparing of law till we had more witt or wealthe." Another day they obtained from Wingfield the key to his coffers, and took all his accounts, note-books, and "owne proper goods," which he could never recover. Thus was I made good prize on all sides.

During one of Smith's absences on the river President Ratcliffe did beat James Read, the blacksmith. Wingfield says the Council were continually beating the men for their own pleasure. Read struck back.

For this he was condemned to be hanged; but "before he turned of the lather," he desired to speak privately with the President, and thereupon accused Mr. Kendall—who had been released from the pinnace when Wingfield was sent aboard—of mutiny. Read escaped. Kendall was convicted of mutiny and shot to death. In arrest of judgment he objected that the President had no authority to pronounce judgment because his name was Sicklemore and not Ratcliffe. This was true, and Mr. Martin pronounced the sentence. In his "True Relation," Smith agrees with this statement of the death of Kendall, and says that he was tried by a jury. It illustrates the general looseness of the "General Historie," written and compiled many years afterwards, that this transaction there appears as follows: "Wingfield and Kendall being in disgrace, seeing all things at random in the absence of Smith, the company's dislike of their President's weakness, and their small love to Martin's never-mending sickness, strengthened themselves with the sailors and other confederates to regain their power, control, and authority, or at least such meanes aboard the pinnace (being fitted to sail as Smith had appointed for trade) to alter her course and to goe for England. Smith unexpectedly returning had the plot discovered to him, much trouble he had to prevent it, till with store of sakre and musket-shot he forced them to stay or sink in the river, which action cost the life of Captain Kendall."

In a following sentence he says: "The President [Ratcliffe] and Captain Archer not long after intended also to have abandoned the country, which project also was curbed and suppressed by Smith." Smith was always suppressing attempts at flight, according to his own story, unconfirmed by any other writers. He had before accused President Wingfield of a design to escape in the pinnace.

Communications were evidently exchanged with Mr. Wingfield on the pinnace, and the President was evidently ill at ease about him. One day he was summoned ashore, but declined to go, and requested an interview with ten gentlemen. To those who came off to him he said that he had determined to go to England to make known the weakness of the colony, that he could not live under the laws and usurpations of the Triumvirate; however, if the President and Mr. Archer would go, he was willing to stay and take his fortune with the colony, or he would contribute one hundred pounds towards taking the colony home. "They did like none of my proffers, but made divers shott at uss in the pynnasse." Thereupon he went ashore and had a conference.

On the 10th of December Captain Smith departed on his famous expedition up the Chickahominy, during which the alleged Pocahontas episode occurred. Mr. Wingfield's condensed account of this journey and captivity we shall refer to hereafter. In Smith's absence President Ratcliffe, contrary to his oath, swore Mr. Archer one of the Council; and Archer was no sooner settled in authority than he sought to take Smith's life. The enmity of this man must be regarded as a long credit mark to Smith. Archer had him indicted upon a chapter in Leviticus (they all wore a garb of piety) for the death of two men who were killed by the Indians on his expedition. "He had had his trials the same daie of his retourne," says Wingfield, "and I believe his hanging the same, or the next daie, so speedy is our law there. But it pleased God to send Captain Newport unto us the same evening, to our unspeakable comfort; whose arrivall saved Mr. Smyth's leif and mine, because he took me out of the pynnasse, and gave me leave to lyve in the towne. Also by his comyng was prevented a parliament, which the newe counsailor, Mr. Recorder, intended thear to summon."

Captain Newport's arrival was indeed opportune. He was the only one of the Council whose character and authority seem to have been generally respected, the only one who could restore any sort of harmony and curb the factious humors of the other leaders. Smith should have all credit for his energy in procuring supplies, for his sagacity in dealing with the Indians, for better sense than most of the other colonists exhibited, and for more fidelity to the objects of the plantation than most of them; but where ability to rule is claimed for him, at this juncture we can but contrast the deference shown by all to Newport with the want of it given to Smith. Newport's presence at once quelled all the uneasy spirits.

Newport's arrival, says Wingfield, "saved Mr Smith's life and mine." Smith's account of the episode is substantially the same. In his "True Relation" he says on his return to the fort "each man with truest signs of joy they could express welcomed me, except Mr. Archer, and some two or three of his, who was then in my absence sworn councilor, though not with the consent of Captain Martin; great blame and imputation was laid upon me by them for the loss of our two men which the Indians slew: insomuch that they purposed to depose me, but in the midst of my miseries, it pleased God to send Captain Newport, who arriving there the same night, so tripled our joy, as for a while those plots against me were deferred, though with much malice against me, which Captain Newport in short time did plainly see." In his "Map of Virginia," the Oxford tract of 1612, Smith does not allude to this; but in the "General Historie" it had assumed a different aspect in his mind, for at the time of writing that he was the irresistible hero, and remembered himself as always nearly omnipotent in Virginia. Therefore, instead of expressions of gratitude to Newport we read this: "Now in Jamestown they were all in combustion, the strongest preparing once more to run away with the pinnace; which with the hazard of his life, with Sakre, falcon and musket shot, Smith forced now the third time to stay or sink. Some no better than they should be, had plotted to put him to death by the Levitical law, for the lives of Robinson and Emry, pretending that the fault was his, that led them to their ends; but he quickly took such order with such Lawyers, that he laid them by the heels till he sent some of them prisoners to England."

Clearly Captain Smith had no authority to send anybody prisoner to England. When Newport returned, April 10th,

Wingfield and Archer went with him. Wingfield no doubt desired to return. Archer was so insolent, seditious, and libelous that he only escaped the halter by the interposition of Newport. The colony was willing to spare both these men, and probably Newport it was who decided they should go. As one of the Council, Smith would undoubtedly favor their going. He says in the "General Historie": "We not having any use of parliaments, plaises, petitions, admirals, recorders, inter-preters, chronologers, courts of plea, or justices of peace, sent Master Wingfield and Captain Archer home with him, that had engrossed all those titles, to seek some better place of employment." Mr. Wingfield never returned. Captain Archer returned in 1609, with the expedition of Gates and Somers, as master of one of the ships.

Newport had arrived with the first supply on the 8th of January, 1608. The day before, according to Wingfield, a fire occurred which destroyed nearly all the town, with the clothing and provisions. According to Smith, who is probably correct in this, the fire did not occur till five or six days after the arrival of the ship. The date is uncertain, and some doubt is also thrown upon the date of the arrival of the ship. It was on the day of Smith's return from captivity: and that captivity lasted about four weeks if the return was January 8th, for he started on the expedition December 10th. Smith subsequently speaks of his captivity lasting six or seven weeks.

In his "General Historie" Smith says the fire happened after the return of the expedition of Newport, Smith, and Scrivener to the Pamunkey: "Good Master Hunt, our Preacher, lost all his library, and all he had but the clothes on his back; yet none ever heard him repine at his loss." This excellent and devoted man is the only one of these first pioneers of whom everybody speaks well, and he deserved all affection and respect.

One of the first labors of Newport was to erect a suitable church. Services had been held under many disadvantages, which Smith depicts in his "Advertisements for Unexperienced Planters," published in London in 1631:

"When I first went to Virginia, I well remember, we did hang an awning (which is an old saile) to three or foure trees to shadow us from the Sunne, our walls were rales of wood, our seats unhewed trees, till we cut plankes, our Pulpit a bar of wood nailed to two neighboring trees, in foule weather we shifted into an old rotten tent, for we had few better, and this came by the way of adventure for me; this was our Church, till we built a homely thing like a barne, set upon Cratchets, covered with rafts, sedge and earth, so was also the walls: the best of our houses of the like curiosity, but the most part farre much worse workmanship, that could neither well defend wind nor raine, yet we had daily Common Prayer morning and evening, every day two Sermons, and every three moneths the holy Communion, till our Minister died, [Robert Hunt] but our Prayers daily, with an Homily on Sundaies."

It is due to Mr. Wingfield, who is about to disappear from Virginia, that something more in his defense against the charges of Smith and the others should be given. It is not possible now to say how the suspicion of his religious soundness arose, but there seems to have been a notion that he had papal tendencies. His grandfather, Sir Richard Wingfield, was buried in Toledo, Spain. His father, Thomas Maria Wingfield, was christened by Queen Mary and Cardinal Pole. These facts perhaps gave rise to the suspicion. He answers them with some dignity and simplicity, and with a little querulousness:

"It is noised that I combyned with the Spanniards to the distruccion of the Collony; that I ame an atheist, because I carryed not a Bible with me, and because I did forbid the preacher to preache; that I affected a kingdome; that I did hide of the comon provision in the ground.

"I confesse I have alwayes admyred any noble vertue and prowesse, as well in the Spanniards (as in other nations): but naturally I have alwayes distrusted and disliked their neighborhoode. I sorted many bookes in my house, to be sent up to me at my goeing to Virginia; amongst them a Bible. They were sent up in a trunk to London, with divers fruite, conserves, and preserves, which I did sett in Mr. Crofts his house in Ratcliff. In my beeing at Virginia, I did understand my trunk was thear broken up, much lost, my sweetmeates eaten at his table, some of my bookes which I missed to be seene in his hands: and whether amongst them my Bible was so ymbeasiled or mislayed by my servants, and not sent me, I knowe not as yet.

"Two or three Sunday mornings, the Indians gave us allarums at our towne. By that tymes they weare answered, the place about us well discovered, and our devyne service ended, the daie was farr spent. The preacher did aske me if it were my pleasure to have a sermon: hee said hee was prepared for it. I made answere, that our men were weary and hungry, and that he did see the time of the daie farr past (for at other tymes bee never made such question, but, the service finished he began his sermon); and that, if it pleased him, wee would spare him till some other tyme. I never failed to take such noates by wrighting out of his doctrine as my capacity could comprehend, unless some raynie day hindred my endeavor. My mynde never swelled with such ympossible mountebank humors as could make me affect any other kingdome than the kingdom of heaven.

"As truly as God liveth, I gave an ould man, then the keeper of the private store, 2 glasses with sallet oyle which I brought with me out of England for my private stoare, and willed him to bury it in the ground, for that I feared the great heate would spoile it. Whatsoever was more, I did never consent unto or know of it, and as truly was it protested unto me, that all the remaynder before mencioned of the oyle, wyne, &c., which the President receyved of me when I was deposed they themselves poored into their owne bellyes.

"To the President's and Counsell's objections I saie that I doe knowe curtesey and civility became a governor. No penny whittle was asked me, but a knife, whereof I have none to spare The Indyans had long before stoallen my knife. Of chickins I never did eat but one, and that in my sicknes. Mr. Ratcliff had before that time tasted Of 4 or 5. I had by my owne huswiferie bred above 37, and the most part of them my owne poultrye; of all which, at my comyng awaie, I did not see three living. I never denyed him (or any other) beare, when I had it. The corne was of the same which we all lived upon.

"Mr. Smyth, in the time of our hungar, had spread a rumor in the Collony, that I did feast myself and my servants out of the comon stoare, with entent (as I gathered) to have stirred the discontented company against me. I told him privately, in Mr. Gosnold's tent, that indeede I had caused half a pint of pease to be sodden with a peese of pork, of my own provision, for a poore old man, which in a sicknes (whereof he died) he much desired; and said, that if out of his malice he had given it out otherwise, that hee did tell a leye. It was proved to his face, that he begged in Ireland like a rogue, without a lycence. To such I would not my nam should be a companyon."

The explanation about the Bible as a part of his baggage is a little far-fetched, and it is evident that that book was not his daily companion. Whether John Smith habitually carried one about with him we are not informed. The whole passage quoted gives us a curious picture of the mind and of the habits of the time. This allusion to John Smith's begging is the only reference we can find to his having been in Ireland. If he was there it must have been in that interim in his own narrative between his return from Morocco and his going to Virginia. He was likely enough to seek adventure there, as the hangers-on of the court in Raleigh's day occasionally did, and perhaps nothing occurred during his visit there that he cared to celebrate. If he went to Ireland he probably got in straits there, for that was his usual luck.

Whatever is the truth about Mr. Wingfield's inefficiency and embezzlement of corn meal, Communion sack, and penny whittles, his enemies had no respect for each other or concord among themselves. It is Wingfield's testimony that Ratcliffe said he would not have been deposed if he had visited Ratcliffe during his sickness. Smith said that Wingfield would not have been deposed except for Archer; that the charges against him were frivolous. Yet, says Wingfield, "I do believe him the first and only practiser in these practices," and he attributed Smith's hostility to the fact that "his name was mentioned in the intended and confessed mutiny by Galthrop." Noother reference is made to this mutiny. Galthrop was one of those who died in the previous August.

One of the best re-enforcements of the first supply was Matthew Scrivener, who was appointed one of the Council. He was a sensible man, and he and Smith worked together in harmony for some time. They were intent upon building up the colony. Everybody else in the camp was crazy about the prospect of gold: there was, says Smith, "no talk, no hope, no work, but dig gold, wash gold, refine gold, load gold, such a bruit of gold that one mad fellow desired to be buried in the sands, lest they should by their art make gold of his bones."

Charles Dudley Warner

He charges that Newport delayed his return to England on account of this gold fever, in order to load his vessel (which remained fourteen weeks when it might have sailed in fourteen days) with gold-dust. Captain Martin seconded Newport in this; Smith protested against it; he thought Newport was no refiner, and it did torment him "to see all necessary business neglected, to fraught such a drunken ship with so much gilded durt." This was the famous load of gold that proved to be iron pyrites.

In speaking of the exploration of the James River as far as the Falls by Newport, Smith, and Percy, we have followed the statements of Percy and the writer of Newport's discovery that they saw the great Powhatan. There is much doubt of this. Smith in his "True Relation" does not say so; in his voyage up the Chickahominy he seems to have seen Powhatan for the first time; and Wingfield speaks of Powhatan, on Smith's return from that voyage, as one "of whom before we had no knowledge." It is conjectured that the one seen at Powhatan's seat near the Falls was a son of the "Emperor." It was partly the exaggeration of the times to magnify discoveries, and partly English love of high titles, that attributed such titles as princes, emperors, and kings to the half-naked barbarians and petty chiefs of Virginia.

In all the accounts of the colony at this period, no mention is made of women, and it is not probable that any went over with the first colonists. The character of the men was not high. Many of them were "gentlemen" adventurers, turbulent spirits, who would not work, who were much better fitted for piratical maraudings than the labor of founding a state. The historian must agree with the impression conveyed by Smith, that it was poor material out of which to make a colony.

# VII

## SMITH TO THE FRONT

It is now time to turn to Smith's personal adventures among the Indians during this period. Almost our only authority is Smith himself, or such presumed writings of his companions as he edited or rewrote. Strachey and others testify to his energy in procuring supplies for the colony, and his success in dealing with the Indians, and it seems likely that the colony would have famished but for his exertions. Whatever suspicion attaches to Smith's relation of his own exploits, it must never be forgotten that he was a man of extraordinary executive ability, and had many good qualities to offset his vanity and impatience of restraint.

After the departure of Wingfield, Captain Smith was constrained to act as Cape Merchant; the leaders were sick or discontented, the rest were in despair, and would rather starve and rot than do anything for their own relief, and the Indian trade was decreasing. Under these circumstances, Smith says in his "True Relation," "I was sent to the mouth of the river, to Kegquoughtan [now Hampton], an Indian Towne, to trade for corn, and try the river for fish." The Indians, thinking them near famished, tantalized them with offers of little bits of bread in exchange for a hatchet or a piece of copper, and Smith offered trifles in return. The next

Charles Dudley Warner

day the Indians were anxious to trade. Smith sent men up to their town, a display of force was made by firing four guns, and the Indians kindly traded, giving fish, oysters, bread, and deer. The town contained eighteen houses, and heaps of grain. Smith obtained fifteen bushels of it, and on his homeward way he met two canoes with Indians, whom he accompanied to their villages on the south side of the river, and got from them fifteen bushels more.

This incident is expanded in the "General Historie." After the lapse of fifteen years Smith is able to remember more details, and to conceive himself as the one efficient man who had charge of everything outside the fort, and to represent his dealings with the Indians in a much more heroic and summary manner. He was not sent on the expedition, but went of his own motion. The account opens in this way: "The new President [Ratcliffe] and Martin, being little beloved, of weake judgement in dangers, and loose industrie in peace, committed the management of all things abroad to Captain Smith; who by his own example, good words, and fair promises, set some to mow, others to binde thatch, some to builde houses, others to thatch them, himselfe always bearing the greatest taske for his own share, so that in short time he provided most of them with lodgings, neglecting any for himselfe. This done, seeing the Salvage superfluities beginne to decrease (with some of his workmen) shipped himself in the Shallop to search the country for trade."

In this narration, when the Indians trifled with Smith he fired a volley at them, ran his boat ashore, and pursued them fleeing towards their village, where were great heaps of corn that he could with difficulty restrain his soldiers [six or seven] from taking. The Indians then assaulted them with a hideous noise: "Sixty or seventy of them, some black, some red, some white, some particoloured, came in a square order, singing and dancing out of the woods, with their Okee (which is an Idol made of skinnes, stuffed with mosse, and painted and hung with chains and copper) borne before them; and in this manner being well armed with clubs, targets, bowes and arrowes, they charged the English that so kindly received them with their muskets loaden with pistol shot, that down fell their God, and divers lay sprawling on the ground; the rest fled againe to the woods, and ere long sent men of their Quiyoughkasoucks [conjurors] to offer peace and redeeme the Okee." Good feeling was restored, and the savages brought the English "venison, turkies, wild fowl, bread all that they had, singing and dancing in sign of friendship till they departed." This fantastical account is much more readable than the former bare narration.

The supplies which Smith brought gave great comfort to the despairing colony, which was by this time reasonably fitted with houses. But it was not long before they again ran short of food. In his first narrative Smith says there were some motions made for the President and Captain Arthur to go over to England and procure a supply, but it was with much ado concluded that the pinnace and the barge should go up the river to Powhatan to trade for corn, and the lot fell to Smith to command the expedition. In his "General Historie" a little different complexion is put upon this. On his return, Smith says, he suppressed an attempt to run away with the pinnace to England. He represents that what food "he carefully provided the rest carelessly spent," and there is probably much truth in his charges that the settlers were idle and improvident. He says also that they were in continual broils at this time. It is in the fall of 1607, just before his famous voyage up the Chickahominy, on which he departed December 10th—that he writes: "The President and Captain Arthur intended not long after to have abandoned the country, which project was curbed and suppressed by Smith. The Spaniard never more greedily desired gold than he victual, nor his soldiers more to abandon the country than he to keep it. But finding plenty of corn in the river of Chickahomania, where hundreds of salvages in divers places stood with baskets expecting his coming, and now the winter approaching, the rivers became covered with swans, geese, ducks, and cranes, that we daily feasted with good bread, Virginia peas, pumpions, and putchamins, fish, fowls, and divers sorts of wild beasts as fat as we could eat them, so that none of our Tuftaffaty humorists desired to go to England."

While the Chickahominy expedition was preparing, Smith made a voyage to Popohanock or Quiyoughcohanock, as it is called on his map, a town on the south side of the river, above Jamestown. Here the women and children fled from their homes and the natives refused to trade. They had plenty of corn, but Smith says he had no commission to spoil them. On his return he called at Paspahegh, a town on the north side of the James, and on the map placed higher than Popohanock, but evidently nearer to Jamestown, as he visited it on his return. He obtained ten bushels of corn of the churlish and treacherous natives, who closely watched and dogged the expedition.

Everything was now ready for the journey to Powhatan. Smith had the barge and eight men for trading and discovery, and the pinnace was to follow to take the supplies at convenient landings. On the 9th of November he set out in the barge to explore the Chickahominy, which is described as emptying into the James at Paspahegh, eight miles above the fort. The pinnace was to ascend the river twenty miles to Point Weanock, and to await Smith there. All the month of November Smith toiled up and down the Chickahominy, discovering and visiting many villages, finding the natives kindly disposed and eager to trade, and possessing abundance of corn. Notwithstanding this abundance, many were still mutinous. At this time occurred the President's quarrel with the blacksmith, who, for assaulting the

President, was condemned to death, and released on disclosing a conspiracy of which Captain Kendall was principal; and the latter was executed in his place. Smith returned from a third voyage to the Chickahominy with more supplies, only to find the matter of sending the pinnace to England still debated.

This project, by the help of Captain Martin, he again quieted and at last set forward on his famous voyage into the country of Powhatan and Pocahontas.

# VIII

## THE FAMOUS CHICKAHOMINY VOYAGE

We now enter upon the most interesting episode in the life of the gallant captain, more thrilling and not less romantic than the captivity in Turkey and the tale of the faithful love of the fair young mistress Charatza Tragabigzanda.

Although the conduct of the lovely Charatza in despatching Smith to her cruel brother in Nalbrits, where he led the life of a dog, was never explained, he never lost faith in her. His loyalty to women was equal to his admiration of them, and it was bestowed without regard to race or complexion. Nor is there any evidence that the dusky Pocahontas, who is about to appear, displaced in his heart the image of the too partial Tragabigzanda. In regard to women, as to his own exploits, seen in the light of memory, Smith possessed a creative imagination. He did not create Pocahontas, as perhaps he may have created the beautiful mistress of Bashaw Bogall, but he invested her with a romantic interest which forms a lovely halo about his own memory.

As this voyage up the Chickahominy is more fruitful in its consequences than Jason's voyage to Colchis; as it exhibits the energy, daring, invention, and various accomplishments of Captain Smith, as warrior, negotiator, poet, and narrator;

as it describes Smith's first and only captivity among the Indians; and as it was during this absence of four weeks from Jamestown, if ever, that Pocahontas interposed to prevent the beating out of Smith's brains with a club, I shall insert the account of it in full, both Smith's own varying relations of it, and such contemporary notices of it as now come to light. It is necessary here to present several accounts, just as they stand, and in the order in which they were written, that the reader may see for himself how the story of Pocahontas grew to its final proportions. The real life of Pocahontas will form the subject of another chapter.

The first of these accounts is taken from "The True Relation," written by Captain John Smith, composed in Virginia, the earliest published work relating to the James River Colony. It covers a period of a little more than thirteen months, from the arrival at Cape Henry on April 26, 1607, to the return of Captain Nelson in the Phoenix, June 2, 1608. The manuscript was probably taken home by Captain Nelson, and it was published in London in 1608. Whether it was intended for publication is doubtful; but at that time all news of the venture in Virginia was eagerly sought, and a narrative of this importance would naturally speedily get into print.

In the several copies of it extant there are variations in the titlepage, which was changed while the edition was being printed. In some the name of Thomas Watson is given as the author, in others "A Gentleman of the Colony," and an apology appears signed "T. H.," for the want of knowledge or inadvertence of attributing it to any one except Captain Smith.

There is no doubt that Smith was its author. He was still in Virginia when it was printed, and the printers made sad work of parts of his manuscript. The question has been raised, in view of the entire omission of the name of Pocahontas in connection with this voyage and captivity, whether the manuscript was not cut by those who published it. The reason given for excision is that the promoters of the Virginia scheme were anxious that nothing should appear to discourage capitalists, or to deter emigrants, and that this story of the hostility and cruelty of Powhatan, only averted by the tender mercy of his daughter, would have an unfortunate effect. The answer to this is that the hostility was exhibited by the captivity and the intimation that Smith was being fatted to be eaten, and this was permitted to stand. It is wholly improbable that an incident so romantic, so appealing to the imagination, in an age when wonder-tales were eagerly welcomed, and which exhibited such tender pity in the breast of a savage maiden, and such paternal clemency in a savage chief, would have been omitted. It was calculated to lend a lively interest to the narration, and would be invaluable as an advertisement of the adventure.

[For a full bibliographical discussion of this point the reader is referred to the reprint of "The True Relation," by Charles Deane, Esq., Boston, 1864, the preface and notes to which are a masterpiece of critical analysis.]

That some portions of "The True Relation" were omitted is possible. There is internal evidence of this in the abrupt manner in which it opens, and in the absence of allusions to the discords during the voyage and on the arrival. Captain Smith was not the man to pass over such questions in silence, as his subsequent caustic letter sent home to the Governor and Council of Virginia shows. And it is probable enough that the London promoters would cut out from the "Relation" complaints and evidence of the seditions and helpless state of the colony. The narration of the captivity is consistent as it stands, and wholly inconsistent with the Pocahontas episode.

We extract from the narrative after Smith's departure from Apocant, the highest town inhabited, between thirty and forty miles up the river, and below Orapaks, one of Powhatan's seats, which also appears on his map. He writes:

"Ten miles higher I discovered with the barge; in the midway a great tree hindered my passage, which I cut in two: heere the river became narrower, 8, 9 or 10 foote at a high water, and 6 or 7 at a lowe: the stream exceeding swift, and the bottom hard channell, the ground most part a low plaine, sandy soyle, this occasioned me to suppose it might issue from some lake or some broad ford, for it could not be far to the head, but rather then I would endanger the barge, yet to have beene able to resolve this doubt, and to discharge the imputating malicious tungs, that halfe suspected I durst not for so long delaying, some of the company, as desirous as myself, we resolved to hier a canow, and returne with the barge to Apocant, there to leave the barge secure, and put ourselves upon the adventure: the country onely a vast and wilde wilderness, and but only that Towne: within three or foure mile we hired a canow, and 2 Indians to row us ye next day a fowling: having made such provision for the barge as was needfull, I left her there to ride, with expresse charge not any to go ashore til my returne. Though some wise men may condemn this too bould attempt of too much indiscretion, yet if they well consider the friendship of the Indians, in conducting me, the desolatenes of the country, the probabilitie of some lacke, and the malicious judges of my actions at home, as also to have some matters of worth to incourage our adventurers in england, might well have caused any honest minde to have done the like, as wel for his own discharge as for the publike good: having 2 Indians for my guide and 2 of our own company, I set forward, leaving 7 in the barge; having discovered 20 miles further in this desart, the river stil kept his depth and bredth, but much more combred with trees; here we went ashore (being some

12 miles higher than ye barge had bene) to refresh our selves, during the boyling of our vituals: one of the Indians I tooke with me, to see the nature of the soile, and to cross the boughts of the river, the other Indian I left with M. Robbinson and Thomas Emry, with their matches light and order to discharge a peece, for my retreat at the first sight of any Indian, but within a quarter of an houre I heard a loud cry, and a hollowing of Indians, but no warning peece, supposing them surprised, and that the Indians had betraid us, presently I seazed him and bound his arme fast to my hand in a garter, with my pistoll ready bent to be revenged on him: he advised me to fly and seemed ignorant of what was done, but as we went discoursing, I was struck with an arrow on the right thigh, but without harme: upon this occasion I espied 2 Indians drawing their bowes, which I prevented in discharging a french pistoll: by that I had charged again 3 or 4 more did the 'like, for the first fell downe and fled: at my discharge they did the like, my hinde I made my barricade, who offered not to strive, 20 or 30 arrowes were shot at me but short, 3 or 4 times I had discharged my pistoll ere the king of Pamauck called Opeckakenough with 200 men, environed me, each drawing their bowe, which done they laid them upon the ground, yet without shot, my hinde treated betwixt them and me of conditions of peace, he discovered me to be the captaine, my request was to retire to ye boate, they demanded my armes, the rest they saide were slaine, onely me they would reserve: the Indian importuned me not to shoot. In retiring being in the midst of a low quagmire, and minding them more than my steps, I stept fast into the quagmire, and also the Indian in drawing me forth: thus surprised, I resolved to trie their mercies, my armes I caste from me, till which none durst approch me: being ceazed on me, they drew me out and led me to the King, I presented him with a compasse diall, describing by my best meanes the use thereof, whereat he so amazedly admired, as he suffered me to proceed in a

discourse of the roundnes of the earth, the course of the sunne, moone, starres and plannets, with kinde speeches and bread he requited me, conducting me where the canow lay and John Robinson slaine, with 20 or 30 arrowes in him. Emry I saw not, I perceived by the abundance of fires all over the woods, at each place I expected when they would execute me, yet they used me with what kindnes they could: approaching their Towne which was within 6 miles where I was taken, onely made as arbors and covered with mats, which they remove as occasion requires: all the women and children, being advertised of this accident came forth to meet, the King well guarded with 20 bow men 5 flanck and rear and each flanck before him a sword and a peece, and after him the like, then a bowman, then I on each hand a boweman, the rest in file in the reare, which reare led forth amongst the trees in a bishion, eache his bowe and a handfull of arrowes, a quiver at his back grimly painted: on eache flanck a sargeant, the one running alwaiss towards the front the other towards the reare, each a true pace and in exceeding good order, this being a good time continued, they caste themselves in a ring with a daunce, and so eache man departed to his lodging, the captain conducting me to his lodging, a quarter of Venison and some ten pound of bread I had for supper, what I left was reserved for me, and sent with me to my lodging: each morning three women presented me three great platters of fine bread, more venison than ten men could devour I had, my gowne, points and garters, my compas and a tablet they gave me again, though 8 ordinarily guarded me, I wanted not what they could devise to content me: and still our longer acquaintance increased our better affection: much they threatened to assault our forte as they were solicited by the King of Paspahegh, who shewed at our fort great signs of sorrow for this mischance: the King took great delight in understanding the manner of our ships and sayling the seas, the earth and skies and of our God: what he knew of the dominions he spared not to acquaint me with, as of certaine men cloathed at a place called Ocanahonun, cloathed like me, the course of our river, and that within 4 or 5 daies journey of the falles, was a great turning of salt water: I desired he would send a messenger to Paspahegh, with a letter I would write, by which they should understand, how kindly they used me, and that I was well, lest they should revenge my death; this he granted and sent three men, in such weather, as in reason were unpossible, by any naked to be indured: their cruell mindes towards the fort I had deverted, in describing the ordinance and the mines in the fields, as also the revenge Captain Newport would take of them at his returne, their intent, I incerted the fort, the people of Ocanahomm and the back sea, this report they after found divers Indians that confirmed: the next day after my letter, came a salvage to my lodging, with his sword to have slaine me, but being by my guard intercepted, with a bowe and arrow he offred to have effected his purpose: the cause I knew not, till the King understanding thereof came and told me of a man a dying wounded with my pistoll: he tould me also of another I had slayne, yet the most concealed they had any hurte: this was the father of him I had slayne, whose fury to prevent, the King presently conducted me to another kingdome, upon the top of the next northerly river, called Youghtanan, having feasted me, he further led me to another branch of the river called Mattapament, to two other hunting townes they led me, and to each of these Countries, a house of the great Emperor of Pewhakan, whom as yet I supposed to be at the Fals, to him I tolde him I must goe, and so returne to Paspahegh, after this foure or five dayes march we returned to Rasawrack, the first towne they brought me too, where binding the mats in bundles, they marched two dayes journey and crossed the River of Youghtanan, where it was as broad as Thames: so conducting me too a place called Menapacute in Pamunke, where ye King inhabited; the next day another King of that nation called Kekataugh, having received some kindness of me at the Fort, kindly invited me to feast at his house, the people from all places flocked to see me, each shewing to content me. By this the great King hath foure or five houses, each containing fourscore or an hundred foote in length, pleasantly seated upon an high sandy hill, from whence you may see westerly a goodly low country, the river before the which his crooked course causeth many great Marshes of exceeding good ground. An hundred houses, and many large plaines are here together inhabited, more abundance of fish and fowle, and a pleasanter seat cannot be imagined: the King with fortie bowmen to guard me, intreated me to discharge my Pistoll, which they there presented me with a mark at six score to strike therewith but to spoil the practice I broke the cocke, whereat they were much discontented though a chaunce supposed. From hence this kind King conducted me to a place called Topahanocke, a kingdome upon another river northward; the cause of this was, that the yeare before, a shippe had beene in the River of Pamunke, who having been kindly entertained by Powhatan their Emperour, they returned thence, and discovered the River of Topahanocke, where being received with like kindnesse, yet he slue the King, and tooke of his people, and they supposed I were bee, but the people reported him a great man that was Captaine, and using mee kindly, the next day we departed. This River of Topahanock, seemeth in breadth not much lesse than that we dwell upon. At the mouth of the River is a Countrey called Cuttata women, upwards is Marraugh tacum Tapohanock, Apparnatuck, and Nantaugs tacum, at Topmanahocks, the head issuing from many Mountains, the next night I lodged at a hunting town of Powhatam's, and the next day arrived at Waranacomoco upon the river of Parnauncke, where the great king is resident: by the way we passed by the top of another little river, which is betwixt the two called Payankatank. The most of this country though Desert, yet exceeding fertil, good timber, most hils and in dales, in each valley a cristall spring.

"Arriving at Weramacomoco, their Emperour, proudly lying upon a Bedstead a foote high upon tenne or twelve Mattes, richly hung with manie Chaynes of great Pearles about his necke, and covered with a great covering of Rahaughcums: At heade sat a woman, at his feete another, on each side sitting upon a Matte upon the ground were raunged his chiefe men on each side the fire, tenne in a ranke and behinde them as many yong women, each a great Chaine of white Beades over their shoulders: their heades painted in redde and with such a grave and Majeslicall countenance, as drove me into admiration to see such state in a naked Salvage, bee kindlv welcomed me with good wordes, and great Platters of sundrie victuals, asiuring mee his friendship and my libertie within foure dayes, bee much delighted in Opechan Conough's relation of what I had described to him, and oft examined me upon the same. Hee asked me the cause of our comming, I tolde him being in fight with the Spaniards our enemie, being over powred, neare put to retreat, and by extreme weather put to this shore, where landing at Chesipiack, the people shot us, but at Kequoughtan they kindly used us, wee by signes demaunded fresh water, they described us up the River was all fresh water, at Paspahegh, also they kindly used us, our Pinnasse being leake wee were inforced to stay to mend her, till Captain Newport my father came to conduct us away. He demaunded why we went further with our Boate, I tolde him, in that I would have occasion to talke of the backe Sea, that on the other side the maine, where was salt water, my father had a childe slaine, which we supposed Monocan his enemie, whose death we intended to revenge. After good deliberation, hee began to describe me the countreys beyond the Falles, with many of the rest, confirming what not only Opechancanoyes, and an Indian which had been prisoner to Pcwhatan had before tolde mee, but some called it five days, some sixe, some eight, where the sayde water dashed amongst many stones and rocks, each storme which caused oft tymes the heade of the River to bee brackish: Anchanachuck he described to bee the people that had slaine my brother, whose death hee would revenge. Hee described also upon the same Sea, a mighty nation called Pocoughtronack, a fierce nation that did eate men and warred with the people of Moyaoncer, and Pataromerke, Nations upon the toppe of the heade of the Bay, under his territories, where the yeare before they had slain an hundred, he signified their crownes were shaven, long haire in the necke, tied on a knot, Swords like Pollaxes.

"Beyond them he described people with short Coates, and Sleeves to the Elbowes, that passed that way in Shippes like ours. Many Kingdomes hee described mee to the heade of the Bay, which seemed to bee a mightie River, issuing from mightie mountaines, betwixt the two seas; the people clothed at Ocamahowan. He also confirmed, and the Southerly Countries also, as the rest, that reported us to be within a day and a halfe of Mangoge, two dayes of Chawwonock, 6 from Roonock, to the South part of the backe sea: he described a countrie called Anone, where they have abundance of Brasse, and houses walled as ours. I requited his discourse, seeing what pride he had in his great and spacious Dominions, seeing that all hee knewe were under his Territories.

"In describing to him the territories of Europe which was subject to our great King whose subject I was, the innumerable multitude of his ships, I gave him to understand the noyse of Trumpets and terrible manner of fighting were under Captain Newport my father, whom I intituled the Meworames which they call King of all the waters, at his greatnesse bee admired and not a little feared; he desired mee to forsake Paspahegh, and to live with him upon his River, a countrie called Capa Howasicke; he promised to give me corne, venison, or what I wanted to feede us, Hatchets and Copper wee should make him, and none should disturbe us.

This request I promised to performe: and thus having with all the kindnes hee could devise, sought to content me, he sent me home with 4 men, one that usually carried my Gonne and Knapsacke after me, two other loded with bread, and one to accompanie me."

The next extract in regard to this voyage is from President Wingfield's "Discourse of Virginia," which appears partly in the form of a diary, but was probably drawn up or at least finished shortly after Wingfield's return to London in May, 1608. He was in Jamestown when Smith returned from his captivity, and would be likely to allude to the romantic story of Pocahontas if Smith had told it on his escape. We quote:

"Decem.—The 10th of December, Mr. Smyth went up the ryver of the Chechohomynies to trade for corne; he was desirous to see the heade of that river; and, when it was not passible with the shallop, he hired a cannow and an Indian to carry him up further. The river the higher grew worse and worse. Then hee went on shoare with his guide, and left Robinson and Emmery, and twoe of our Men, in the cannow; which were presently slayne by the Indians, Pamaonke's men, and hee himself taken prysoner, and, by the means of his guide, his lief was saved; and Pamaonche, haveing him prisoner, carryed him to his neybors wyroances, to see if any of them knew him for one of those which had bene, some two or three eeres before us, in a river amongst them Northward, and taken awaie some Indians from them by force. At last he brought him to the great Powaton (of whome before wee had no knowledg), who sent him home to our towne the 8th of January."

The next contemporary document to which we have occasion to refer is Smith's Letter to the Treasurer and Council of Virginia in England, written in Virginia after the arrival of Newport there in September, 1608, and probably sent home by him near the close of that year. In this there is no occasion for a reference to Powhatan or his daughter, but he says in it: "I have sent you this Mappe of the Bay and Rivers, with an annexed Relation of the Countryes and Nations that inhabit them as you may see at large." This is doubtless the "Map of Virginia," with a description of the country, published some two or three years after Smith's return to England, at Oxford, 1612. It is a description of the country and people, and contains little narrative. But with this was published, as an appendix, an account of the proceedings of the Virginia colonists from 1606 to 1612, taken out of the writings of Thomas Studley and several others who had been residents in Virginia. These several discourses were carefully edited by William Symonds, a doctor of divinity and a man of learning and repute, evidently at the request of Smith. To the end of the volume Dr. Symonds appends a note addressed to Smith, saying: "I return you the fruit of my labors, as Mr. Cranshaw requested me, which I bestowed in reading the discourses and hearing the relations of such as have walked and observed the land of Virginia with you." These narratives by Smith's companions, which he made a part of his Oxford book, and which passed under his eye and had his approval, are uniformly not only friendly to him, but eulogistic of him, and probably omit no incident known to the writers which would do him honor or add interest to him as a knight of romance. Nor does it seem probable that Smith himself would have omitted to mention the dramatic scene of the prevented execution if it had occurred to him. If there had been a reason in the minds of others in 1608 why it should not appear in the "True Relation," that reason did not exist for Smith at this time, when the discords and discouragements of the colony were fully known. And by this time the young girl Pocahontas had become well known to the colonists at Jamestown. The account of this Chickahominy voyage given in this volume, published in 1612, is signed by Thomas Studley, and is as follows:

"The next voyage he proceeded so farre that with much labour by cutting of trees in sunder he made his passage, but when his Barge could passe no farther, he left her in a broad bay out of danger of shot, commanding none should go ashore till his returne; himselfe with 2 English and two Salvages went up higher in a Canowe, but he was not long absent, but his men went ashore, whose want of government gave both occasion and opportunity to the Salvages to surprise one George Casson, and much failed not to have cut of the boat and all the rest. Smith little dreaming of that accident, being got to the marshes at the river's head, 20 miles in the desert, had his 2 men slaine (as is supposed) sleeping by the Canowe, whilst himselfe by fowling sought them victual, who finding he was beset by 200 Salvages, 2 of them he slew, stil defending himselfe with the aid of a Salvage his guid (whome bee bound to his arme and used as his buckler), till at last slipping into a bogmire they tooke him prisoner: when this news came to the fort much was their sorrow for his losse, fewe expecting what ensued. A month those Barbarians kept him prisoner, many strange triumphs and conjurations they made of him, yet he so demeaned himselfe amongst them, as he not only diverted them from surprising the Fort, but procured his own liberty, and got himselfe and his company such estimation amongst them, that those Salvages admired him as a demi-God. So returning safe to the Fort, once more staied the pinnas her flight for England, which til his returne could not set saile, so extreme was the weather and so great the frost."

The first allusion to the salvation of Captain Smith by Pocahontas occurs in a letter or "little booke" which he wrote to Queen Anne in 1616, about the time of the arrival in England of the Indian Princess, who was then called the Lady Rebecca, and was wife of John Rolfe, by whom she had a son, who accompanied them. Pocahontas had by this time become a person of some importance. Her friendship had been of substantial service to the colony. Smith had acknowledged this in his "True Relation," where he referred to her as the "nonpareil" of Virginia. He was kind-hearted and naturally magnanimous, and would take some pains to do the Indian convert a favor, even to the invention of an incident that would make her attractive. To be sure, he was vain as well as inventive, and here was an opportunity to attract the attention of his sovereign and increase his own importance by connecting his name with hers in a romantic manner. Still, we believe that the main motive that dictated this epistle was kindness to Pocahontas. The sentence that refers to her heroic act is this: "After some six weeks [he was absent only four weeks] fatting amongst those Salvage Countries, at the minute of my execution she hazarded the beating out of her own braines to save mine, and not only that, but so prevailed with her father [of whom he says, in a previous paragraph, 'I received from this great Salvage exceeding great courtesie'], that I was safely conducted to Jamestown."

This guarded allusion to the rescue stood for all known account of it, except a brief reference to it in his "New England's Trials" of 1622, until the appearance of Smith's "General Historie" in London, 1624. In the first edition of "New England's Trials," 1620, there is no reference to it. In the enlarged edition of 1622, Smith gives a new version to his capture, as resulting from "the folly of them that fled," and says: "God made Pocahontas, the King's daughter the means to deliver me."

The "General Historie" was compiled—as was the custom in making up such books at the time from a great variety of sources. Such parts of it as are not written by Smith—and these constitute a considerable portion of the history—bear marks here and there of his touch. It begins with his description of Virginia, which appeared in the Oxford tract of 1612; following this are the several narratives by his comrades, which formed the appendix of that tract. The one that concerns us here is that already quoted, signed Thomas Studley. It is reproduced here as "written by Thomas Studley, the first Cape Merchant in Virginia, Robert Fenton, Edward Harrington, and I. S." [John Smith]. It is, however, considerably extended, and into it is interjected a detailed account of the captivity and the story of the stones, the clubs, and the saved brains.

It is worthy of special note that the "True Relation" is not incorporated in the "General Historie." This is the more remarkable because it was an original statement, written when the occurrences it describes were fresh, and is much more in detail regarding many things that happened during the period it covered than the narratives that Smith uses in the "General Historie." It was his habit to use over and over again his own publications. Was this discarded because it contradicted the Pocahontas story—because that story could not be fitted into it as it could be into the Studley relation?

It should be added, also, that Purchas printed an abstract of the Oxford tract in his "Pilgrimage," in 1613, from material furnished him by Smith. The Oxford tract was also republished by Purchas in his "Pilgrimes," extended by new matter in manuscript supplied by Smith. The "Pilgrimes" did not appear till 1625, a year after the "General Historie," but was in preparation long before. The Pocahontas legend appears in the "Pilgrimes," but not in the earlier "Pilgrimage."

We have before had occasion to remark that Smith's memory had the peculiarity of growing stronger and more minute in details the further he was removed in point of time from any event he describes. The revamped narrative is worth quoting in full for other reasons. It exhibits Smith's skill as a writer and his capacity for rising into poetic moods. This is the story from the "General Historie":

"The next voyage hee proceeded so farre that with much labour by cutting of trees in sunder he made his passage, but when his Barge could pass no farther, he left her in a broad bay out of danger of shot, commanding none should goe ashore till his return: himselfe with two English and two Salvages went up higher in a Canowe, but he was not long absent, but his men went ashore, whose want of government, gave both occasion and opportunity to the Salvages to surprise one George Cassen, whom they slew, and much failed not to have cut of the boat and all the rest. Smith little dreaming of that accident, being got to the marshes at the river's head, twentie myles in the desert, had his two men slaine (as is supposed) sleeping by the Canowe, whilst himselfe by fowling sought them victuall, who finding he was beset with 200 Salvages, two of them hee slew, still defending himself with the ayd of a Salvage his guide, whom he bound to his arme with his garters, and used him as a buckler, yet he was shot in his thigh a little, and had many arrowes stucke in his cloathes but no great hurt, till at last they tooke him prisoner. When this newes came to Jamestowne, much was their sorrow for his losse, fewe expecting what ensued. Sixe or seven weekes those Barbarians kept him prisoner, many strange triumphes and conjurations they made of him, yet hee so demeaned himselfe amongst them, as he not onely diverted them from surprising the Fort, but procured his owne libertie, and got himself and his company such estimation amongst them, that those Salvages admired him more than their owne Quiyouckosucks. The manner how they used and delivered him, is as followeth.

"The Salvages having drawne from George Cassen whether Captaine Smith was gone, prosecuting that opportunity they followed him with 300 bowmen, conducted by the King of

Pamaunkee, who in divisions searching the turnings of the river, found Robinson and Entry by the fireside, those they shot full of arrowes and slew. Then finding the Captaine as is said, that used the Salvage that was his guide as his shield (three of them being slaine and divers others so gauld) all the rest would not come neere him. Thinking thus to have returned to his boat, regarding them, as he marched, more then his way, slipped up to the middle in an oasie creeke and his Salvage with him, yet durst they not come to him till being neere dead with cold, he threw away his armes. Then according to their composition they drew him forth and led him to the fire, where his men were slaine. Diligently they chafed his benumbed limbs. He demanding for their Captaine, they shewed him Opechankanough, King of Pamaunkee, to whom he gave a round Ivory double compass Dyall. Much they marvailed at the playing of the Fly and Needle, which they could see so plainly, and yet not touch it, because of the glass that covered them. But when he demonstrated by that Globe-like Jewell, the roundnesse of the earth and skies, the sphaere of the Sunne, Moone, and Starres, and how the Sunne did chase the night round about the world continually: the greatnesse of the Land and Sea, the diversitie of Nations, varietie of Complexions, and how we were to them Antipodes, and many other such like matters, they all stood as amazed with admiration. Notwithstanding within an houre after they tyed him to a tree, and as many as could stand about him prepared to shoot him, but the King holding up the Compass in his hand, they all laid downe their Bowes and Arrowes, and in a triumphant manner led him to Orapaks, where he was after their manner kindly feasted and well used.

"Their order in conducting him was thus: Drawing themselves all in fyle, the King in the middest had all their Peeces and Swords borne before him. Captaine Smith was led after him by three great Salvages, holding him fast by each arme:

and on each side six went in fyle with their arrowes nocked. But arriving at the Towne (which was but onely thirtie or fortie hunting houses made of Mats, which they remove as they please, as we our tents) all the women and children staring to behold him, the souldiers first all in file performe the forme of a Bissom so well as could be: and on each flanke, officers as Serieants to see them keepe their orders. A good time they continued this exercise, and then cast themselves in a ring, dauncing in such severall Postures, and singing and yelling out such hellish notes and screeches: being strangely painted, every one his quiver of arrowes, and at his backe a club: on his arme a Fox or an Otters skinne, or some such matter for his vambrace: their heads and shoulders painted red, with oyle and Pocones mingled together, which Scarlet like colour made an exceeding handsome shew, his Bow in his hand, and the skinne of a Bird with her wings abroad dryed, tyed on his head, a peece of copper, a white shell, a long feather, with a small rattle growing at the tayles of their snaks tyed to it, or some such like toy. All this time Smith and the King stood in the middest guarded, as before is said, and after three dances they all departed. Smith they conducted to a long house, where thirtie or fortie tall fellowes did guard him, and ere long more bread and venison were brought him then would have served twentie men. I thinke his stomacke at that time was not very good; what he left they put in baskets and tyed over his head. About midnight they set the meat again before him, all this time not one of them would eat a bit with him, till the next morning they brought him as much more, and then did they eate all the old, and reserved the new as they had done the other, which made him think they would fat him to eat him. Yet in this desperate estate to defend him from the cold, one Maocassater brought him his gowne, in requitall of some beads and toyes Smith had given him at his first arrival in Firginia.

"Two days a man would have slaine him (but that the guard prevented it) for the death of his sonne, to whom they conducted him to recover the poore man then breathing his last. Smith told them that at James towne he had a water would doe it if they would let him fetch it, but they would not permit that: but made all the preparations they could to assault James towne, craving his advice, and for recompence he should have life, libertie, land, and women. In part of a Table booke he writ his mind to them at the Fort, what was intended, how they should follow that direction to affright the messengers, and without fayle send him such things as he writ for. And an Inventory with them. The difficultie and danger he told the Salvaves, of the Mines, great gunnes, and other Engins, exceedingly affrighted them, yet according to his request they went to James towne in as bitter weather as could be of frost and snow, and within three days returned with an answer.

"But when they came to James towne, seeing men sally out as he had told them they would, they fled: yet in the night they came again to the same place where he had told them they should receive an answer, and such things as he had promised them, which they found accordingly, and with which they returned with no small expedition, to the wonder of them all that heard it, that he could either divine or the paper could speake. Then they led him to the Youthtanunds, the Mattapanients, the Payankatanks, the Nantaughtacunds and Onawmanients, upon the rivers of Rapahanock and Patawomek, over all those rivers and backe againe by divers other severall Nations, to the King's habitation at Pamaunkee, where they entertained him with most strange and fearefull conjurations;

'As if neare led to hell,
Amongst the Devils to dwell.'

"Not long after, early in a morning, a great fire was made in a long house, and a mat spread on the one side as on the other; on the one they caused him to sit, and all the guard went out of the house, and presently came skipping in a great grim fellow, all painted over with coale mingled with oyle; and many Snakes and Wesels skins stuffed with mosse, and all their tayles tyed together, so as they met on the crowne of his head in a tassell; and round about the tassell was a Coronet of feathers, the skins hanging round about his head, backe, and shoulders, and in a manner covered his face; with a hellish voyce and a rattle in his hand. With most strange gestures and passions he began his invocation, and environed the fire with a circle of meale; which done three more such like devils came rushing in with the like antique tricks, painted halfe blacke, halfe red: but all their eyes were painted white, and some red stroakes like Mutchato's along their cheekes: round about him those fiends daunced a pretty while, and then came in three more as ugly as the rest; with red eyes and stroakes over their blacke faces, at last they all sat downe right against him; three of them on the one hand of the chiefe Priest, and three on the other. Then all with their rattles began a song, which ended, the chiefe Priest layd downe five wheat cornes: then strayning his arms and hands with such violence that he sweat, and his veynes swelled, he began a short Oration: at the conclusion they all gave a short groane; and then layd downe three graines more. After that began their song againe, and then another Oration, ever laying down so many cornes as before, til they had twice incirculed the fire; that done they tooke a bunch of little stickes prepared for that purpose, continuing still their devotion, and at the end of every song and Oration they layd downe a sticke betwixt the divisions of Corne. Til night, neither he nor they did either eate or drinke, and then they feasted merrily, and with the best provisions they could make. Three dayes they used this Ceremony: the meaning whereof they told him was to know if he intended them well

Charles Dudley Warner

or no. The circle of meale signified their Country, the circles of corne the bounds of the Sea, and the stickes his Country. They imagined the world to be flat and round, like a trencher, and they in the middest. After this they brought him a bagge of gunpowder, which they carefully preserved till the next spring, to plant as they did their corne, because they would be acquainted with the nature of that seede. Opitchapam, the King's brother, invited him to his house, where with many platters of bread, foule, and wild beasts, as did environ him, he bid him wellcome: but not any of them would eate a bit with him, but put up all the remainder in Baskets. At his returne to Opechancanoughs, all the King's women and their children flocked about him for their parts, as a due by Custome, to be merry with such fragments.

"But his waking mind in hydeous dreames did oft see wondrous shapes
Of bodies strange, and huge in growth, and of stupendious makes."

"At last they brought him to Meronocomoco, where was Powhatan their Emperor. Here more than two hundred of those grim Courtiers stood wondering at him, as he had beene a monster, till Powhatan and his trayne had put themselves in their greatest braveries. Before a fire upon a seat like a bedstead, he sat covered with a great robe, made of Rarowcun skinnes and all the tayles hanging by. On either hand did sit a young wench of sixteen or eighteen years, and along on each side the house, two rowes of men, and behind them as many women, with all their heads and shoulders painted red; many of their heads bedecked with the white downe of Birds; but everyone with something: and a great chayne of white beads about their necks. At his entrance before the King, all the people gave a great shout. The Queene of Appamatuck was appointed to bring him water to wash his hands, and another brought him a bunch of feathers, instead of a Towell to dry them: having feasted him after their best barbarous manner they could. A long consultation was held, but the conclusion was two great stones were brought before Powhatan; then as many as could layd hands on him, dragged him to them, and thereon laid his head, and being ready with their clubs, to beate out his braines. Pocahontas, the King's dearest daughter, when no entreaty could prevaile, got his head in her armes, and laid her owne upon his to save him from death: whereat the Emperour was contented he should live to make him hatchets, and her bells, beads, and copper: for they thought him as well of all occupations as themselves. For the King himselfe will make his owne robes, shooes, bowes, arrowes, pots, plant, hunt, or doe any thing so well as the rest.

'They say he bore a pleasant shew,
But sure his heart was sad
For who can pleasant be, and rest,
That lives in feare and dread.
And having life suspected, doth
If still suspected lead.'"

"Two days after, Powhatan having disguised himselfe in the most fearfullest manner he could, caused Capt. Smith to be brought forth to a great house in the woods and there upon a mat by the fire to be left alone. Not long after from behinde a mat that divided the house, was made the most dolefullest noyse he ever heard: then Powhatan more like a devill than a man with some two hundred more as blacke as himseffe, came unto him and told him now they were friends, and presently he should goe to James town, to send him two great gunnes, and a gryndstone, for which he would give him the country of Capahowojick, and for ever esteeme him as his sonn Nantaquoud. So to James towne with 12 guides Powhatan sent him. That night they quartered in the woods, he still expecting (as he had done all this long time of his imprisonment) every houre to be put to one death or other; for all their feasting. But almightie God (by his divine providence) had mollified the hearts of those sterne Barbarians with compassion. The next morning betimes they came to the Fort, where Smith having used the salvages with what kindnesse he could, he shewed Rawhunt, Powhatan's trusty servant, two demiculverings and a millstone to carry Powhatan; they found them somewhat too heavie; but when they did see him discharge them, being loaded with stones, among the boughs of a great tree loaded with Isickles, the yce and branches came so tumbling downe, that the poore Salvages ran away halfe dead with feare. But at last we regained some conference with them and gave them such toys: and sent to Powhatan, his women, and children such presents, and gave them in generall full content. Now in James Towne they were all in combustion, the strongest preparing once more to run away with the Pinnace; which with the hazard of his life, with Sakre falcon and musketshot, Smith forced now the third time to stay or sinke. Some no better then they should be had plotted with the President, the next day to have put him to death by the Leviticall law, for the lives of Robinson and Emry, pretending the fault was his that had led them to their ends; but he quickly tooke such order with such Lawyers, that he layed them by the heeles till he sent some of them prisoners for England. Now ever once in four or five dayes, Pocahontas with her attendants, brought him so much provision, that saved many of their lives, that els for all this had starved with hunger.

'Thus from numbe death our good God sent reliefe,
The sweete asswager of all other griefe.'

"His relation of the plenty he had scene, especially at Werawocomoco, and of the state and bountie of Powhatan (which till that time was unknowne), so revived their dead spirits (especially the love of Pocahontas) as all men's feare was abandoned."

We should like to think original, in the above, the fine passage, in which Smith, by means of a simple compass dial, demonstrated the roundness of the earth, and skies, the sphere of the sun, moon, and stars, and how the sun did chase the night round about the world continually; the greatness of the land and sea, the diversity of nations, variety of complexions, and how we were to them antipodes, so that the Indians stood amazed with admiration.

Captain Smith up to his middle in a Chickahominy swamp, discoursing on these high themes to a Pamunkey Indian, of whose language Smith was wholly ignorant, and who did not understand a word of English, is much more heroic, considering the adverse circumstances, and appeals more to the imagination, than the long-haired Iopas singing the song of Atlas, at the banquet given to AEneas, where Trojans and Tyrians drained the flowing bumpers while Dido drank long draughts of love. Did Smith, when he was in the neighborhood of Carthage pick up some such literal translations of the song of Atlas' as this:

> "He sang the wandering moon, and the labors of the Sun;
> From whence the race of men and flocks; whence rain and lightning;
> Of Arcturus, the rainy Hyades, and the twin Triones;
> Why the winter suns hasten so much to touch themselves in the ocean,
> And what delay retards the slow nights."

The scene of the rescue only occupies seven lines and the reader feels that, after all, Smith has not done full justice to it. We cannot, therefore, better conclude this romantic episode than by quoting the description of it given with an elaboration of language that must be, pleasing to the shade of

Smith, by John Burke in his History of Virginia:

"Two large stones were brought in, and placed at the feet of the emperor; and on them was laid the head of the prisoner; next a large club was brought in, with which Powhatan, for whom, out of respect, was reserved this honor, prepared to crush the head of his captive. The assembly looked on with sensations of awe, probably not unmixed with pity for the fate of an enemy whose bravery had commanded their admiration, and in whose misfortunes their hatred was possibly forgotten.

"The fatal club was uplifted: the breasts of the company already by anticipation felt the dreadful crash, which was to bereave the wretched victim of life: when the young and beautiful Pocahontas, the beloved daughter of the emperor, with a shriek of terror and agony threw herself on the body of Smith; Her hair was loose, and her eyes streaming with tears, while her whole manner bespoke the deep distress and agony of her bosom. She cast a beseeching look at her furious and astonished father, deprecating his wrath, and imploring his pity and the life of his prisoner, with all the eloquence of mute but impassioned sorrow.

"The remainder of this scene is honorable to Powhatan. It will remain a lasting monument, that tho' different principles of action, and the influence of custom, have given to the manners and opinions of this people an appearance neither amiable nor virtuous, they still retain the noblest property of human character, the touch of pity and the feeling of humanity.

"The club of the emperor was still uplifted; but pity had touched his bosom, and his eye was every moment losing its fierceness; he looked around to collect his fortitude, or perhaps to find an excuse for his weakness in the faces of his attendants. But every eye was suffused with the sweetly contagious softness. The generous savage no longer hesitated. The compassion of the rude state is neither ostentatious nor dilating: nor does it insult its object by the exaction of impossible conditions. Powhatan lifted his grateful and delighted daughter, and the captive, scarcely yet assured of safety, from the earth...."

"The character of this interesting woman, as it stands in the concurrent accounts of all our historians, is not, it is with confidence affirmed, surpassed by any in the whole range of history; and for those qualities more especially which do honor to our nature—an humane and feeling heart, an ardor and unshaken constancy in her attachments—she stands almost without a rival.

"At the first appearance of the Europeans her young heart was impressed with admiration of the persons and manners of the strangers; but it is not during their prosperity that she displays her attachment. She is not influenced by awe of their greatness, or fear of their resentment, in the assistance she affords them. It was during their severest distresses, when their most celebrated chief was a captive in their hands, and was dragged through the country as a spectacle for the sport and derision of their people, that she places herself between him and destruction.

"The spectacle of Pocahontas in an attitude of entreaty, with her hair loose, and her eyes streaming with tears, supplicating with her enraged father for the life of Captain Smith when he was about to crush the head of his prostrate victim with a club, is a situation equal to the genius of Raphael. And when the royal savage directs his ferocious glance for a moment from his victim to reprove his weeping daughter, when softened by her distress his eye loses its fierceness, and he gives his captive to her tears, the painter will discover a new occasion for exercising his talents."

The painters have availed themselves of this opportunity. In one picture Smith is represented stiffly extended on the greensward (of the woods), his head resting on a stone, appropriately clothed in a dresscoat, knee-breeches, and silk stockings; while Powhatan and the other savages stand ready for murder, in full-dress parade costume; and Pocahontas, a full-grown woman, with long, disheveled hair, in the sentimental dress and attitude of a Letitia E. Landon of the period, is about to cast herself upon the imperiled and well-dressed Captain.

Must we, then, give up the legend altogether, on account of the exaggerations that have grown up about it, our suspicion of the creative memory of Smith, and the lack of all contemporary allusion to it? It is a pity to destroy any pleasing story of the past, and especially to discharge our hard struggle for a foothold on this continent of the few elements of romance. If we can find no evidence of its truth that stands the test of fair criticism, we may at least believe that it had some slight basis on which to rest. It is not at all improbable that Pocahontas, who was at that time a precocious maid of perhaps twelve or thirteen years of age (although Smith mentions her as a child of ten years old when she came to the camp after his release), was touched with compassion for the captive, and did influence her father to treat him kindly.

## IX

## SMITH'S WAY WITH THE INDIANS

As we are not endeavoring to write the early history of Virginia, but only to trace Smith's share in it, we proceed with his exploits after the arrival of the first supply, consisting of near a hundred men, in two ships, one commanded by Captain Newport and the other by Captain Francis Nelson. The latter, when in sight of Cape Henry, was driven by a storm back to the West Indies, and did not arrive at James River with his vessel, the Phoenix, till after the departure of Newport for England with his load of "golddust," and Master Wingfield and Captain Arthur.

In his "True Relation," Smith gives some account of his exploration of the Pamunkey River, which he sometimes calls the "Youghtamand," upon which, where the water is salt, is the town of Werowocomoco. It can serve no purpose in elucidating the character of our hero to attempt to identify all the places he visited.

It was at Werowocomoco that Smith observed certain conjurations of the medicine men, which he supposed had reference to his fate. From ten o'clock in the morning till six at night, seven of the savages, with rattles in their hands, sang and danced about the fire, laying down grains of corn in circles, and with vehement actions, casting cakes of deer suet, deer, and tobacco into the fire, howling without ceasing. One of them was "disfigured with a great skin, his head hung around with little skins of weasels and other vermin, with a crownlet of feathers on his head, painted as ugly as the devil." So fat they fed him that he much doubted they intended to sacrifice him to the Quiyoughquosicke, which is a superior power they worship: a more uglier thing cannot be described. These savages buried their dead with great sorrow and weeping, and they acknowledge no resurrection. Tobacco they offer to the water to secure a good passage in foul weather. The descent of the crown is to the first heirs of the king's sisters, "for the kings have as many women as they will, the subjects two, and most but one."

After Smith's return, as we have read, he was saved from a plot to take his life by the timely arrival of Captain Newport. Somewhere about this time the great fire occurred. Smith was now one of the Council; Martin and Matthew Scrivener, just named, were also councilors. Ratcliffe was still President. The savages, owing to their acquaintance with and confidence in Captain Smith, sent in abundance of provision. Powhatan sent once or twice a week "deer, bread, raugroughcuns (probably not to be confounded with the rahaughcuns [raccoons] spoken of before, but probably 'rawcomens,' mentioned in the Description of Virginia), half for Smith, and half for his father, Captain Newport." Smith had, in his intercourse with the natives, extolled the greatness of Newport, so that they conceived him to be the chief and all the rest his children, and regarded him as an oracle, if not a god.

Powhatan and the rest had, therefore, a great desire to see this mighty person. Smith says that the President and Council greatly envied his reputation with the Indians, and wrought upon them to believe, by giving in trade four times as much as the price set by Smith, that their authority exceeded his as much as their bounty.

We must give Smith the credit of being usually intent upon the building up of the colony, and establishing permanent and livable relations with the Indians, while many of his companions in authority seemed to regard the adventure as a temporary occurrence, out of which they would make what personal profit they could. The new-comers on a vessel always demoralized the trade with the Indians, by paying extravagant prices. Smith's relations with Captain Newport were peculiar. While he magnified him to the Indians as the great power, he does not conceal his own opinion of his ostentation and want of shrewdness. Smith's attitude was that of a priest who puts up for the worship of the vulgar an idol, which he knows is only a clay image stuffed with straw.

In the great joy of the colony at the arrival of the first supply, leave was given to sailors to trade with the Indians, and the new-comers soon so raised prices that it needed a pound of copper to buy a quantity of provisions that before had been obtained for an ounce. Newport sent great presents to Powhatan, and, in response to the wish of the "Emperor," prepared to visit him. "A great coyle there was to set him forward," says Smith. Mr. Scrivener and Captain Smith, and a guard of thirty or forty, accompanied him. On this expedition they found the mouth of the Pamaunck (now York) River. Arriving at Werowocomoco, Newport, fearing treachery, sent Smith with twenty men to land and make a preliminary visit. When they came ashore they found a network of creeks which were crossed by very shaky bridges, constructed of crotched sticks and poles, which had so much the appearance of traps that Smith would not cross them until many of the Indians had preceded him, while he kept others with him as hostages. Three hundred savages conducted him to Powhatan, who received him in great state.

Before his house were ranged forty or fifty great platters of fine bread. Entering his house, "with loude tunes they made all signs of great joy." In the first account Powhatan is represented as surrounded by his principal women and chief men, "as upon a throne at the upper end of the house, with such majesty as I cannot express, nor yet have often seen, either in Pagan or Christian." In the later account he is "sitting upon his bed of mats, his pillow of leather embroidered (after their rude manner with pearls and white beads), his attire a fair robe of skins as large as an Irish mantel; at his head and feet a handsome young woman; on each side of his house sat twenty of his concubines, their heads and shoulders painted red, with a great chain of white beads about each of their necks. Before those sat his chiefest men in like order in his arbor-like house." This is the scene that figures in the old copper-plate engravings. The Emperor welcomed Smith with a kind countenance, caused him to sit beside him, and with pretty discourse they renewed their old acquaintance. Smith presented him with a suit of red cloth, a white greyhound, and a hat. The Queen of Apamatuc, a comely young savage, brought him water, a turkeycock, and bread to eat. Powhatan professed great content with Smith, but desired to see his father, Captain Newport. He inquired also with a merry countenance after the piece of ordnance that Smith had promised to send him, and Smith, with equal jocularity, replied that he had offered the men four demi-culverins, which they found too heavy to carry. This night they quartered with Powhatan, and were liberally feasted, and entertained with singing, dancing, and orations.

The next day Captain Newport came ashore. The two monarchs exchanged presents. Newport gave Powhatan a white boy thirteen years old, named Thomas Savage. This boy remained with the Indians and served the colony many years as an interpreter. Powhatan gave Newport in return a bag of beans and an Indian named Namontack for his servant. Three or four days they remained, feasting, dancing, and trading with the Indians.

In trade the wily savage was more than a match for Newport. He affected great dignity; it was unworthy such great werowances to dicker; it was not agreeable to his greatness in a peddling manner to trade for trifles; let the great Newport lay down his commodities all together, and Powhatan would take what he wished, and recompense him with a proper return. Smith, who knew the Indians and their ostentation, told Newport that the intention was to cheat him, but his interference was resented. The result justified Smith's suspicion. Newport received but four bushels of corn when he should have had twenty hogsheads. Smith then tried his hand at a trade. With a few blue beads, which he represented as of a rare substance, the color of the skies, and worn by the greatest kings in the world, he so inflamed the desire of Powhatan that he was half mad to possess such strange jewels, and gave for them 200 to 300 bushels of corn, "and yet," says Smith, "parted good friends."

At this time Powhatan, knowing that they desired to invade or explore Monacan, the country above the Falls, proposed an expedition, with men and boats, and "this faire tale had almost made Captain Newport undertake by this means to discover the South Sea," a project which the adventurers had always in mind. On this expedition they sojourned also with the King of Pamaunke.

Captain Newport returned to England on the 10th of April. Mr. Scrivener and Captain Smith were now in fact the sustainers of the colony. They made short expeditions of exploration. Powhatan and other chiefs still professed friendship and sent presents, but the Indians grew more and more offensive, lurking about and stealing all they could lay hands on. Several of them were caught and confined in the fort, and, guarded, were conducted to the morning and evening prayers. By threats and slight torture, the captives were made to confess the hostile intentions of Powhatan and the other chiefs, which was to steal their weapons and then overpower the colony. Rigorous measures were needed to keep the Indians in check, but the command from England not to offend the savages was so strict that Smith dared not chastise them as they deserved. The history of the colony all this spring of 1608 is one of labor and discontent, of constant annoyance from the Indians, and expectations of attacks. On the 20th of April, while they were hewing trees and setting corn, an alarm was given which sent them all to their arms. Fright was turned into joy by the sight of the Phoenix, with Captain Nelson and his company, who had been for three months detained in the West Indies, and given up for lost.

Being thus re-enforced, Smith and Scrivener desired to explore the country above the Falls, and got ready an expedition. But this, Martin, who was only intent upon loading the return ship with "his phantastical gold," opposed, and Nelson did not think he had authority to allow it, unless they would bind themselves to pay the hire of the ships. The project was therefore abandoned. The Indians continued their depredations. Messages daily passed between the fort and the Indians, and treachery was always expected. About this time the boy Thomas Savage was returned, with his chest and clothing.

The colony had now several of the Indians detained in the fort. At this point in the "True Relation" occurs the first mention of Pocahontas. Smith says: "Powhatan, understanding we detained certain Salvages, sent his daughter, a child of tenne years old, which not only for feature, countenance, and proportion much exceeded any of his people, but for wit and spirit, the only nonpareil of his country." She was accompanied by his trusty messenger

Rawhunt, a crafty and deformed savage, who assured Smith how much Powhatan loved and respected him and, that he should not doubt his kindness, had sent his child, whom he most esteemed, to see him, and a deer, and bread besides for a present; "desiring us that the boy might come again, which he loved exceedingly, his little daughter he had taught this lesson also: not taking notice at all of the Indians that had been prisoners three days, till that morning that she saw their fathers and friends come quietly and in good terms to entreat their liberty."

Opechancanough (the King of "Pamauk") also sent asking the release of two that were his friends; and others, apparently with confidence in the whites, came begging for the release of the prisoners. "In the afternoon they being gone, we guarded them [the prisoners] as before to the church, and after prayer gave them to Pocahuntas, the King's daughter, in regard to her father's kindness in sending her: after having well fed them, as all the time of their imprisonment, we gave them their bows, arrows, or what else they had, and with much content sent them packing; Pocahuntas, also, we requited with such trifles as contented her, to tell that we had used the Paspaheyans very kindly in so releasing them."

This account would show that Pocahontas was a child of uncommon dignity and self-control for her age. In his letter to Queen Anne, written in 1616, he speaks of her as aged twelve or thirteen at the time of his captivity, several months before this visit to the fort.

The colonists still had reasons to fear ambuscades from the savages lurking about in the woods. One day a Paspahean came with a glittering mineral stone, and said he could show them great abundance of it. Smith went to look for this mine, but was led about hither and thither in the woods till he lost his patience and was convinced that the Indian was fooling him, when he gave him twenty lashes with a rope, handed him his bows and arrows, told him to shoot if he dared, and let him go. Smith had a prompt way with the Indians. He always traded "squarely" with them, kept his promises, and never hesitated to attack or punish them when they deserved it. They feared and respected him.

The colony was now in fair condition, in good health, and contented; and it was believed, though the belief was not well founded, that they would have lasting peace with the Indians. Captain Nelson's ship, the Phoenix, was freighted with cedar wood, and was despatched for England June 8, 1608. Captain Martin, "always sickly and unserviceable, and desirous to enjoy the credit of his supposed art of finding the gold mine," took passage. Captain Nelson probably carried Smith's "True Relation."

# X

## DISCOVERY OF THE CHESAPEAKE

On the same, day that Nelson sailed for England, Smith set out to explore the Chesapeake, accompanying the Phoenix as far as Cape Henry, in a barge of about three tons. With him went Dr. Walter Russell, six gentlemen, and seven soldiers. The narrative of the voyage is signed by Dr. Russell, Thomas Momford, gentleman, and Anas Todkill, soldier. Master Scrivener remained at the fort, where his presence was needed to keep in check the prodigal waste of the stores upon his parasites by President Ratcliffe.

The expedition crossed the bay at "Smith's Isles," named after the Captain, touched at Cape Charles, and coasted along the eastern shore. Two stout savages hailed them from Cape Charles, and directed them to Accomack, whose king proved to be the most comely and civil savage they had yet encountered.

He told them of a strange accident that had happened. The parents of two children who had died were moved by some phantasy to revisit their dead carcasses, "whose benumbed bodies reflected to the eyes of the beholders such delightful countenances as though they had regained their vital spirits." This miracle drew a great part of the King's people to behold

Charles Dudley Warner

them, nearly all of whom died shortly afterward. These people spoke the language of Powhatan. Smith explored the bays, isles, and islets, searching for harbors and places of habitation. He was a born explorer and geographer, as his remarkable map of Virginia sufficiently testifies. The company was much tossed about in the rough waves of the bay, and had great difficulty in procuring drinking-water. They entered the Wighcocomoco, on the east side, where the natives first threatened and then received them with songs, dancing, and mirth. A point on the mainland where they found a pond of fresh water they named "Poynt Ployer in honer of the most honorable house of Monsay, in Britaine, that in an extreme extremitie once relieved our Captain." This reference to the Earl of Ployer, who was kind to Smith in his youth, is only an instance of the care with which he edited these narratives of his own exploits, which were nominally written by his companions.

The explorers were now assailed with violent storms, and at last took refuge for two days on some uninhabited islands, which by reason of the ill weather and the hurly-burly of thunder, lightning, wind, and rain, they called "Limbo." Repairing their torn sails with their shirts, they sailed for the mainland on the east, and ran into a river called Cuskarawook (perhaps the present Annomessie), where the inhabitants received them with showers of arrows, ascending the trees and shooting at them. The next day a crowd came dancing to the shore, making friendly signs, but Smith, suspecting villainy, discharged his muskets into them. Landing toward evening, the explorers found many baskets and much blood, but no savages. The following day, savages to the number, the account wildly says, of two or three thousand, came to visit them, and were very friendly. These tribes Smith calls the Sarapinagh, Nause, Arseek, and Nantaquak, and says they are the best merchants of that coast. They told him of a great nation, called the

Massawomeks, of whom he set out in search, passing by the Limbo, and coasting the west side of Chesapeake Bay. The people on the east side he describes as of small stature.

They anchored at night at a place called Richard's Cliffs, north of the Pawtuxet, and from thence went on till they reached the first river navigable for ships, which they named the Bolus, and which by its position on Smith's map may be the Severn or the Patapsco.

The men now, having been kept at the oars ten days, tossed about by storms, and with nothing to eat but bread rotten from the wet, supposed that the Captain would turn about and go home. But he reminded them how the company of Ralph Lane, in like circumstances, importuned him to proceed with the discovery of Moratico, alleging that they had yet a dog that boiled with sassafrks leaves would richly feed them. He could not think of returning yet, for they were scarce able to say where they had been, nor had yet heard of what they were sent to seek. He exhorted them to abandon their childish fear of being lost in these unknown, large waters, but he assured them that return he would not, till he had seen the Massawomeks and found the Patowomek.

On the 16th of June they discovered the River Patowomek (Potomac), seven miles broad at the mouth, up which they sailed thirty miles before they encountered any inhabitants. Four savages at length appeared and conducted them up a creek where were three or four thousand in ambush, "so strangely painted, grimed, and disguised, shouting, yelling, and crying as so many spirits from hell could not have showed more terrible." But the discharge of the firearms and the echo in the forest so appeased their fury that they threw down their bows, exchanged hostages, and kindly used the strangers. The Indians told him that Powhatan had commanded them to betray them, and the serious charge is added that Powhatan, "so directed from the discontents at Jamestown because our Captain did cause them to stay in their country against their wills." This reveals the suspicion and thoroughly bad feeling existing among the colonists.

The expedition went up the river to a village called Patowomek, and thence rowed up a little River Quiyough (Acquia Creek?) in search of a mountain of antimony, which they found. The savages put this antimony up in little bags and sold it all over the country to paint their bodies and faces, which made them look like Blackamoors dusted over with silver. Some bags of this they carried away, and also collected a good amount of furs of otters, bears, martens, and minks. Fish were abundant, "lying so thick with their heads above water, as for want of nets (our barge driving among them) we attempted to catch them with a frying-pan; but we found it a bad instrument to catch fish with; neither better fish, more plenty, nor more variety for small fish, had any of us ever seen in any place, so swimming in the water, but they are not to be caught with frying-pans."

In all his encounters and quarrels with the treacherous savages Smith lost not a man; it was his habit when he encountered a body of them to demand their bows, arrows, swords, and furs, and a child or two as hostages.

Having finished his discovery he returned. Passing the mouth of the Rappahannock, by some called the Tappahannock, where in shoal water were many fish lurking in the weeds, Smith had his first experience of the Stingray. It chanced that the Captain took one of these fish from his sword, "not knowing her condition, being much the fashion of a Thornbeck, but a long tayle like a riding rodde whereon the middest is a most poysonne sting of two or three inches long, bearded like a saw on each side, which she struck into the wrist of his arme neare an inch and a half." The arm and shoulder swelled so much, and the torment was so great, that "we all with much sorrow concluded his funerale, and prepared his grave in an island by, as himself directed." But it "pleased God by a precious oyle Dr. Russell applied to it that his tormenting paine was so assuged that he ate of that fish to his supper."

Setting sail for Jamestown, and arriving at Kecoughtan, the sight of the furs and other plunder, and of Captain Smith wounded, led the Indians to think that he had been at war with the Massawomeks; which opinion Smith encouraged. They reached Jamestown July 21st, in fine spirits, to find the colony in a mutinous condition, the last arrivals all sick, and the others on the point of revenging themselves on the silly President, who had brought them all to misery by his riotous consumption of the stores, and by forcing them to work on an unnecessary pleasure-house for himself in the woods. They were somewhat appeased by the good news of the discovery, and in the belief that their bay stretched into the South Sea; and submitted on condition that Ratclifte should be deposed and Captain Smith take upon himself the government, "as by course it did belong." He consented, but substituted Mr. Scrivener, his dear friend, in the presidency, distributed the provisions, appointed honest men to assist Mr. Scrivener, and set out on the 24th, with twelve men, to finish his discovery.

He passed by the Patowomek River and hasted to the River Bolus, which he had before visited. In the bay they fell in with seven or eight canoes full of the renowned Massawomeks, with whom they had a fight, but at length these savages became friendly and gave them bows, arrows, and skins. They were at war with the Tockwoghes. Proceeding up the River Tockwogh, the latter Indians received them with friendship, because they had the weapons which they supposed had been captured in a fight with the Massawomeks. These Indians had hatchets, knives, pieces of iron and brass, they reported came from the Susquesahanocks, a mighty people, the enemies of the Massawomeks, living at the head of the bay. As Smith in his barge could not ascend to them, he sent an interpreter to request a visit from them. In three or four days sixty of these giant-like people came down with presents of venison, tobacco-pipes three feet in length, baskets, targets, and bows and arrows. Some further notice is necessary of this first appearance of the Susquehannocks, who became afterwards so well known, by reason of their great stature and their friendliness. Portraits of these noble savages appeared in De Bry's voyages, which were used in Smith's map, and also by Strachey. These beautiful copperplate engravings spread through Europe most exaggerated ideas of the American savages.

"Our order," says Smith, "was daily to have prayers, with a psalm, at which solemnity the poor savages wondered." When it was over the Susquesahanocks, in a fervent manner, held up their hands to the sun, and then embracing the Captain, adored him in like manner. With a furious manner and "a hellish voyce" they began an oration of their loves, covered him with their painted bear-skins, hung a chain of white beads about his neck, and hailed his creation as their governor and protector, promising aid and victuals if he would stay and help them fight the Massawomeks. Much they told him of the Atquanachuks, who live on the Ocean Sea, the Massawomeks and other people living on a great water beyond the mountain (which Smith understood to be some great lake or the river of Canada), and that they received their hatchets and other commodities from the French. They mourned greatly at Smith's departure. Of Powhatan they knew nothing but the name.

Strachey, who probably enlarges from Smith his account of the same people, whom he calls Sasquesahanougs, says they were well-proportioned giants, but of an honest and simple disposition. Their language well beseemed their proportions, "sounding from them as it were a great voice in a vault or cave, as an ecco." The picture of one of these chiefs is given in De Bry, and described by Strachey," the calf of whose leg was three-quarters of a yard about, and all the rest of his limbs so answerable to the same proportions that he seemed the goodliest man they ever saw."

It would not entertain the reader to follow Smith in all the small adventures of the exploration, during which he says he went about 3,000 miles (three thousand miles in three or four weeks in a rowboat is nothing in Smith's memory), "with such watery diet in these great waters and barbarous countries." Much hardship he endured, alternately skirmishing and feasting with the Indians; many were the tribes he struck an alliance with, and many valuable details he added to the geographical knowledge of the region. In all this exploration Smith showed himself skillful as he was vigorous and adventurous.

He returned to James River September 7th. Many had died, some were sick, Ratcliffe, the late President, was a prisoner for mutiny, Master Scrivener had diligently gathered the harvest, but much of the provisions had been spoiled by rain. Thus the summer was consumed, and nothing had been accomplished except Smith's discovery.

Charles Dudley Warner

# XI

## SMITH'S PRESIDENCY AND PROWESS

On the 10th of September, by the election of the Council and the request of the company, Captain Smith received the letters-patent, and became President. He stopped the building of Ratcliffe's "palace," repaired the church and the storehouse, got ready the buildings for the supply expected from England, reduced the fort to a "five square form," set and trained the watch and exercised the company every Saturday on a plain called Smithfield, to the amazement of the on-looking Indians.

Captain Newport arrived with a new supply of seventy persons. Among them were Captain Francis West, brother to Lord Delaware, Captain Peter Winne, and Captain Peter Waldo, appointed on the Council, eight Dutchmen and Poles, and Mistress Forest and Anne Burrows her maid, the first white women in the colony.

Smith did not relish the arrival of Captain Newport nor the instructions under which he returned. He came back commanded to discover the country of Monacan (above the Falls) and to perform the ceremony of coronation on the Emperor Powhatan.

How Newport got this private commission when he had returned to England without a lump of gold, nor any certainty of the South Sea, or one of the lost company sent out by Raleigh; and why he brought a "fine peeced barge" which must be carried over unknown mountains before it reached the South Sea, he could not understand. "As for the coronation of Powhatan and his presents of basin and ewer, bed, bedding, clothes, and such costly novelties, they had been much better well spared than so ill spent, for we had his favor and better for a plain piece of copper, till this stately kind of soliciting made him so much overvalue himself that he respected us as much as nothing at all." Smith evidently understood the situation much better than the promoters in England; and we can quite excuse him in his rage over the foolishness and greed of most of his companions. There was little nonsense about Smith in action, though he need not turn his hand on any man of that age as a boaster.

To send out Poles and Dutchmen to make pitch, tar, and glass would have been well enough if the colony had been firmly established and supplied with necessaries; and they might have sent two hundred colonists instead of seventy, if they had ordered them to go to work collecting provisions of the Indians for the winter, instead of attempting this strange discovery of the South Sea, and wasting their time on a more strange coronation. "Now was there no way," asks Smith, "to make us miserable," but by direction from England to perform this discovery and coronation, "to take that time, spend what victuals we had, tire and starve our men, having no means to carry victuals, ammunition, the hurt or the sick, but on their own backs?"

Smith seems to have protested against all this nonsense, but though he was governor, the Council overruled him. Captain Newport decided to take one hundred and twenty men, fearing to go with a less number and journey to

Werowocomoco to crown Powhatan. In order to save time Smith offered to take a message to Powhatan, and induce him to come to Jamestown and receive the honor and the presents. Accompanied by only four men he crossed by land to Werowocomoco, passed the Pamaunkee (York) River in a canoe, and sent for Powhatan, who was thirty miles off. Meantime Pocahontas, who by his own account was a mere child, and her women entertained Smith in the following manner:

"In a fayre plaine they made a fire, before which, sitting upon a mat, suddenly amongst the woods was heard such a hydeous noise and shreeking that the English betook themselves to their armes, and seized upon two or three old men, by them supposing Powhatan with all his power was come to surprise them. But presently Pocahontas came, willing him to kill her if any hurt were intended, and the beholders, which were men, women and children, satisfied the Captaine that there was no such matter. Then presently they were presented with this anticke: Thirty young women came naked out of the woods, only covered behind and before with a few greene leaves, their bodies all painted, some of one color, some of another, but all differing; their leader had a fayre payre of Bucks hornes on her head, and an Otters skinne at her girdle, and another at her arme, a quiver of arrows at her backe, a bow and arrows in her hand; the next had in her hand a sword, another a club, another a pot-sticke: all horned alike; the rest every one with their several devises. These fiends with most hellish shouts and cries, rushing from among the trees, cast themselves in a ring about the fire, singing and dancing with most excellent ill-varietie, oft falling into their infernal passions, and solemnly again to sing and dance; having spent nearly an hour in this Mascarado, as they entered, in like manner they departed.

"Having reaccommodated themselves, they solemnly invited

him to their lodgings, where he was no sooner within the house, but all these Nymphs more tormented him than ever, with crowding, pressing, and hanging about him, most tediously crying, 'Love you not me? Love you not me?' This salutation ended, the feast was set, consisting of all the Salvage dainties they could devise: some attending, others singing and dancing about them: which mirth being ended, with fire brands instead of torches they conducted him to his lodging."

The next day Powhatan arrived. Smith delivered up the Indian Namontuck, who had just returned from a voyage to England—whither it was suspected the Emperor wished him to go to spy out the weakness of the English tribe—and repeated Father Newport's request that Powhatan would come to Jamestown to receive the presents and join in an expedition against his enemies, the Monacans.

Powhatan's reply was worthy of his imperial highness, and has been copied ever since in the speeches of the lords of the soil to the pale faces: "If your king has sent me present, I also am a king, and this is my land: eight days I will stay to receive them. Your father is to come to me, not I to him, nor yet to your fort, neither will I bite at such a bait; as for the Monacans, I can revenge my own injuries."

This was the lofty potentate whom Smith, by his way of management, could have tickled out of his senses with a glass bead, and who would infinitely have preferred a big shining copper kettle to the misplaced honor intended to be thrust upon him, but the offer of which puffed him up beyond the reach of negotiation. Smith returned with his message. Newport despatched the presents round by water a hundred miles, and the Captains, with fifty soldiers, went over land to Werowocomoco, where occurred the ridiculous ceremony of the coronation, which Smith describes with much humor. "The next day," he says, "was appointed for the coronation. Then the presents were brought him, his bason and ewer, bed and furniture set up, his scarlet cloke and apparel, with much adoe put on him, being persuaded by Namontuck they would not hurt him. But a foule trouble there was to make him kneel to receive his Crown; he not knowing the majesty nor wearing of a Crown, nor bending of the knee, endured so many persuasions, examples and instructions as tyred them all. At last by bearing hard on his shoulders, he a little stooped, and three having the crown in their hands put it on his head, when by the warning of a pistoll the boats were prepared with such a volley of shot that the king start up in a horrible feare, till he saw all was well. Then remembering himself to congratulate their kindness he gave his old shoes and his mantell to Captain Newport!"

The Monacan expedition the King discouraged, and refused to furnish for it either guides or men. Besides his old shoes, the crowned monarch charitably gave Newport a little heap of corn, only seven or eight bushels, and with this little result the absurd expedition returned to Jamestown.

Shortly after Captain Newport with a chosen company of one hundred and twenty men (leaving eighty with President Smith in the fort) and accompanied by Captain Waldo, Lieutenant Percy, Captain Winne, Mr. West, and Mr. Scrivener, who was eager for adventure, set off for the discovery of Monacan. The expedition, as Smith predicted, was fruitless: the Indians deceived them and refused to trade, and the company got back to Jamestown, half of them sick, all grumbling, and worn out with toil, famine, and discontent.

Smith at once set the whole colony to work, some to make glass, tar, pitch, and soap-ashes, and others he conducted five miles down the river to learn to fell trees and make clapboards. In this company were a couple of gallants, lately come over, Gabriel Beadle and John Russell, proper gentle-men, but unused to hardships, whom Smith has immortalized by his novel cure of their profanity. They took gayly to the rough life, and entered into the attack on the forest so pleasantly that in a week they were masters of chopping: "making it their delight to hear the trees thunder as they fell, but the axes so often blistered their tender fingers that many times every third blow had a loud othe to drown the echo; for remedie of which sinne the President devised how to have every man's othes numbered, and at night for every othe to have a Canne of water powred downe his sleeve, with which every offender was so washed (himself and all), that a man would scarce hear an othe in a weake." In the clearing of our country since, this excellent plan has fallen into desuetude, for want of any pious Captain Smith in the logging camps.

These gentlemen, says Smith, did not spend their time in wood-logging like hirelings, but entered into it with such spirit that thirty of them would accomplish more than a hundred of the sort that had to be driven to work; yet, he sagaciously adds, "twenty good workmen had been better than them all."

Returning to the fort, Smith, as usual, found the time consumed and no provisions got, and Newport's ship lying idle at a great charge. With Percy he set out on an expedition for corn to the Chickahominy, which the insolent Indians, knowing their want, would not supply. Perceiving that it was Powhatan's policy to starve them (as if it was the business of the Indians to support all the European vagabonds and adventurers who came to dispossess them of their country), Smith gave out that he came not so much for corn as to revenge his imprisonment and the death of his men murdered by the Indians, and proceeded to make war. This high-handed treatment made the savages sue for peace, and furnish, although they complained of want themselves, owing to a bad harvest, a hundred bushels of corn.

This supply contented the company, who feared nothing so much as starving, and yet, says Smith, so envied him that they would rather hazard starving than have him get reputation by his vigorous conduct. There is no contemporary account of that period except this which Smith indited. He says that Newport and Ratcliffe conspired not only to depose him but to keep him out of the fort; since being President they could not control his movements, but that their horns were much too short to effect it.

At this time in the "old Taverne," as Smith calls the fort, everybody who had money or goods made all he could by trade; soldiers, sailors, and savages were agreed to barter, and there was more care to maintain their damnable and private trade than to provide the things necessary for the colony. In a few weeks the whites had bartered away nearly all the axes, chisels, hoes, and picks, and what powder, shot, and pikeheads they could steal, in exchange for furs, baskets, young beasts and such like commodities. Though the supply of furs was scanty in Virginia, one master confessed he had got in one voyage by this private trade what he sold in England for thirty pounds. "These are the Saint-seeming Worthies of Virginia," indignantly exclaims the President, "that have, notwithstanding all this, meate, drinke, and wages." But now they began to get weary of the country, their trade being prevented. "The loss, scorn, and misery was the poor officers, gentlemen and careless governors, who were bought and sold." The adventurers were cheated, and all their actions overthrown by false information and unwise directions.

Master Scrivener was sent with the barges and pinnace to Werowocomoco, where by the aid of Namontuck he procured a little corn, though the savages were more ready to fight than to trade. At length Newport's ship was loaded with clapboards, pitch, tar, glass, frankincense (?) and soapashes, and despatched to England. About two hundred men were left in the colony. With Newport, Smith sent his famous letter to the Treasurer and Council in England. It is so good a specimen of Smith's ability with the pen, reveals so well his sagacity and knowledge of what a colony needed, and exposes so clearly the ill-management of the London promoters, and the condition of the colony, that we copy it entire. It appears by this letter that Smith's "Map of Virginia," and his description of the country and its people, which were not published till 1612, were sent by this opportunity. Captain Newport sailed for England late in the autumn of 1608. The letter reads:

RIGHT HONORABLE, ETC.:

I received your letter wherein you write that our minds are so set upon faction, and idle conceits in dividing the country without your consents, and that we feed you but with ifs and ands, hopes and some few proofes; as if we would keepe the mystery of the businesse to ourselves: and that we must expressly follow your instructions sent by Captain Newport: the charge of whose voyage amounts to neare two thousand pounds, the which if we cannot defray by the ships returne we are likely to remain as banished men. To these particulars I humbly intreat your pardons if I offend you with my rude answer.

For our factions, unless you would have me run away and leave the country, I cannot prevent them; because I do make many stay that would else fly away whither. For the Idle letter sent to my Lord of Salisbury, by the President and his confederates, for dividing the country, &c., what it was I know not, for you saw no hand of mine to it; nor ever dream't I of any such matter. That we feed you with hopes,

&c. Though I be no scholar, I am past a schoolboy; and I desire but to know what either you and these here doe know, but that I have learned to tell you by the continuall hazard of my life. I have not concealed from you anything I know; but I feare some cause you to believe much more than is true.

Expressly to follow your directions by Captain Newport, though they be performed, I was directly against it; but according to our commission, I was content to be overouled by the major part of the Councill, I feare to the hazard of us all; which now is generally confessed when it is too late. Onely Captaine Winne and Captaine Walclo I have sworne of the Councill, and crowned Powhattan according to your instructions.

For the charge of the voyage of two or three thousand pounds we have not received the value of one hundred pounds, and for the quartered boat to be borne by the souldiers over the falls. Newport had 120 of the best men he could chuse. If he had burnt her to ashes, one might have carried her in a bag, but as she is, five hundred cannot to a navigable place above the falls. And for him at that time to find in the South Sea a mine of gold; or any of them sent by Sir Walter Raleigh; at our consultation I told them was as likely as the rest. But during this great discovery of thirtie miles (which might as well have been done by one man, and much more, for the value of a pound of copper at a seasonable tyme), they had the pinnace and all the boats with them but one that remained with me to serve the fort. In their absence I followed the new begun works of Pitch and Tarre, Glasse, Sope-ashes, Clapboord, whereof some small quantities we have sent you. But if you rightly consider what an infinite toyle it is in Russia and Swethland, where the woods arc propcr for naught els, and though there be the helpe both of man and beast in those ancient common-wealths, which many an hundred years have used it, yet thousands of those poor people can scarce get necessaries to live, but from hand to mouth, and though your factors there can buy as much in a week as will fraught you a ship, or as much as you please, you must not expect from us any such matter, which are but as many of ignorant, miserable soules, that are scarce able to get wherewith to live, and defend ourselves against the inconstant Salvages: finding but here and there a tree fit for the purpose, and want all things else the Russians have. For the Coronation of Powhattan, by whose advice you sent him such presents, I know not; but this give me leave to tell you, I feare they will be the confusion of us all ere we heare from you again. At your ships arrivall, the Salvages harvest was newly gathered, and we going to buy it, our owne not being halve sufficient for so great a number. As for the two ships loading of corne Newport promised to provide us from Powhattan, he brought us but fourteen bushels; and from the Monacans nothing, but the most of the men sicke and neare famished. From your ship we had not provision in victuals worth twenty pound, and we are more than two hundred to live upon this, the one halfe sicke, the other little better. For the saylers (I confesse), they daily make good cheare, but our dyet is a little meale and water, and not sufficient of that. Though there be fish in the Sea, fowles in the ayre, and beasts in the woods, their bounds are so large, they so wilde, and we so weake and ignorant, we cannot much trouble them. Captaine Newport we much suspect to be the Author of these inventions. Now that you should know, I have made you as great a discovery as he, for less charge than he spendeth you every meale; I had sent you this mappe of the Countries and Nations that inhabit them, as you may see at large. Also two barrels of stones, and such as I take to be good. Iron ore at the least; so divided, as by their notes you may see in what places I found them. The souldiers say many of your officers maintaine their families out of that you sent us, and that Newport hath an hundred pounds a year for carrying newes. For every master you have yet sent can find the way as well as he, so that an hundred pounds might be spared, which is more than we have all, that helps to pay him wages. Cap. Ratliffe is now called Sicklemore, a poore counterfeited Imposture. I have sent you him home least the Company should cut his throat. What he is, now every one can tell you: if he and Archer returne againe, they are sufficient to keep us always in factions. When you send againe I entreat you rather send but thirty carpenters, husbandmen, gardiners, fishermen, blacksmiths, masons, and diggers up of trees roots, well provided, then a thousand of such as we have; for except wee be able both to lodge them, and feed them, the most will consume with want of necessaries before they can be made good for anything. Thus if you please to consider this account, and the unnecessary wages to Captaine Newport, or his ships so long lingering and staying here (for notwithstanding his boasting to leave us victuals for 12 months, though we had 89 by this discovery lame and sicke, and but a pinte of corne a day for a man, we were constrained to give him three hogsheads of that to victuall him homeward), or yet to send into Germany or Poleland for glassemen and the rest, till we be able to sustaine ourselves, and releeve them when they come. It were better to give five hundred pound a ton for those grosse Commodities in Denmarke, then send for them hither, till more necessary things be provided. For in over-toyling our weake and unskilfull bodies, to satisfy this desire of present profit, we can scarce ever recover ourselves from one supply to another. And I humbly intreat you hereafter, let us have what we should receive, and not stand to the Saylers courtesie to leave us what they please, els you may charge us what you will, but we not you with anything. These are the causes that have kept us in Virginia from laying such a foundation that ere this might have given much better content and satisfaction, but as yet you must not look for any profitable returning. So I humbly rest.

After the departure of Newport, Smith, with his accustomed resolution, set to work to gather supplies for the winter. Corn had to be extorted from the Indians by force. In one expedition to Nansemond, when the Indians refused to trade, Smith fired upon them, and then landed and burned one of their houses; whereupon they submitted and loaded his three boats with corn. The ground was covered with ice and snow, and the nights were bitterly cold. The device for sleeping warm in the open air was to sweep the snow away from the ground and build a fire; the fire was then raked off from the heated earth and a mat spread, upon which the whites lay warm, sheltered by a mat hung up on the windward side, until the ground got cold, when they builded a fire on another place. Many a cold winter night did the explorers endure this hardship, yet grew fat and lusty under it.

About this time was solemnized the marriage of John Laydon and Anne Burrows, the first in Virginia. Anne was the maid of Mistress Forrest, who had just come out to grow up with the country, and John was a laborer who came with the first colony in 1607. This was actually the "First Family of Virginia," about which so much has been eloquently said.

Provisions were still wanting. Mr. Scrivener and Mr. Percy returned from an expedition with nothing. Smith proposed to surprise Powhatan, and seize his store of corn, but he says he was hindered in this project by Captain Winne and Mr. Scrivener (who had heretofore been considered one of Smith's friends), whom he now suspected of plotting his ruin in England.

Powhatan on his part sent word to Smith to visit him, to send him men to build a house, give him a grindstone, fifty swords, some big guns, a cock and a hen, much copper and beads, in return for which he would load his ship with corn. Without any confidence in the crafty savage, Smith humored him by sending several workmen, including four Dutchmen, to build him a house. Meantime with two barges and the pinnace and forty-six men, including Lieutenant Percy, Captain Wirt, and Captain William Phittiplace, on the 29th of December he set out on a journey to the Pamaunky, or York, River.

The first night was spent at "Warraskogack," the king of which warned Smith that while Powhatan would receive him kindly he was only seeking an opportunity to cut their throats and seize their arms. Christmas was kept with extreme winds, rain, frost and snow among the savages at Kecoughton, where before roaring fires they made merry with plenty of oysters, fish, flesh, wild fowls and good bread. The President and two others went gunning for birds, and brought down one hundred and forty-eight fowls with three shots.

Ascending the river, on the 12th of January they reached Werowocomoco. The river was frozen half a mile from the shore, and when the barge could not come to land by reason of the ice and muddy shallows, they effected a landing by wading. Powhatan at their request sent them venison, turkeys, and bread; the next day he feasted them, and then inquired when they were going, ignoring his invitation to them to come. Hereupon followed a long game of fence between Powhatan and Captain Smith, each trying to overreach the other, and each indulging profusely in lies and pledges. Each professed the utmost love for the other.

Smith upbraided him with neglect of his promise to supply them with corn, and told him, in reply to his demand for weapons, that he had no arms to spare. Powhatan asked him, if he came on a peaceful errand, to lay aside his weapons, for he had heard that the English came not so much for trade as to invade his people and possess his country, and the people did not dare to bring in their corn while the English were around.

Powhatan seemed indifferent about the building. The Dutchmen who had come to build Powhatan a house liked the Indian plenty better than the risk of starvation with the colony, revealed to Powhatan the poverty of the whites, and plotted to betray them, of which plot Smith was not certain till six months later. Powhatan discoursed eloquently on the advantage of peace over war: "I have seen the death of all my people thrice," he said, "and not any one living of those three generations but myself; I know the difference of peace and war better than any in my country. But I am now old and ere long must die." He wanted to leave his brothers and sisters in peace. He heard that Smith came to destroy his country. He asked him what good it would do to destroy them that provided his food, to drive them into the woods where they must feed on roots and acorns; "and be so hunted by you that I can neither rest, eat nor sleep, but my tired men must watch, and if a twig but break every one crieth, there cometh Captain Smith!" They might live in peace, and trade, if Smith would only lay aside his arms. Smith, in return, boasted of his power to get provisions, and said that he had only been restrained from violence by his love for Powhatan; that the Indians came armed to Jamestown, and it was the habit of the whites to wear their arms. Powhatan then contrasted the liberality of Newport, and told Smith that while he had used him more kindly than any other chief, he had received from him (Smith) the least kindness of any.

Believing that the palaver was only to get an opportunity to cut his throat, Smith got the savages to break the ice in order to bring up the barge and load it with corn, and gave orders for his soldiers to land and surprise Powhatan; meantime, to allay his suspicions, telling him the lie that next day he would lay aside his arms and trust Powhatan's promises. But

Charles Dudley Warner

Powhatan was not to be caught with such chaff. Leaving two or three women to talk with the Captain he secretly fled away with his women, children, and luggage. When Smith perceived this treachery he fired into the "naked devils" who were in sight. The next day Powhatan sent to excuse his flight, and presented him a bracelet and chain of pearl and vowed eternal friendship.

With matchlocks lighted, Smith forced the Indians to load the boats; but as they were aground, and could not be got off till high water, he was compelled to spend the night on shore. Powhatan and the treacherous Dutchmen are represented as plotting to kill Smith that night. Provisions were to be brought him with professions of friendship, and Smith was to be attacked while at supper. The Indians, with all the merry sports they could devise, spent the time till night, and then returned to Powhatan.

The plot was frustrated in the providence of God by a strange means. "For Pocahuntas his dearest jewele and daughter in that dark night came through the irksome woods, and told our Captaine good cheer should be sent us by and by; but Powhatan and all the power he could make would after come and kill us all, if they that brought it could not kill us with our own weapons when we were at supper. Therefore if we would live she wished us presently to be gone. Such things as she delighted in he would have given her; but with the tears rolling down her cheeks she said she durst not to be seen to have any; for if Powhatan should know it, she were but dead, and so she ran away by herself as she came."

[This instance of female devotion is exactly paralleled in D'Albertis's "New Guinea." Abia, a pretty Biota girl of seventeen, made her way to his solitary habitation at the peril of her life, to inform him that the men of Rapa would shortly bring him insects and other presents, in order to get near him without suspicion, and then kill him. He tried to reward the brave girl by hanging a gold chain about her neck, but she refused it, saying it would betray her. He could only reward her with a fervent kiss, upon which she fled. Smith omits that part of the incident.]

In less than an hour ten burly fellows arrived with great platters of victuals, and begged Smith to put out the matches (the smoke of which made them sick) and sit down and eat. Smith, on his guard, compelled them to taste each dish, and then sent them back to Powhatan. All night the whites watched, but though the savages lurked about, no attack was made. Leaving the four Dutchmen to build Powhatan's house, and an Englishman to shoot game for him, Smith next evening departed for Pamaunky.

No sooner had he gone than two of the Dutchmen made their way overland to Jamestown, and, pretending Smith had sent them, procured arms, tools, and clothing. They induced also half a dozen sailors, "expert thieves," to accompany them to live with Powhatan; and altogether they stole, besides powder and shot, fifty swords, eight pieces, eight pistols, and three hundred hatchets. Edward Boynton and Richard Savage, who had been left with Powhatan, seeing the treachery, endeavored to escape, but were apprehended by the Indians.

At Pamaunky there was the same sort of palaver with Opechancanough, the king, to whom Smith the year before had expounded the mysteries of history, geography, and astronomy. After much fencing in talk, Smith, with fifteen companions, went up to the King's house, where presently he found himself betrayed and surrounded by seven hundred armed savages, seeking his life. His company being dismayed, Smith restored their courage by a speech, and then, boldly charging the King with intent to murder him, he challenged him to a single combat on an island in the river, each to use his own arms, but Smith to be as naked as the King. The King still professed friendship, and laid a great present at the door, about which the Indians lay in ambush to kill Smith. But this hero, according to his own account, took prompt measures. He marched out to the King where he stood guarded by fifty of his chiefs, seized him by his long hair in the midst of his men, and pointing a pistol at his breast led, him trembling and near dead with fear amongst all his people. The King gave up his arms, and the savages, astonished that any man dare treat their king thus, threw down their bows. Smith, still holding the King by the hair, made them a bold address, offering peace or war. They chose peace.

In the picture of this remarkable scene in the "General Historie," the savage is represented as gigantic in stature, big enough to crush the little Smith in an instant if he had but chosen. Having given the savages the choice to load his ship with corn or to load it himself with their dead carcasses, the Indians so thronged in with their commodities that Smith was tired of receiving them, and leaving his comrades to trade, he lay down to rest. When he was asleep the Indians, armed some with clubs, and some with old English swords, entered into the house. Smith awoke in time, seized his arms, and others coming to his rescue, they cleared the house.

While enduring these perils, sad news was brought from Jamestown. Mr. Scrivener, who had letters from England (writes Smith) urging him to make himself Caesar or nothing, declined in his affection for Smith, and began to exercise extra authority. Against the advice of the others, he needs must make a journey to the Isle of Hogs, taking with him in the boat Captain Waldo, Anthony Gosnoll (or Gosnold, believed to be a relative of Captain Bartholomew Gosnold), and eight others. The boat was overwhelmed in a storm, and sunk, no one knows how or where. The savages were the first to discover the bodies of the lost. News of this disaster was brought to Captain Smith (who did not disturb the rest by making it known) by Richard Wiffin, who encountered great dangers on the way. Lodging overnight at Powhatan's, he saw great preparations for war, and found himself in peril. Pocahontas hid him for a time, and by her means, and extraordinary bribes, in three days' travel he reached Smith.

Powhatan, according to Smith, threatened death to his followers if they did not kill Smith. At one time swarms of natives, unarmed, came bringing great supplies of provisions; this was to put Smith off his guard, surround him with hundreds of savages, and slay him by an ambush. But he also laid in ambush and got the better of the crafty foe with a superior craft. They sent him poisoned food, which made his company sick, but was fatal to no one. Smith apologizes for temporizing with the Indians at this time, by explaining that his purpose was to surprise Powhatan and his store of provisions. But when they stealthily stole up to the seat of that crafty chief, they found that those "damned Dutchmen" had caused Powhatan to abandon his new house at Werowocomoco, and to carry away all his corn and provisions.

The reward of this wearisome winter campaign was two hundred weight of deer-suet and four hundred and seventy-nine bushels of corn for the general store. They had not to show such murdering and destroying as the Spaniards in their "relations," nor heaps and mines of gold and silver; the land of Virginia was barbarous and ill-planted, and without precious jewels, but no Spanish relation could show, with such scant means, so much country explored, so many natives reduced to obedience, with so little bloodshed.

# XII

## TRIALS OF THE SETTLEMENT

Without entering at all into the consideration of the character of the early settlers of Virginia and of Massachusetts, one contrast forces itself upon the mind as we read the narratives of the different plantations. In Massachusetts there was from the beginning a steady purpose to make a permanent settlement and colony, and nearly all those who came over worked, with more or less friction, with this end before them. The attempt in Virginia partook more of the character of a temporary adventure. In Massachusetts from the beginning a commonwealth was in view. In Virginia, although the London promoters desired a colony to be fixed that would be profitable to themselves, and many of the adventurers, Captain Smith among them, desired a permanent planting, a great majority of those who went thither had only in mind the advantages of trade, the excitement of a free and licentious life, and the adventure of something new and startling. It was long before the movers in it gave up the notion of discovering precious metals or a short way to the South Sea. The troubles the primitive colony endured resulted quite as much from its own instability of purpose, recklessness, and insubordination as from the hostility of the Indians. The majority spent their time in idleness, quarreling, and plotting mutiny.

The ships departed for England in December, 1608. When Smith returned from his expedition for food in the winter of 1609, he found that all the provision except what he had gathered was so rotted from the rain, and eaten by rats and worms, that the hogs would scarcely eat it. Yet this had been the diet of the soldiers, who had consumed the victuals and accomplished nothing except to let the savages have the most of the tools and a good part of the arms.

Taking stock of what he brought in, Smith found food enough to last till the next harvest, and at once organized the company into bands of ten or fifteen, and compelled them to go to work. Six hours a day were devoted to labor, and the remainder to rest and merry exercises. Even with this liberal allowance of pastime a great part of the colony still sulked. Smith made them a short address, exhibiting his power in the letters-patent, and assuring them that he would enforce discipline and punish the idle and froward; telling them that those that did not work should not eat, and that the labor of forty or fifty industrious men should not be consumed to maintain a hundred and fifty idle loiterers. He made a public table of good and bad conduct; but even with this inducement the worst had to be driven to work by punishment or the fear of it.

The Dutchmen with Powhatan continued to make trouble, and confederates in the camp supplied them with powder and shot, swords and tools. Powhatan kept the whites who were with him to instruct the Indians in the art of war. They expected other whites to join them, and those not coming, they sent Francis, their companion, disguised as an Indian, to find out the cause. He came to the Glass house in the woods a mile from Jamestown, which was the rendezvous for all their villainy. Here they laid an ambush of forty men for Smith, who hearing of the Dutchman, went thither to apprehend him. The rascal had gone, and Smith, sending

Charles Dudley Warner

twenty soldiers to follow and capture him, started alone from the Glass house to return to the fort. And now occurred another of those personal adventures which made Smith famous by his own narration.

On his way he encountered the King of Paspahegh, "a most strong, stout savage," who, seeing that Smith had only his falchion, attempted to shoot him. Smith grappled him; the savage prevented his drawing his blade, and bore him into the river to drown him. Long they struggled in the water, when the President got the savage by the throat and nearly strangled him, and drawing his weapon, was about to cut off his head, when the King begged his life so pitifully, that Smith led him prisoner to the fort and put him in chains.

In the pictures of this achievement, the savage is represented as about twice the size and stature of Smith; another illustration that this heroic soul was never contented to take one of his size.

The Dutchman was captured, who, notwithstanding his excuses that he had escaped from Powhatan and did not intend to return, but was only walking in the woods to gather walnuts, on the testimony of Paspahegh of his treachery, was also "laid by the heels." Smith now proposed to Paspahegh to spare his life if he would induce Powhatan to send back the renegade Dutchmen. The messengers for this purpose reported that the Dutchmen, though not detained by Powhatan, would not come, and the Indians said they could not bring them on their backs fifty miles through the woods. Daily the King's wives, children, and people came to visit him, and brought presents to procure peace and his release. While this was going on, the King, though fettered, escaped. A pursuit only resulted in a vain fight with the Indians. Smith then made prisoners of two Indians who seemed to be hanging around the camp, Kemps and Tussore, "the two most exact villains in all the country," who would betray their own king and kindred for a piece of copper, and sent them with a force of soldiers, under Percy, against Paspahegh. The expedition burned his house, but did not capture the fugitive. Smith then went against them himself, killed six or seven, burned their houses, and took their boats and fishing wires. Thereupon the savages sued for peace, and an amnesty was established that lasted as long as Smith remained in the country.

Another incident occurred about this time which greatly raised Smith's credit in all that country. The Chicahomanians, who always were friendly traders, were great thieves. One of them stole a Pistol, and two proper young fellows, brothers, known to be his confederates, were apprehended. One of them was put in the dungeon and the other sent to recover the pistol within twelve hours, in default of which his brother would be hanged. The President, pitying the wretched savage in the dungeon, sent him some victuals and charcoal for a fire. "Ere midnight his brother returned with the pistol, but the poor savage in the dungeon was so smothered with the smoke he had made, and so piteously burnt, that we found him dead. The other most lamentably bewailed his death, and broke forth in such bitter agonies, that the President, to quiet him, told him that if hereafter they would not steal, he would make him alive again; but he (Smith) little thought he could be recovered." Nevertheless, by a liberal use of aqua vitae and vinegar the Indian was brought again to life, but "so drunk and affrighted that he seemed lunatic, the which as much tormented and grieved the other as before to see him dead." Upon further promise of good behavior Smith promised to bring the Indian out of this malady also, and so laid him by a fire to sleep. In the morning the savage had recovered his perfect senses, his wounds were dressed, and the brothers with presents of copper were sent away well contented. This was spread among the savages for a miracle, that Smith could make a man alive that was dead. He narrates a second incident which served to give the Indians a wholesome fear of the whites: "Another ingenious savage of Powhatan having gotten a great bag of powder and the back of an armour at Werowocomoco, amongst a many of his companions, to show his extraordinary skill, he did dry it on the back as he had seen the soldiers at Jamestown. But he dried it so long, they peeping over it to see his skill, it took fire, and blew him to death, and one or two more, and the rest so scorched they had little pleasure any more to meddle with gunpowder."

"These and many other such pretty incidents," says Smith, "so amazed and affrighted Powhatan and his people that from all parts they desired peace;" stolen articles were returned, thieves sent to Jamestown for punishment, and the whole country became as free for the whites as for the Indians.

And now ensued, in the spring of 1609, a prosperous period of three months, the longest season of quiet the colony had enjoyed, but only a respite from greater disasters. The friendship of the Indians and the temporary subordination of the settlers we must attribute to Smith's vigor, shrewdness, and spirit of industry. It was much easier to manage the Indian's than the idle and vicious men that composed the majority of the settlement.

In these three months they manufactured three or four lasts (fourteen barrels in a last) of tar, pitch, and soap-ashes, produced some specimens of glass, dug a well of excellent sweet water in the fort, which they had wanted for two years, built twenty houses, repaired the church, planted thirty or forty acres of ground, and erected a block-house on the neck of the island, where a garrison was stationed to trade with the savages and permit neither whites nor Indians to pass except on the President's order. Even the domestic animals partook the industrious spirit: "of three sowes in eighteen months increased 60 and od Pigs; and neare 500 chickings brought up themselves without having any meat given them." The hogs were transferred to Hog Isle, where another block house was built and garrisoned, and the garrison were permitted to take "exercise" in cutting down trees and making clapboards and wainscot. They were building a fort on high ground, intended for an easily defended retreat, when a woful discovery put an end to their thriving plans.

Upon examination of the corn stored in casks, it was found half-rotten, and the rest consumed by rats, which had bred in thousands from the few which came over in the ships. The colony was now at its wits end, for there was nothing to eat except the wild products of the country. In this prospect of famine, the two Indians, Kemps and Tussore, who had been kept fettered while showing the whites how to plant the fields, were turned loose; but they were unwilling to depart from such congenial company. The savages in the neighborhood showed their love by bringing to camp, for sixteen days, each day at least a hundred squirrels, turkeys, deer, and other wild beasts. But without corn, the work of fortifying and building had to be abandoned, and the settlers dispersed to provide victuals. A party of sixty or eighty men under Ensign Laxon were sent down the river to live on oysters; some twenty went with Lieutenant Percy to try fishing at Point Comfort, where for six weeks not a net was cast, owing to the sickness of Percy, who had been burnt with gunpowder; and another party, going to the Falls with Master West, found nothing to eat but a few acorns.

Up to this time the whole colony was fed by the labors of thirty or forty men: there was more sturgeon than could be devoured by dog and man; it was dried, pounded, and mixed with caviare, sorrel, and other herbs, to make bread; bread was also made of the "Tockwhogh" root, and with the fish and these wild fruits they lived very well. But there were one hundred and fifty of the colony who would rather starve or eat each other than help gather food. These "distracted, gluttonous loiterers" would have sold anything they had—tools, arms, and their houses—for anything the savages would bring them to eat. Hearing that there was a basket of corn at Powhatan's, fifty miles away, they would have exchanged all their property for it. To satisfy their factious humors, Smith succeeded in getting half of it: "they would have sold their souls," he says, for the other half, though not sufficient to last them a week.

The clamors became so loud that Smith punished the ringleader, one Dyer, a crafty fellow, and his ancient maligner, and then made one of his conciliatory addresses. Having shown them how impossible it was to get corn, and reminded them of his own exertions, and that he had always shared with them anything he had, he told them that he should stand their nonsense no longer; he should force the idle to work, and punish them if they railed; if any attempted to escape to Newfoundland in the pinnace they would arrive at the gallows; the sick should not starve; every man able must work, and every man who did not gather as much in a day as he did should be put out of the fort as a drone.

Such was the effect of this speech that of the two hundred only seven died in this pinching time, except those who were drowned; no man died of want. Captain Winne and Master Leigh had died before this famine occurred. Many of the men were billeted among the savages, who used them well, and stood in such awe of the power at the fort that they dared not wrong the whites out of a pin. The Indians caught Smith's humor, and some of the men who ran away to seek Kemps and Tussore were mocked and ridiculed, and had applied to them—Smith's law of "who cannot work must not eat;" they were almost starved and beaten nearly to death. After amusing himself with them, Kemps returned the fugitives, whom Smith punished until they were content to labor at home, rather than adventure to live idly among the savages, "of whom," says our shrewd chronicler, "there was more hope to make better christians and good subjects than the one half of them that counterfeited themselves both." The Indians were in such subjection that any who were punished at the fort would beg the President not to tell their chief, for they would be again punished at home and sent back for another round.

We hear now of the last efforts to find traces of the lost colony of Sir Walter Raleigh. Master Sicklemore returned from the Chawwonoke (Chowan River) with no tidings of them; and Master Powell, and Anas Todkill who had been conducted to the Mangoags, in the regions south of the James, could learn nothing but that they were all dead. The king of this country was a very proper, devout, and friendly man; he acknowledged that our God exceeded his as much as our guns did his bows and arrows, and asked the President to pray his God for him, for all the gods of the Mangoags were angry.

The Dutchmen and one Bentley, another fugitive, who were with Powhatan, continued to plot against the colony, and the President employed a Swiss, named William Volday, to go and regain them with promises of pardon. Volday turned out to be a hypocrite, and a greater rascal than the others. Many of the discontented in the fort were brought into the scheme, which was, with Powhatan's aid, to surprise and destroy Jamestown. News of this getting about in the fort, there was a demand that the President should cut off these Dutchmen. Percy and Cuderington, two gentlemen, volunteered to do it; but Smith sent instead Master Wiffin and Jeffrey Abbot, to go and stab them or shoot them. But the Dutchmen were too shrewd to be caught, and Powhatan sent a conciliatory message that he did not detain the Dutchmen, nor hinder the slaying of them.

While this plot was simmering, and Smith was surrounded by treachery inside the fort and outside, and the savages were being taught that King James would kill Smith because he had used the Indians so unkindly, Captain Argall and Master Thomas Sedan arrived out in a well-furnished vessel, sent by Master Cornelius to trade and fish for sturgeon. The wine and other good provision of the ship were so opportune to the necessities of the colony that the President seized them. Argall lost his voyage; his ship was revictualed and sent back to England, but one may be sure that this event was so represented as to increase the fostered dissatisfaction with Smith in London. For one reason or another, most of the persons who returned had probably carried a bad report of him. Argall brought to Jamestown from London a report of great complaints of him for his dealings with the savages and not returning ships freighted with the products of the country. Misrepresented in London, and unsupported and conspired against in Virginia, Smith felt his fall near at hand. On the face of it he was the victim of envy and the rascality of incompetent and bad men; but whatever his capacity for dealing with savages, it must be confessed that he lacked something which conciliates success with one's own people. A new commission was about to be issued, and a great supply was in preparation under Lord De La Ware.

# XIII

## SMITH'S LAST DAYS IN VIRGINIA

The London company were profoundly dissatisfied with the results of the Virginia colony. The South Sea was not discovered, no gold had turned up, there were no valuable products from the new land, and the promoters received no profits on their ventures. With their expectations, it is not to be wondered at that they were still further annoyed by the quarreling amongst the colonists themselves, and wished to begin over again.

A new charter, dated May 23, 1609, with enlarged powers, was got from King James. Hundreds of corporators were named, and even thousands were included in the various London trades and guilds that were joined in the enterprise. Among the names we find that of Captain John Smith. But he was out of the Council, nor was he given then or ever afterward any place or employment in Virginia, or in the management of its affairs. The grant included all the American coast two hundred miles north and two hundred miles south of Point Comfort, and all the territory from the coast up into the land throughout from sea to sea, west and northwest. A leading object of the project still being (as we have seen it was with Smith's precious crew at Jamestown) the conversion and reduction of the natives to the true religion, no one was permitted in the colony who had not taken the oath of supremacy.

Under this charter the Council gave a commission to Sir Thomas West, Lord Delaware, Captain-General of Virginia; Sir Thomas Gates, Lieutenant-General; Sir George Somers, Admiral; Captain Newport, Vice-Admiral; Sir Thomas Dale, High Marshal; Sir Frederick Wainman, General of the Horse, and many other officers for life.

With so many wealthy corporators money flowed into the treasury, and a great expedition was readily fitted out. Towards the end of May, 1609, there sailed from England nine ships and five hundred people, under the command of Sir Thomas Gates, Sir George Somers, and Captain Newport. Each of these commanders had a commission, and the one who arrived first was to call in the old commission; as they could not agree, they all sailed in one ship, the Sea Venture.

This brave expedition was involved in a contest with a hurricane; one vessel was sunk, and the Sea Venture, with the three commanders, one hundred and fifty men, the new commissioners, bills of lading, all sorts of instructions, and much provision, was wrecked on the Bermudas. With this company was William Strachey, of whom we shall hear more hereafter. Seven vessels reached Jamestown, and brought, among other annoyances, Smith's old enemy, Captain Ratcliffe, alias Sicklemore, in command of a ship. Among the company were also Captains Martin, Archer, Wood, Webbe, Moore, King, Davis, and several gentlemen of good means, and a crowd of the riff-raff of London. Some of these Captains whom Smith had sent home, now returned with new pretensions, and had on the voyage prejudiced the company against him. When the fleet was first espied, the President thought it was Spaniards, and prepared to defend himself, the Indians promptly coming to his assistance.

This hurricane tossed about another expedition still more famous, that of Henry Hudson, who had sailed from England on his third voyage toward Nova Zembla March 25th, and in July and August was beating down the Atlantic coast. On the 18th of August he entered the Capes of Virginia, and sailed a little way up the Bay. He knew he was at the mouth of the James River, "where our Englishmen are," as he says. The next day a gale from the northeast made him fear being driven aground in the shallows, and he put to sea. The storm continued for several days. On the 21st "a sea broke over the fore-course and split it;" and that night something more ominous occurred: "that night [the chronicle records] our cat ran crying from one side of the ship to the other, looking overboard, which made us to wonder, but we saw nothing." On the 26th they were again off the bank of Virginia, and in the very bay and in sight of the islands they had seen on the 18th. It appeared to Hudson "a great bay with rivers," but too shallow to explore without a small boat. After lingering till the 29th, without any suggestion of ascending the James, he sailed northward and made the lucky stroke of river exploration which immortalized him.

It seems strange that he did not search for the English colony, but the adventurers of that day were independent actors, and did not care to share with each other the glories of discovery.

The first of the scattered fleet of Gates and Somers came in on the 11th, and the rest straggled along during the three or four days following. It was a narrow chance that Hudson missed them all, and one may imagine that the fate of the Virginia colony and of the New York settlement would have been different if the explorer of the Hudson had gone up the James.

No sooner had the newcomers landed than trouble began.

They would have deposed Smith on report of the new commission, but they could show no warrant. Smith professed himself willing to retire to England, but, seeing the new commission did not arrive, held on to his authority, and began to enforce it to save the whole colony from anarchy. He depicts the situation in a paragraph: "To a thousand mischiefs these lewd Captains led this lewd company, wherein were many unruly gallants, packed thither by their friends to escape ill destinies, and those would dispose and determine of the government, sometimes to one, the next day to another; today the old commission must rule, tomorrow the new, the next day neither; in fine, they would rule all or ruin all; yet in charity we must endure them thus to destroy us, or by correcting their follies, have brought the world's censure upon us to be guilty of their blouds. Happie had we beene had they never arrived, and we forever abandoned, as we were left to our fortunes; for on earth for their number was never more confusion or misery than their factions occasioned." In this company came a boy, named Henry Spelman, whose subsequent career possesses considerable interest.

The President proceeded with his usual vigor: he "laid by the heels" the chief mischief-makers till he should get leisure to punish them; sent Mr. West with one hundred and twenty good men to the Falls to make a settlement; and despatched Martin with near as many and their proportion of provisions to Nansemond, on the river of that name emptying into the James, obliquely opposite Point Comfort.

Lieutenant Percy was sick and had leave to depart for England when he chose. The President's year being about expired, in accordance with the charter, he resigned, and Captain Martin was elected President. But knowing his inability, he, after holding it three hours, resigned it to Smith, and went down to Nansemond. The tribe used him kindly, but he was so frightened with their noisy demonstration of mirth that he surprised and captured the poor naked King with his houses, and began fortifying his position, showing so much fear that the savages were emboldened to attack him, kill some of his men, release their King, and carry off a thousand bushels of corn which had been purchased, Martin not offering to intercept them. The frightened Captain sent to Smith for aid, who despatched to him thirty good shot. Martin, too chicken-hearted to use them, came back with them to Jamestown, leaving his company to their fortunes. In this adventure the President commends the courage of one George Forrest, who, with seventeen arrows sticking into him and one shot through him, lived six or seven days.

Meantime Smith, going up to the Falls to look after Captain West, met that hero on his way to Jamestown. He turned him back, and found that he had planted his colony on an unfavorable flat, subject not only to the overflowing of the river, but to more intolerable inconveniences. To place him more advantageously the President sent to Powhatan, offering to buy the place called Powhatan, promising to defend him against the Monacans, to pay him in copper, and make a general alliance of trade and friendship.

But "those furies," as Smith calls West and his associates, refused to move to Powhatan or to accept these conditions. They contemned his authority, expecting all the time the new commission, and, regarding all the Monacans' country as full of gold, determined that no one should interfere with them in the possession of it. Smith, however, was not intimidated from landing and attempting to quell their mutiny. In his "General Historie" it is written "I doe more than wonder to think how onely with five men he either durst or would adventure as he did (knowing how greedy they were of his bloud) to come amongst them." He landed and ordered the arrest of the chief disturbers, but the crowd hustled him off. He seized one of their boats and escaped to the ship which contained the provision. Fortunately the sailors were friendly and saved his life, and a considerable number of the better sort, seeing the malice of Ratcliffe and Archer, took Smith's part.

Out of the occurrences at this new settlement grew many of the charges which were preferred against Smith. According to the "General Historie" the company of Ratcliffe and Archer was a disorderly rabble, constantly tormenting the Indians, stealing their corn, robbing their gardens, beating them, and breaking into their houses and taking them prisoners. The Indians daily complained to the President that these "protectors" he had given them were worse enemies than the Monacans, and desired his pardon if they defended themselves, since he could not punish their tormentors. They even proposed to fight for him against them. Smith says that after spending nine days in trying to restrain them, and showing them how they deceived themselves with "great guilded hopes of the South Sea Mines," he abandoned them to their folly and set sail for Jamestown.

No sooner was he under way than the savages attacked the fort, slew many of the whites who were outside, rescued their friends who were prisoners, and thoroughly terrified the garrison. Smith's ship happening to go aground half a league below, they sent off to him, and were glad to submit on any terms to his mercy. He "put by the heels" six or seven of the chief offenders, and transferred the colony to Powhatan, where were a fort capable of defense against all the savages in Virginia, dry houses for lodging, and two hundred acres of ground ready to be planted. This place, so strong and delightful in situation, they called Non-such. The savages appeared and exchanged captives, and all became friends again.

At this moment, unfortunately, Captain West returned. All

the victuals and munitions having been put ashore, the old factious projects were revived. The soft-hearted West was made to believe that the rebellion had been solely on his account. Smith, seeing them bent on their own way, took the row-boat for Jamestown. The colony abandoned the pleasant Non-such and returned to the open air at West's Fort. On his way down, Smith met with the accident that suddenly terminated his career in Virginia.

While he was sleeping in his boat his powder-bag was accidentally fired; the explosion tore the flesh from his body and thighs, nine or ten inches square, in the most frightful manner. To quench the tormenting fire, frying him in his clothes, he leaped into the deep river, where, ere they could recover him, he was nearly drowned. In this pitiable condition, without either surgeon or surgery, he was to go nearly a hundred miles.

It is now time for the appearance upon the scene of the boy Henry Spelman, with his brief narration, which touches this period of Smith's life. Henry Spelman was the third son of the distinguished antiquarian, Sir Henry Spelman, of Coughan, Norfolk, who was married in 1581. It is reasonably conjectured that he could not have been over twenty-one when in May, 1609, he joined the company going to Virginia. Henry was evidently a scapegrace, whose friends were willing to be rid of him. Such being his character, it is more than probable that he was shipped bound as an apprentice, and of course with the conditions of apprentice-ship in like expeditions of that period—to be sold or bound out at the end of the voyage to pay for his passage. He remained for several years in Virginia, living most of the time among the Indians, and a sort of indifferent go between of the savages and the settlers. According to his own story it was on October 20, 1609, that he was taken up the river to Powhatan by Captain Smith, and it was in April, 1613, that he was rescued from his easy-setting captivity on the Potomac by Captain Argall. During his sojourn in Virginia, or more probably shortly after his return to England, he wrote a brief and bungling narration of his experiences in the colony, and a description of Indian life. The MS. was not printed in his time, but mislaid or forgotten. By a strange series of chances it turned up in our day, and was identified and prepared for the press in 1861. Before the proof was read, the type was accidentally broken up and the MS. again mislaid. Lost sight of for several years, it was recovered and a small number of copies of it were printed at London in 1872, edited by Mr. James F. Hunnewell.

Spelman's narration would be very important if we could trust it. He appeared to have set down what he saw, and his story has a certain simplicity that gains for it some credit. But he was a reckless boy, unaccustomed to weigh evidence, and quite likely to write as facts the rumors that he heard. He took very readily to the ways of Indian life. Some years after, Spelman returned to Virginia with the title of Captain, and in 1617 we find this reference to him in the "General Historie": "Here, as at many other times, we are beholden to Capt. Henry Spilman, an interpreter, a gentleman that lived long time in this country, and sometimes a prisoner among the Salvages, and done much good service though but badly rewarded." Smith would probably not have left this on record had he been aware of the contents of the MS. that Spelman had left for after-times.

Spelman begins his Relation, from which I shall quote substantially, without following the spelling or noting all the interlineations, with the reason for his emigration, which was, "being in displeasure of my friends, and desirous to see other countries." After a brief account of the voyage and the joyful arrival at Jamestown, the Relation continues:

"Having here unloaded our goods and bestowed some senight or fortnight in viewing the country, I was carried by Capt. Smith, our President, to the Falls, to the little Powhatan, where, unknown to me, he sold me to him for a town called Powhatan; and, leaving me with him, the little Powhatan, he made known to Capt. West how he had bought a town for them to dwell in. Whereupon Capt. West, growing angry because he had bestowed cost to begin a town in another place, Capt. Smith desiring that Capt. West would come and settle himself there, but Capt. West, having bestowed cost to begin a town in another place, misliked it, and unkindness thereupon arising between them, Capt. Smith at that time replied little, but afterward combined with Powhatan to kill Capt. West, which plot took but small effect, for in the meantime Capt. Smith was apprehended and sent aboard for England."

That this roving boy was "thrown in" as a makeweight in the trade for the town is not impossible; but that Smith combined with Powhatan to kill Captain West is doubtless West's perversion of the offer of the Indians to fight on Smith's side against him.

According to Spelman's Relation, he stayed only seven or eight days with the little Powhatan, when he got leave to go to Jamestown, being desirous to see the English and to fetch the small articles that belonged to him. The Indian King agreed to wait for him at that place, but he stayed too long, and on his return the little Powhatan had departed, and Spelman went back to Jamestown. Shortly after, the great Powhatan sent Thomas Savage with a present of venison to President Percy. Savage was loath to return alone, and Spelman was appointed to go with him, which he did willingly, as victuals were scarce in camp. He carried some copper and a hatchet, which he presented to Powhatan, and that Emperor treated him and his comrade very kindly, seating them at his own mess-table. After some three weeks of this life, Powhatan sent this guileless youth down to decoy the English into his hands, promising to freight a ship with corn if they would visit him. Spelman took the message and brought back the English reply, whereupon Powhatan laid the plot which resulted in the killing of Captain Ratcliffe and thirty-eight men, only two of his company escaping to Jamestown. Spelman gives two versions of this incident. During the massacre Spelman says that Powhatan sent him and Savage to a town some sixteen miles away. Smith's "General Historie" says that on this occasion "Pocahuntas saved a boy named Henry Spilman that lived many years afterward, by her means, among the Patawomekes." Spelman says not a word about Pocahuntas. On the contrary, he describes the visit of the King of the Patawomekes to Powhatan; says that the King took a fancy to him; that he and Dutch Samuel, fearing for their lives, escaped from Powhatan's town; were pursued; that Samuel was killed, and that Spelman, after dodging about in the forest, found his way to the Potomac, where he lived with this good King Patomecke at a place called Pasptanzie for more than a year. Here he seems to have passed his time agreeably, for although he had occasional fights with the squaws of Patomecke, the King was always his friend, and so much was he attached to the boy that he would not give him up to Captain Argall without some copper in exchange.

When Smith returned wounded to Jamestown, he was physically in no condition to face the situation. With no medical attendance, his death was not improbable. He had no strength to enforce discipline nor organize expeditions for supplies; besides, he was acting under a commission whose virtue had expired, and the mutinous spirits rebelled against his authority. Ratcliffe, Archer, and the others who were awaiting trial conspired against him, and Smith says he would have been murdered in his bed if the murderer's heart had not failed him when he went to fire his pistol at the defenseless sick man. However, Smith was forced to yield to circumstances. No sooner had he given out that he would depart for England than they persuaded Mr. Percy to stay and act as President, and all eyes were turned in expectation of favor upon the new commanders. Smith being thus divested of authority, the most of the colony turned against him; many preferred charges, and began to collect testimony. "The ships were detained three weeks to get up proofs of his ill-conduct"—"time and charges," says Smith, dryly, "that might much better have been spent."

It must have enraged the doughty Captain, lying thus helpless, to see his enemies triumph, the most factious of the disturbers in the colony in charge of affairs, and become his accusers. Even at this distance we can read the account with little patience, and should have none at all if the account were not edited by Smith himself. His revenge was in his good fortune in setting his own story afloat in the current of history. The first narrative of these events, published by Smith in his Oxford tract of 1612, was considerably remodeled and changed in his "General Historie" of 1624. As we have said before, he had a progressive memory, and his opponents ought to be thankful that the pungent Captain did not live to work the story over a third time.

It is no doubt true, however, that but for the accident to our hero, he would have continued to rule till the arrival of Gates and Somers with the new commissions; as he himself says, "but had that unhappy blast not happened, he would quickly have qualified the heat of those humors and factions, had the ships but once left them and us to our fortunes; and have made that provision from among the salvages, as we neither feared Spaniard, Salvage, nor famine: nor would have left Virginia nor our lawful authority, but at as dear a price as we had bought it, and paid for it."

He doubtless would have fought it out against all comers; and who shall say that he does not merit the glowing eulogy on himself which he inserts in his General History? "What shall I say but this, we left him, that in all his proceedings made justice his first guide, and experience his second, ever hating baseness, sloth, pride, and indignity, more than any dangers; that upon no danger would send them where he would not lead them himself; that would never see us want what he either had or could by any means get us; that would rather want than borrow; or starve than not pay; that loved action more than words, and hated falsehood and covetousness worse than death; whose adventures were our lives, and whose loss our deaths."

A handsomer thing never was said of another man than Smith could say of himself, but he believed it, as also did many of his comrades, we must suppose. He suffered detraction enough, but he suffered also abundant eulogy both in verse and prose. Among his eulogists, of course, is not the factious Captain Ratcliffe. In the English Colonial State papers, edited by Mr. Noel Sainsbury, is a note, dated Jamestown, October 4, 1609, from Captain "John Radclyffe comenly called," to the Earl of Salisbury, which contains this remark upon Smith's departure after the arrival of the last supply: "They heard that all the Council were dead but Capt. [John] Smith, President, who reigned sole Governor, and is now sent home to answer some misdemeanor."

Captain Archer also regards this matter in a different light from that in which Smith represents it. In a letter from Jamestown, written in August, he says:

"In as much as the President [Smith], to strengthen his authority, accorded with the variances and gave not any due respect to many worthy gentlemen that were in our ships, wherefore they generally, with my consent, chose Master

West, my Lord De La Ware's brother, their Governor or President de bene esse, in the absence of Sir Thomas Gates, or if he be miscarried by sea, then to continue till we heard news from our counsell in England. This choice of him they made not to disturb the old President during his term, but as his authority expired, then to take upon him the sole government, with such assistants of the captains or discreet persons as the colony afforded.

"Perhaps you shall have it blamed as a mutinie by such as retaine old malice, but Master West, Master Piercie, and all the respected gentlemen of worth in Virginia, can and will testify otherwise upon their oaths. For the King's patent we ratified, but refused to be governed by the President—that is, after his time was expired and only subjected ourselves to Master West, whom we labor to have next President."

It is clear from this statement that the attempt was made to supersede Smith even before his time expired, and without any authority (since the new commissions were still with Gates and Somers in Bermuda), for the reason that Smith did not pay proper respect to the newly arrived "gentlemen." Smith was no doubt dictatorial and offensive, and from his point of view he was the only man who understood Virginia, and knew how successfully to conduct the affairs of the colony. If this assumption were true it would be none the less disagreeable to the new-comers.

At the time of Smith's deposition the colony was in prosperous condition. The "General Historie" says that he left them "with three ships, seven boats, commodities ready to trade, the harvest newly gathered, ten weeks' provision in store, four hundred ninety and odd persons, twenty-four pieces of ordnance, three hundred muskets, snaphances and fire-locks, shot, powder, and match sufficient, curats, pikes, swords, and morrios, more than men; the Salvages, their language and habitations well known to a hundred well-trained and expert soldiers; nets for fishing; tools of all kinds to work; apparel to supply our wants; six mules and a horse; five or six hundred swine; as many hens and chickens; some goats; some sheep; what was brought or bred there remained." Jamestown was also strongly palisaded and contained some fifty or sixty houses; besides there were five or six other forts and plantations, "not so sumptuous as our succerers expected, they were better than they provided any for us."

These expectations might well be disappointed if they were founded upon the pictures of forts and fortifications in Virginia and in the Somers Islands, which appeared in De Bry and in the "General Historie," where they appear as massive stone structures with all the finish and elegance of the European military science of the day.

Notwithstanding these ample provisions for the colony, Smith had small expectation that it would thrive without him. "They regarding nothing," he says, "but from hand to mouth, did consume what we had, took care for nothing but to perfect some colorable complaint against Captain Smith."

Nor was the composition of the colony such as to beget high hopes of it. There was but one carpenter, and three others that desired to learn, two blacksmiths, ten sailors; those called laborers were for the most part footmen, brought over to wait upon the adventurers, who did not know what a day's work was—all the real laborers were the Dutchmen and Poles and some dozen others. "For all the rest were poor gentlemen, tradesmen, serving men, libertines, and such like, ten times more fit to spoil a commonwealth than either begin one or help to maintain one. For when neither the fear of God, nor the law, nor shame, nor displeasure of their friends could rule them here, there is small hope ever to bring one in twenty of them to be good there." Some of them proved more industrious than was expected; "but ten good workmen would have done more substantial work in a day than ten of them in a week."

The disreputable character of the majority of these colonists is abundantly proved by other contemporary testimony. In the letter of the Governor and Council of Virginia to the London Company, dated Jamestown, July 7, 1610, signed by Lord De La Ware, Thomas Gates, George Percy, Ferd. Wenman, and William Strachey, and probably composed by Strachey, after speaking of the bountiful capacity of the country, the writer exclaims: "Only let me truly acknowledge there are not one hundred or two of deboisht hands, dropt forth by year after year, with penury and leysure, ill provided for before they come, and worse governed when they are here, men of such distempered bodies and infected minds, whom no examples daily before their eyes, either of goodness or punishment, can deterr from their habituall impieties, or terrifie from a shameful death, that must be the carpenters and workmen in this so glorious a building."

The chapter in the "General Historie" relating to Smith's last days in Virginia was transferred from the narrative in the appendix to Smith's "Map of Virginia," Oxford, 1612, but much changed in the transfer. In the "General Historie" Smith says very little about the nature of the charges against him. In the original narrative signed by Richard Pots and edited by Smith, there are more details of the charges. One omitted passage is this: "Now all those Smith had either whipped or punished, or in any way disgraced, had free power and liberty to say or sweare anything, and from a whole armful of their examinations this was concluded."

Another omitted passage relates to the charge, to which reference is made in the "General Historie," that Smith proposed to marry Pocahontas:

"Some propheticall spirit calculated he had the salvages in such subjection, he would have made himself a king by marrying Pocahuntas, Powhatan's daughter. It is true she was the very nonpareil of his kingdom, and at most not past thirteen or fourteen years of age. Very oft she came to our fort with what she could get for Capt. Smith, that ever loved and used all the country well, but her especially he ever much respected, and she so well requited it, that when her father intended to have surprised him, she by stealth in the dark night came through the wild woods and told him of it. But her marriage could in no way have entitled him by any right to the kingdom, nor was it ever suspected he had such a thought, or more regarded her or any of them than in honest reason and discretion he might. If he would he might have married her, or have done what he listed. For there were none that could have hindered his determination."

It is fair, in passing, to remark that the above allusion to the night visit of Pocahontas to Smith in this tract of 1612 helps to confirm the story, which does not appear in the previous narration of Smith's encounter with Powhatan at Werowocomoco in the same tract, but is celebrated in the "General Historie." It is also hinted plainly enough that Smith might have taken the girl to wife, Indian fashion.

# XIV

## THE COLONY WITHOUT SMITH

It was necessary to follow for a time the fortune of the Virginia colony after the departure of Captain Smith. Of its disasters and speedy decline there is no more doubt than there is of the opinion of Smith that these were owing to his absence. The savages, we read in his narration, no sooner knew he was gone than they all revolted and spoiled and murdered all they encountered.

The day before Captain Smith sailed, Captain Davis arrived in a small pinnace with sixteen men. These, with a company from the fort under Captain Ratcliffe, were sent down to Point Comfort. Captain West and Captain Martin, having lost their boats and half their men among the savages at the Falls, returned to Jamestown. The colony now lived upon what Smith had provided, "and now they had presidents with all their appurtenances." President Percy was so sick he could neither go nor stand. Provisions getting short, West and Ratcliffe went abroad to trade, and Ratcliffe and twenty-eight of his men were slain by an ambush of Powhatan's, as before related in the narrative of Henry Spelman. Powhatan cut off their boats, and refused to trade, so that Captain West set sail for England. What ensued cannot be more vividly told than in the "General Historie":

"Now we all found the losse of Capt. Smith, yea his greatest maligners could now curse his losse; as for corne provision and contribution from the salvages, we had nothing but mortall wounds, with clubs and arrowes; as for our hogs, hens, goats, sheep, horse, or what lived, our commanders, officers and salvages daily consumed them, some small proportions sometimes we tasted, till all was devoured; then swords, arms, pieces or anything was traded with the salvages, whose cruell fingers were so oft imbrued in our blouds, that what by their crueltie, our Governor's indiscretion, and the losse of our ships, of five hundred within six months after Capt. Smith's departure, there remained not past sixty men, women and children, most miserable and poore creatures; and those were preserved for the most part, by roots, herbes, acorns, walnuts, berries, now and then a little fish; they that had starch in these extremities made no small use of it, yea, even the very skinnes of our horses. Nay, so great was our famine, that a salvage we slew and buried, the poorer sort took him up again and eat him, and so did divers one another boyled, and stewed with roots and herbs. And one amongst the rest did kill his wife, poudered her and had eaten part of her before it was knowne, for which he was executed, as he well deserved; now whether she was better roasted, boyled, or carbonaded, I know not, but of such a dish as powdered wife I never heard of. This was that time, which still to this day we called the starving time; it were too vile to say and scarce to be believed what we endured; but the occasion was our owne, for want of providence, industrie and government, and not the barreness and defect of the country as is generally supposed."

This playful allusion to powdered wife, and speculation as to how she was best cooked, is the first instance we have been able to find of what is called "American humor," and Captain Smith has the honor of being the first of the "American humorists" who have handled subjects of this kind with such pleasing gayety.

It is to be noticed that this horrible story of cannibalism and wife-eating appears in Smith's "General Historie" of 1624, without a word of contradiction or explanation, although the company as early as 1610 had taken pains to get at the facts, and Smith must have seen their "Declaration," which supposes the story was started by enemies of the colony. Some reported they saw it, some that Captain Smith said so, and some that one Beadle, the lieutenant of Captain Davis, did relate it. In "A True Declaration of the State of the Colonie in Virginia," published by the advice and direction of the Council of Virginia, London, 1610, we read:

"But to clear all doubt, Sir Thomas Yates thus relateth the tragedie:

"There was one of the company who mortally hated his wife, and therefore secretly killed her, then cut her in pieces and hid her in divers parts of his house: when the woman was missing, the man suspected, his house searched, and parts of her mangled body were discovered, to excuse himself he said that his wife died, that he hid her to satisfie his hunger, and that he fed daily upon her. Upon this his house was again searched, when they found a good quantitie of meale, oatmeale, beanes and pease. Hee therefore was arraigned, confessed the murder, and was burned for his horrible villainy."

This same "True Declaration," which singularly enough does not mention the name of Captain Smith, who was so prominent an actor in Virginia during the period to which it relates, confirms all that Smith said as to the character of the colonists, especially the new supply which landed in the eight vessels with Ratcliffe and Archer. "Every man overvalueing his own strength would be a commander; every man underprizing another's value, denied to be commanded." They were negligent and improvident. "Every man sharked for his

Charles Dudley Warner

present bootie, but was altogether careless of succeeding penurie." To idleness and faction was joined treason. About thirty "unhallowed creatures," in the winter of 1610, some five months before the arrival of Captain Gates, seized upon the ship Swallow, which had been prepared to trade with the Indians, and having obtained corn conspired together and made a league to become pirates, dreaming of mountains of gold and happy robberies. By this desertion they weakened the colony, which waited for their return with the provisions, and they made implacable enemies of the Indians by their violence. "These are that scum of men," which, after roving the seas and failing in their piracy, joined themselves to other pirates they found on the sea, or returned to England, bound by a mutual oath to discredit the land, and swore they were drawn away by famine. "These are they that roared at the tragicall historie of the man eating up his dead wife in Virginia"—"scandalous reports of a viperous generation."

If further evidence were wanting, we have it in "The New Life of Virginia," published by authority of the Council, London, 1612. This is the second part of the "Nova Britannia," published in London, 1609. Both are prefaced by an epistle to Sir Thomas Smith, one of the Council and treasurer, signed "R. I." Neither document contains any allusion to Captain John Smith, or the part he played in Virginia. The "New Life of Virginia," after speaking of the tempest which drove Sir Thomas Gates on Bermuda, and the landing of the eight ships at Jamestown, says: "By which means the body of the plantation was now augmented with such numbers of irregular persons that it soon became as so many members without a head, who as they were bad and evil affected for the most part before they went hence; so now being landed and wanting restraint, they displayed their condition in all kinds of looseness, those chief and wisest guides among them (whereof there were not many) did nothing but bitterly contend who should be first to command the rest, the common sort, as is ever seen in such cases grew factious and disordered out of measure, in so much as the poor colony seemed (like the Colledge of English fugitives in Rome) as a hostile camp within itself; in which distemper that envious man stept in, sowing plentiful tares in the hearts of all, which grew to such speedy confusion, that in few months ambition, sloth and idleness had devoured the fruit of former labours, planting and sowing were clean given over, the houses decayed, the church fell to ruin, the store was spent, the cattle consumed, our people starved, and the Indians by wrongs and injuries made our enemies.... As for those wicked Impes that put themselves a shipboard, not knowing otherwise how to live in England; or those ungratious sons that daily vexed their fathers hearts at home, and were therefore thrust upon the voyage, which either writing thence, or being returned back to cover their own leudnes, do fill mens ears with false reports of their miserable and perilous life in Virginia, let the imputation of misery be to their idleness, and the blood that was spilt upon their own heads that caused it."

Sir Thomas Gates affirmed that after his first coming there he had seen some of them eat their fish raw rather than go a stone's cast to fetch wood and dress it.

The colony was in such extremity in May, 1610, that it would have been extinct in ten days but for the arrival of Sir Thomas Gates and Sir George Somers and Captain Newport from the Bermudas. These gallant gentlemen, with one hundred and fifty souls, had been wrecked on the Bermudas in the Sea Venture in the preceding July. The terrors of the hurricane which dispersed the fleet, and this shipwreck, were much dwelt upon by the writers of the time, and the Bermudas became a sort of enchanted islands, or realms of the imagination. For three nights, and three days that were as black as the nights, the water logged Sea Venture was scarcely kept afloat by bailing. We have a vivid picture of the stanch Somers sitting upon the poop of the ship, where he sat three days and three nights together, without much meat and little or no sleep, conning the ship to keep her as upright as he could, until he happily descried land. The ship went ashore and was wedged into the rocks so fast that it held together till all were got ashore, and a good part of the goods and provisions, and the tackling and iron of the ship necessary for the building and furnishing of a new ship.

This good fortune and the subsequent prosperous life on the island and final deliverance was due to the noble Somers, or Sommers, after whom the Bermudas were long called "Sommers Isles," which was gradually corrupted into "The Summer Isles." These islands of Bermuda had ever been accounted an enchanted pile of rocks and a desert inhabitation for devils, which the navigator and mariner avoided as Scylla and Charybdis, or the devil himself. But this shipwrecked company found it the most delightful country in the world, the climate was enchanting, delicious fruits abounded, the waters swarmed with fish, some of them big enough to nearly drag the fishers into the sea, while whales could be heard spouting and nosing about the rocks at night; birds fat and tame and willing to be eaten covered all the bushes, and such droves of wild hogs covered the island that the slaughter of them for months seemed not to diminish their number. The friendly disposition of the birds seemed most to impress the writer of the "True Declaration of Virginia." He remembers how the ravens fed Elias in the brook Cedron; "so God provided for our disconsolate people in the midst of the sea by foules; but with an admirable difference; unto Elias the ravens brought meat, unto our men the foules brought (themselves) for meate: for when they whistled, or made any strange noyse, the foules would come and sit on their shoulders, they would suffer themselves to be taken and weighed by our men, who would make choice of the fairest and fattest and let flie the leane and lightest, an accident [the chronicler exclaims], I take it [and everybody will take it], that cannot be paralleled by any Historie, except when God sent abundance of Quayles to feed his Israel in the barren wilderness."

The rescued voyagers built themselves comfortable houses on the island, and dwelt there nine months in good health and plentifully fed. Sunday was carefully observed, with sermons by Mr. Buck, the chaplain, an Oxford man, who was assisted in the services by Stephen Hopkins, one of the Puritans who were in the company. A marriage was celebrated between Thomas Powell, the cook of Sir George Somers, and Elizabeth Persons, the servant of Mrs. Horlow. Two children were also born, a boy who was christened Bermudas and a girl Bermuda. The girl was the child of Mr. John Rolfe and wife, the Rolfe who was shortly afterward to become famous by another marriage. In order that nothing should be wanting to the ordinary course of a civilized community, a murder was committed. In the company were two Indians, Machumps and Namontack, whose acquaintance we have before made, returning from England, whither they had been sent by Captain Smith. Falling out about something, Machumps slew Namontack, and having made a hole to bury him, because it was too short he cut off his legs and laid them by him. This proceeding Machumps concealed till he was in Virginia.

Somers and Gates were busy building two cedar ships, the Deliverer, of eighty tons, and a pinnace called the Patience. When these were completed, the whole company, except two scamps who remained behind and had adventures enough for a three-volume novel, embarked, and on the 16th of May sailed for Jamestown, where they arrived on the 23d or 24th, and found the colony in the pitiable condition before described. A few famished settlers watched their coming.

The church bell was rung in the shaky edifice, and the emaciated colonists assembled and heard the "zealous and sorrowful prayer" of Chaplain Buck. The commission of Sir Thomas Gates was read, and Mr. Percy retired from the governorship.

The town was empty and unfurnished, and seemed like the ruin of some ancient fortification rather than the habitation of living men. The palisades were down; the ports open; the gates unhinged; the church ruined and unfrequented; the houses empty, torn to pieces or burnt; the people not able to step into the woods to gather fire-wood; and the Indians killing as fast without as famine and pestilence within. William Strachey was among the new-comers, and this is the story that he despatched as Lord Delaware's report to England in July. On taking stock of provisions there was found only scant rations for sixteen days, and Gates and Somers determined to abandon the plantation, and, taking all on board their own ships, to make their way to Newfoundland, in the hope of falling in with English vessels. Accordingly, on the 7th of June they got on board and dropped down the James.

Meantime the news of the disasters to the colony, and the supposed loss of the Sea Venture, had created a great excitement in London, and a panic and stoppage of subscriptions in the company. Lord Delaware, a man of the highest reputation for courage and principle, determined to go himself, as Captain-General, to Virginia, in the hope of saving the fortunes of the colony. With three ships and one hundred and fifty persons, mostly artificers, he embarked on the 1st of April, 1610, and reached the Chesapeake Bay on the 5th of June, just in time to meet the forlorn company of Gates and Somers putting out to sea.

They turned back and ascended to Jamestown, when landing

on Sunday, the 10th, after a sermon by Mr. Buck, the commission of Lord Delaware was read, and Gates turned over his authority to the new Governor. He swore in as Council, Sir Thomas Gates, Lieutenant-General; Sir George Somers, Admiral; Captain George Percy; Sir Ferdinando Wenman, Marshal; Captain Christopher Newport, and William Strachey, Esq., Secretary and Recorder.

On the 19th of June the brave old sailor, Sir George Somers, volunteered to return to the Bermudas in his pinnace to procure hogs and other supplies for the colony. He was accompanied by Captain Argall in the ship Discovery. After a rough voyage this noble old knight reached the Bermudas. But his strength was not equal to the memorable courage of his mind. At a place called Saint George he died, and his men, confounded at the death of him who was the life of them all, embalmed his body and set sail for England. Captain Argall, after parting with his consort, without reaching the Bermudas, and much beating about the coast, was compelled to return to Jamestown.

Captain Gates was sent to England with despatches and to procure more settlers and more supplies. Lord Delaware remained with the colony less than a year; his health failing, he went in pursuit of it, in March, 1611, to the West Indies. In June of that year Gates sailed again, with six vessels, three hundred men, one hundred cows, besides other cattle, and provisions of all sorts. With him went his wife, who died on the passage, and his daughters. His expedition reached the James in August. The colony now numbered seven hundred persons. Gates seated himself at Hampton, a "delicate and necessary site for a city."

Percy commanded at Jamestown, and Sir Thomas Dale went up the river to lay the foundations of Henrico.

We have no occasion to follow further the fortunes of the Virginia colony, except to relate the story of Pocahontas under her different names of Amonate, Matoaka, Mrs. Rolfe, and Lady Rebecca.

# XV

## NEW ENGLAND ADVENTURES

Captain John Smith returned to England in the autumn of 1609, wounded in body and loaded with accusations of misconduct, concocted by his factious companions in Virginia. There is no record that these charges were ever considered by the London Company. Indeed, we cannot find that the company in those days ever took any action on the charges made against any of its servants in Virginia. Men came home in disgrace and appeared to receive neither vindication nor condemnation. Some sunk into private life, and others more pushing and brazen, like Ratcliffe, the enemy of Smith, got employment again after a time. The affairs of the company seem to have been conducted with little order or justice.

Whatever may have been the justice of the charges against Smith, he had evidently forfeited the good opinion of the company as a desirable man to employ. They might esteem his energy and profit by his advice and experience, but they did not want his services. And in time he came to be considered an enemy of the company.

Unfortunately for biographical purposes, Smith's life is pretty much a blank from 1609 to 1614. When he ceases to write about himself he passes out of sight. There are scarcely any contemporary allusions to his existence at this time. We may assume, however, from our knowledge of his restlessness, ambition, and love of adventure, that he was not idle. We may assume that he besieged the company with his plans for the proper conduct of the settlement of Virginia; that he talked at large in all companies of his discoveries, his exploits, which grew by the relating, and of the prospective greatness of the new Britain beyond the Atlantic. That he wearied the Council by his importunity and his acquaintances by his hobby, we can also surmise. No doubt also he was considered a fanatic by those who failed to comprehend the greatness of his schemes, and to realize, as he did, the importance of securing the new empire to the English before it was occupied by the Spanish and the French. His conceit, his boasting, and his overbearing manner, which no doubt was one of the causes why he was unable to act in harmony with the other adventurers of that day, all told against him. He was that most uncomfortable person, a man conscious of his own importance, and out of favor and out of money.

Yet Smith had friends, and followers, and men who believed in him. This is shown by the remarkable eulogies in verse from many pens, which he prefixes to the various editions of his many works. They seem to have been written after reading the manuscripts, and prepared to accompany the printed volumes and tracts. They all allude to the envy and detraction to which he was subject, and which must have amounted to a storm of abuse and perhaps ridicule; and they all tax the English vocabulary to extol Smith, his deeds, and his works. In putting forward these tributes of admiration and affection, as well as in his constant allusion to the ill requital of his services, we see a man fighting for his reputation, and conscious of the necessity of doing so. He is ever turning back, in whatever he writes, to rehearse his exploits and to defend his motives.

The London to which Smith returned was the London of Shakespeare's day; a city dirty, with ill-paved streets unlighted at night, no sidewalks, foul gutters, wooden houses, gable ends to the street, set thickly with small windows from which slops and refuse were at any moment of the day or night liable to be emptied upon the heads of the passers by; petty little shops in which were beginning to be displayed the silks and luxuries of the continent; a city crowded and growing rapidly, subject to pestilences and liable to sweeping conflagrations. The Thames had no bridges, and hundreds of boats plied between London side and Southwark, where were most of the theatres, the bull-baitings, the bear-fighting, the public gardens, the residences of the hussies, and other amusements that Bankside, the resort of all classes bent on pleasure, furnished high or low. At no time before or since was there such fantastical fashion in dress, both in cut and gay colors, nor more sumptuousness in costume or luxury in display among the upper classes, and such squalor in low life. The press teemed with tracts and pamphlets, written in language "as plain as a pikestaff," against the immoralities of the theatres, those "seminaries of vice," and calling down the judgment of God upon the cost and the monstrosities of the dress of both men and women; while the town roared on its way, warned by sermons, and instructed in its chosen path by such plays and masques as Ben Jonson's "Pleasure reconciled to Virtue."

The town swarmed with idlers, and with gallants who wanted advancement but were unwilling to adventure their ease to obtain it. There was much lounging in apothecaries' shops to smoke tobacco, gossip, and hear the news. We may be sure that Smith found many auditors for his adventures and his complaints. There was a good deal of interest in the New World, but mainly still as a place where gold and other wealth might be got without much labor, and as a possible short cut to the South Sea and Cathay. The vast number of

Londoners whose names appear in the second Virginia charter shows the readiness of traders to seek profit in adventure. The stir for wider freedom in religion and government increased with the activity of exploration and colonization, and one reason why James finally annulled the Virginia, charter was because he regarded the meetings of the London Company as opportunities of sedition.

Smith is altogether silent about his existence at this time. We do not hear of him till 1612, when his "Map of Virginia" with his description of the country was published at Oxford. The map had been published before: it was sent home with at least a portion of the description of Virginia. In an appendix appeared (as has been said) a series of narrations of Smith's exploits, covering the rime he was in Virginia, written by his companions, edited by his friend Dr. Symonds, and carefully overlooked by himself.

Failing to obtain employment by the Virginia company, Smith turned his attention to New England, but neither did the Plymouth company avail themselves of his service. At last in 1614 he persuaded some London merchants to fit him out for a private trading adventure to the coast of New England. Accordingly with two ships, at the charge of Captain Marmaduke Roydon, Captain George Langam, Mr. John Buley, and William Skelton, merchants, he sailed from the Downs on the 3d of March, 1614, and in the latter part of April "chanced to arrive in New England, a part of America at the Isle of Monahiggan in 43 1/2 of Northerly latitude." This was within the territory appropriated to the second (the Plymouth) colony by the patent of 1606, which gave leave of settlement between the 38th and 44th parallels.

Smith's connection with New England is very slight, and mainly that of an author, one who labored for many years to excite interest in it by his writings. He named several points, and made a map of such portion of the coast as he saw, which was changed from time to time by other observations. He had a remarkable eye for topography, as is especially evident by his map of Virginia. This New England coast is roughly indicated in Venazzani's Plot Of 1524, and better on Mercator's of a few years later, and in Ortelius's "Theatrum Orbis Terarum" of 1570; but in Smith's map we have for the first time a fair approach to the real contour.

Of Smith's English predecessors on this coast there is no room here to speak. Gosnold had described Elizabeth's Isles, explorations and settlements had been made on the coast of Maine by Popham and Weymouth, but Smith claims the credit of not only drawing the first fair map of the coast, but of giving the name "New England" to what had passed under the general names of Virginia, Canada, Norumbaga, etc.

Smith published his description of New England June 18, 1616, and it is in that we must follow his career. It is dedicated to the "high, hopeful Charles, Prince of Great Britain," and is prefaced by an address to the King's Council for all the plantations, and another to all the adventurers into New England. The addresses, as usual, call attention to his own merits. "Little honey [he writes] hath that hive, where there are more drones than bees; and miserable is that land where more are idle than are well employed. If the endeavors of these vermin be acceptable, I hope mine may be excusable: though I confess it were more proper for me to be doing what I say than writing what I know. Had I returned rich I could not have erred; now having only such food as came to my net, I must be taxed. But, I would my taxers were as ready to adventure their purses as I, purse, life, and all I have; or as diligent to permit the charge, as I know they are vigilant to reap the fruits of my labors." The value of the fisheries he had demonstrated by his catch; and he says, looking, as usual, to large results, "but because I speak so much of fishing, if any mistake me for such a devote fisher, as I dream of nought else, they mistake me. I know a ring of gold from a grain of barley as well as a goldsmith; and nothing is there to be had which fishing doth hinder, but further us to obtain."

John Smith first appears on the New England coast as a whale fisher. The only reference to his being in America in Josselyn's "Chronological Observations of America" is under the wrong year, 1608: "Capt. John Smith fished now for whales at Monhiggen." He says: "Our plot there was to take whales, and made tryall of a Myne of gold and copper;" these failing they were to get fish and furs. Of gold there had been little expectation, and (he goes on) "we found this whale fishing a costly conclusion; we saw many, and spent much time in chasing them; but could not kill any; they being a kind of Jubartes, and not the whale that yeeldes finnes and oyle as we expected." They then turned their attention to smaller fish, but owing to their late arrival and "long lingering about the whale"—chasing a whale that they could not kill because it was not the right kind—the best season for fishing was passed. Nevertheless, they secured some 40,000 cod—the figure is naturally raised to 60,000 when Smith retells the story fifteen years afterwards.

But our hero was a born explorer, and could not be content with not examining the strange coast upon which he found himself. Leaving his sailors to catch cod, he took eight or nine men in a small boat, and cruised along the coast, trading wherever he could for furs, of which he obtained above a thousand beaver skins; but his chance to trade was limited by the French settlements in the east, by the presence of one of Popham's ships opposite Monhegan, on the main, and by a couple of French vessels to the westward. Having examined the coast from Penobscot to Cape Cod, and gathered a profitable harvest from the sea, Smith returned in his vessel, reaching the Downs within six months after his departure. This was his whole experience in New England, which ever afterwards he regarded as particularly his discovery, and spoke of as one of his children, Virginia being the other.

With the other vessel Smith had trouble. He accuses its master, Thomas Hunt, of attempting to rob him of his plots and observations, and to leave him "alone on a desolate isle, to the fury of famine, And all other extremities." After Smith's departure the rascally Hunt decoyed twenty-seven unsuspecting savages on board his ship and carried them off to Spain, where he sold them as slaves. Hunt sold his furs at a great profit. Smith's cargo also paid well: in his letter to Lord Bacon in 1618 he says that with forty-five men he had cleared L 1,500 in less than three months on a cargo of dried fish and beaver skins—a pound at that date had five times the purchasing power of a pound now.

The explorer first landed on Monhegan, a small island in sight of which in the war of 1812 occurred the lively little seafight of the American Wasp and the British Frolic, in which the Wasp was the victor, but directly after, with her prize, fell into the hands of an English seventy-four.

He made certainly a most remarkable voyage in his open boat. Between Penobscot and Cape Cod (which he called Cape James) he says he saw forty several habitations, and sounded about twenty-five excellent harbors. Although Smith accepted the geographical notion of his time, and thought that Florida adjoined India, he declared that Virginia was not an island, but part of a great continent, and he comprehended something of the vastness of the country he was coasting along, "dominions which stretch themselves into the main, God doth know how many thousand miles, of which one could no more guess the extent and products than a stranger sailing betwixt England and France could tell what was in Spain, Italy, Germany, Bohemia, Hungary, and the rest." And he had the prophetic vision, which he more than once refers to, of one of the greatest empires of the world that would one day arise here. Contrary to the opinion that prevailed then and for years after, he declared also that New England was not an island.

Smith describes with considerable particularity the coast, giving the names of the Indian tribes, and cataloguing the native productions, vegetable and animal. He bestows his favorite names liberally upon points and islands—few of which were accepted. Cape Ann he called from his charming Turkish benefactor, "Cape Tragabigzanda"; the three islands in front of it, the "Three Turks' Heads"; and the Isles of Shoals he simply describes: "Smyth's Isles are a heape together, none neare them, against Acconimticus." Cape Cod, which appears upon all the maps before Smith's visit as "Sandy" cape, he says "is only a headland of high hills of sand, overgrown with shrubbie pines, hurts [whorts, whortleberries] and such trash; but an excellent harbor for all weathers. This Cape is made by the maine Sea on the one side, and a great bay on the other in the form of a sickle."

A large portion of this treatise on New England is devoted to an argument to induce the English to found a permanent colony there, of which Smith shows that he would be the proper leader. The main staple for the present would be fish, and he shows how Holland has become powerful by her fisheries and the training of hardy sailors. The fishery would support a colony until it had obtained a good foothold, and control of these fisheries would bring more profit to England than any other occupation. There are other reasons than gain that should induce in England the large ambition of founding a great state, reasons of religion and humanity, erecting towns, peopling countries, informing the ignorant, reforming things unjust, teaching virtue, finding employment for the idle, and giving to the mother country a kingdom to attend her. But he does not expect the English to indulge in such noble ambitions unless he can show a profit in them.

"I have not [he says] been so ill bred but I have tasted of plenty and pleasure, as well as want and misery; nor doth a necessity yet, nor occasion of discontent, force me to these endeavors; nor am I ignorant that small thank I shall have for my pains; or that many would have the world imagine them to be of great judgment, that can but blemish these my designs, by their witty objections and detractions; yet (I hope) my reasons and my deeds will so prevail with some, that I shall not want employment in these affairs to make the most blind see his own senselessness and incredulity; hoping that gain will make them affect that which religion, charity and the common good cannot.... For I am not so simple to think that ever any other motive than wealth will ever erect there a Commonwealth; or draw company from their ease and humours at home, to stay in New England to effect any purpose."

But lest the toils of the new settlement should affright his readers, our author draws an idyllic picture of the simple pleasures which nature and liberty afford here freely, but which cost so dearly in England. Those who seek vain pleasure in England take more pains to enjoy it than they would spend in New England to gain wealth, and yet have not half such sweet content. What pleasure can be more, he exclaims, when men are tired of planting vines and fruits and ordering gardens, orchards and building to their mind, than "to recreate themselves before their owne doore, in their owne boates upon the Sea, where man, woman and child, with a small hooke and line, by angling, may take divers sorts of excellent fish at their pleasures? And is it not pretty sport, to pull up two pence, six pence, and twelve pence as fast as you can hale and veere a line?... And what sport doth yield more pleasing content, and less hurt or charge than angling with a hooke, and crossing the sweet ayre from Isle to Isle, over the silent streams of a calme Sea? wherein the most curious may finde pleasure, profit and content."

Smith made a most attractive picture of the fertility of the soil and the fruitfulness of the country. Nothing was too trivial to be mentioned. "There are certain red berries called Alkermes which is worth ten shillings a pound, but of these hath been sold for thirty or forty shillings the pound, may yearly be gathered a good quantity." John Josselyn, who was much of the time in New England from 1638 to 1671 and saw more marvels there than anybody else ever imagined, says, "I have sought for this berry he speaks of, as a man should for a needle in a bottle of hay, but could never light upon it; unless that kind of Solomon's seal called by the English treacle-berry should be it."

Towards the last of August, 1614, Smith was back at Plymouth. He had now a project of a colony which he imparted to his friend Sir Ferdinand Gorges. It is difficult from Smith's various accounts to say exactly what happened to him next. It would appear that he declined to go with an expedition of four ship which the Virginia company despatched in 1615, and incurred their ill-will by refusing, but he considered himself attached to the western or Plymouth company. Still he experienced many delays from them: they promised four ships to be ready at Plymouth; on his arrival "he found no such matter," and at last he embarked in a private expedition, to found a colony at the expense of Gorges, Dr. Sutliffe, Bishop o Exeter, and a few gentlemen in London. In January 1615, he sailed from Plymouth with a ship Of 20 tons, and another of 50. His intention was, after the fishing was over, to remain in New England with only fifteen men and begin a colony.

These hopes were frustrated. When only one hundred and twenty leagues out all the masts of his vessels were carried away in a storm, and it was only by diligent pumping that he was able to keep his craft afloat and put back to Plymouth. Thence on the 24th of June he made another start in a vessel of sixty tons with thirty men. But ill-luck still attended him. He had a queer adventure with pirates. Lest the envious world should not believe his own story, Smith had Baker, his steward, and several of his crew examined before a magistrate at Plymouth, December 8, 1615, who support his story by their testimony up to a certain point.

It appears that he was chased two days by one Fry, an English pirate, in a greatly superior vessel, heavily armed and manned. By reason of the foul weather the pirate could not board Smith, and his master, mate, and pilot, Chambers, Minter, and Digby, importuned him to surrender, and that he should send a boat to the pirate, as Fry had no boat. This singular proposal Smith accepted on condition Fry would not take anything that would cripple his voyage, or send more men aboard (Smith furnishing the boat) than he allowed. Baker confessed that the quartermaster and Chambers received gold of the pirates, for what purpose it does not appear. They came on board, but Smith would not come out of his cabin to entertain them, "although a great many of them had been his sailors, and for his love would have wafted us to the Isle of Flowers."

Having got rid of the pirate Fry by this singular manner of receiving gold from him, Smith's vessel was next chased by two French pirates at Fayal. Chambers, Minter, and Digby again desired Smith to yield, but he threatened to blow up his ship if they did not stand to the defense; and so they got clear of the French pirates. But more were to come.

At "Flowers" they were chased by four French men-of-war.

Again Chambers, Minter, and Digby importuned Smith to yield, and upon the consideration that he could speak French, and that they were Protestants of Rochelle and had the King's commission to take Spaniards, Portuguese, and pirates, Smith, with some of his company, went on board one of the French ships. The next day the French plundered Smith's vessel and distributed his crew among their ships, and for a week employed his boat in chasing all the ships that came in sight. At the end of this bout they surrendered her again to her crew, with victuals but no weapons. Smith exhorted his officers to proceed on their voyage for fish, either to New England or Newfoundland. This the officers declined to do at first, but the soldiers on board compelled them, and thereupon Captain Smith busied himself in collecting from the French fleet and sending on board his bark various commodities that belonged to her—powder, match, books, instruments, his sword and dagger, bedding, aquavite, his commission, apparel, and many other things. These articles Chambers and the others divided among themselves, leaving Smith, who was still on board the Frenchman, only his waistcoat and breeches. The next day, the weather being foul, they ran so near the Frenchman as to endanger their yards, and Chambers called to Captain Smith to come aboard or he would leave him. Smith ordered him to send a boat; Chambers replied that his boat was split, which was a lie, and told him to come off in the Frenchman's boat. Smith said he could not command that, and so they parted. The English bark returned to Plymouth, and Smith was left on board the French man-of-war.

Smith himself says that Chambers had persuaded the French admiral that if Smith was let to go on his boat he would revenge himself on the French fisheries on the Banks.

For over two months, according to his narration, Smith was kept on board the Frenchman, cruising about for prizes, "to manage their fight against the Spaniards, and be in a prison when they took any English." One of their prizes was a sugar caraval from Brazil; another was a West Indian worth two hundred thousand crowns, which had on board fourteen coffers of wedges of silver, eight thousand royals of eight, and six coffers of the King of Spain's treasure, besides the pillage and rich coffers of many rich passengers. The French captain, breaking his promise to put Smith ashore at Fayal, at length sent him towards France on the sugar caravel. When near the coast, in a night of terrible storm, Smith seized a boat and escaped. It was a tempest that wrecked all the vessels on the coast, and for twelve hours Smith was drifting about in his open boat, in momentary expectation of sinking, until he was cast upon the oozy isle of "Charowne," where the fowlers picked him up half dead with water, cold, and hunger, and he got to Rochelle, where he made complaint to the Judge of Admiralty. Here he learned that the rich prize had been wrecked in the storm and the captain and half the crew drowned. But from the wreck of this great prize thirty-six thousand crowns' worth of jewels came ashore. For his share in this Smith put in his claim with the English ambassador at Bordeaux. The Captain was hospitably treated by the Frenchmen. He met there his old friend Master Crampton, and he says: "I was more beholden to the Frenchmen that escaped drowning in the man-of-war, Madam Chanoyes of Rotchell, and the lawyers of Burdeaux, than all the rest of my countrymen I met in France." While he was waiting there to get justice, he saw the "arrival of the King's great marriage brought from Spain." This is all his reference to the arrival of Anne of Austria, eldest daughter of Philip III., who had been betrothed to Louis XIII. in 1612, one of the double Spanish marriages which made such a commotion in France.

Leaving his business in France unsettled (forever), Smith returned to Plymouth, to find his reputation covered with infamy and his clothes, books, and arms divided among the mutineers of his boat. The chiefest of these he "laid by the heels," as usual, and the others confessed and told the singular tale we have outlined. It needs no comment, except that Smith had a facility for unlucky adventures unequaled among the uneasy spirits of his age. Yet he was as buoyant as a cork, and emerged from every disaster with more enthusiasm for himself and for new ventures. Among the many glowing tributes to himself in verse that Smith prints with this description is one signed by a soldier, Edw. Robinson, which begins:

"Oft thou hast led, when I brought up the Rere,
In bloody wars where thousands have been slaine."

This common soldier, who cannot help breaking out in poetry when he thinks of Smith, is made to say that Smith was his captain "in the fierce wars of Transylvania," and he apostrophizes him:

"Thou that to passe the worlds foure parts dost deeme
No more, than ewere to goe to bed or drinke,
And all thou yet hast done thou dost esteeme
As nothing.

"For mee: I not commend but much admire
Thy England yet unknown to passers by-her,
For it will praise itselfe in spight of me:
Thou, it, it, thou, to all posteritie."

# XVI

## NEW ENGLAND'S TRIALS

Smith was not cast down by his reverses. No sooner had he laid his latest betrayers by the heels than he set himself resolutely to obtain money and means for establishing a colony in New England, and to this project and the cultivation in England of interest in New England he devoted the rest of his life.

His Map and Description of New England was published in 1616, and he became a colporteur of this, beseeching everywhere a hearing for his noble scheme. It might have been in 1617, while Pocahontas was about to sail for Virginia, or perhaps after her death, that he was again in Plymouth, provided with three good ships, but windbound for three months, so that the season being past, his design was frustrated, and his vessels, without him, made a fishing expedition to Newfoundland.

It must have been in the summer of this year that he was at Plymouth with divers of his personal friends, and only a hundred pounds among them all. He had acquainted the nobility with his projects, and was afraid to see the Prince Royal before he had accomplished anything, "but their great promises were nothing but air to prepare the voyage against

Charles Dudley Warner

the next year." He spent that summer in the west of England, visiting "Bristol, Exeter, Bastable? Bodman, Perin, Foy, Milborow, Saltash, Dartmouth, Absom, Pattnesse, and the most of the gentry in Cornwall and Devonshire, giving them books and maps," and inciting them to help his enterprise.

So well did he succeed, he says, that they promised him twenty sail of ships to go with him the next year, and to pay him for his pains and former losses. The western commissioners, in behalf of the company, contracted with him, under indented articles, "to be admiral of that country during my life, and in the renewing of the letters-patent so to be nominated"; half the profits of the enterprise to be theirs, and half to go to Smith and his companions.

Nothing seems to have come out of this promising induction except the title of "Admiral of New England," which Smith straightway assumed and wore all his life, styling himself on the title-page of everything he printed, "Sometime Governor of Virginia and Admiral of New England." As the generous Captain had before this time assumed this title, the failure of the contract could not much annoy him. He had about as good right to take the sounding name of Admiral as merchants of the west of England had to propose to give it to him.

The years wore away, and Smith was beseeching aid, republishing his works, which grew into new forms with each issue, and no doubt making himself a bore wherever he was known. The first edition of "New England's Trials"—by which he meant the various trials and attempts to settle New England was published in 1620. It was to some extent a repetition of his "Description" of 1616. In it he made no reference to Pocahontas. But in the edition of 1622, which is dedicated to Charles, Prince of Wales, and considerably enlarged, he drops into this remark about his experience at Jamestown: "It Is true in our greatest extremitie they shot me, slue three of my men, and by the folly of them that fled tooke me prisoner; yet God made Pocahontas the king's daughter the meanes to deliver me: and thereby taught me to know their treacheries to preserve the rest. [This is evidently an allusion to the warning Pocahontas gave him at Werowocomoco.] It was also my chance in single combat to take the king of Paspahegh prisoner, and by keeping him, forced his subjects to work in chains till I made all the country pay contribution having little else whereon to live."

This was written after he had heard of the horrible massacre of 1622 at Jamestown, and he cannot resist the temptation to draw a contrast between the present and his own management. He explains that the Indians did not kill the English because they were Christians, but to get their weapons and commodities. How different it was when he was in Virginia. "I kept that country with but 38, and had not to eat but what we had from the savages. When I had ten men able to go abroad, our commonwealth was very strong: with such a number I ranged that unknown country 14 weeks: I had but 18 to subdue them all." This is better than Sir John Falstaff. But he goes on: "When I first went to those desperate designes it cost me many a forgotten pound to hire men to go, and procrastination caused more run away than went." "Twise in that time I was President." [It will be remembered that about the close of his first year he gave up the command, for form's sake, to Capt. Martin, for three hours, and then took it again.] "To range this country of New England in like manner, I had but eight, as is said, and amongst their bruite conditions I met many of their silly encounters, and without any hurt, God be thanked." The valiant Captain had come by this time to regard himself as the inventor and discoverer of Virginia and New England, which were explored and settled at the cost of his private pocket, and which he is not ashamed to say cannot fare well in his absence. Smith, with all his good opinion of himself, could not have imagined how delicious his character would be to readers in after-times. As he goes on he warms up: "Thus you may see plainly the yearly success from New England by Virginia, which hath been so costly to this kingdom and so dear to me.

"By that acquaintance I have with them I may call them my children [he spent between two and three months on the New England coast] for they have been my wife, my hawks, my hounds, my cards, my dice, and total my best content, as indifferent to my heart as my left hand to my right.... Were there not one Englishman remaining I would yet begin again as I did at the first; not that I have any secret encouragement for any I protest, more than lamentable experiences; for all their discoveries I can yet hear of are but pigs of my sowe: nor more strange to me than to hear one tell me he hath gone from Billingate and discovered Greenwich!"

As to the charge that he was unfortunate, which we should think might have become current from the Captain's own narratives, he tells his maligners that if they had spent their time as he had done, they would rather believe in God than in their own calculations, and peradventure might have had to give as bad an account of their actions. It is strange they should tax him before they have tried what he tried in Asia, Europe, and America, where he never needed to importune for a reward, nor ever could learn to beg: "These sixteen years I have spared neither pains nor money, according to my ability, first to procure his majesty's letters patent, and a Company here to be the means to raise a company to go with me to Virginia [this is the expedition of 1606 in which he was without command] as is said: which beginning here and there cost me near five years work, and more than 500 pounds of my own estate, besides all the dangers, miseries and encumbrances I endured gratis, where I stayed till I left 500 better provided than ever I was: from which blessed Virgin (ere I returned) sprung the fortunate habitation of

Somer Isles." "Ere I returned" is in Smith's best vein. The casual reader would certainly conclude that the Somers Isles were somehow due to the providence of John Smith, when in fact he never even heard that Gates and Smith were shipwrecked there till he had returned to England, sent home from Virginia. Neill says that Smith ventured L 9 in the Virginia company! But he does not say where he got the money.

New England, he affirms, hath been nearly as chargeable to him and his friends: he never got a shilling but it cost him a pound. And now, when New England is prosperous and a certainty, "what think you I undertook when nothing was known, but that there was a vast land." These are some of the considerations by which he urges the company to fit out an expedition for him: "thus betwixt the spur of desire and the bridle of reason I am near ridden to death in a ring of despair; the reins are in your hands, therefore I entreat you to ease me."

The Admiral of New England, who since he enjoyed the title had had neither ship, nor sailor, nor rod of land, nor cubic yard of salt water under his command, was not successful in his several "Trials." And in the hodge-podge compilation from himself and others, which he had put together shortly after,—the "General Historie," he pathetically exclaims: "Now all these proofs and this relation, I now called New England's Trials. I caused two or three thousand of them to be printed, one thousand with a great many maps both of Virginia and New England, I presented to thirty of the chief companies in London at their Halls, desiring either generally or particularly (them that would) to imbrace it and by the use of a stock of five thousand pounds to ease them of the superfluity of most of their companies that had but strength and health to labor; near a year I spent to understand their resolutions, which was to me a greater toil and torment, than to have been in New England about my business but with bread and water, and what I could get by my labor; but in conclusion, seeing nothing would be effected I was contented as well with this loss of time and change as all the rest."

In his "Advertisements" he says that at his own labor, cost, and loss he had "divulged more than seven thousand books and maps," in order to influence the companies, merchants and gentlemen to make a plantation, but "all availed no more than to hew Rocks with Oister-shels."

His suggestions about colonizing were always sensible. But we can imagine the group of merchants in Cheapside gradually dissolving as Smith hove in sight with his maps and demonstrations.

In 1618, Smith addressed a letter directly to Lord Bacon, to which there seems to have been no answer. The body of it was a condensation of what he had repeatedly written about New England, and the advantage to England of occupying the fisheries. "This nineteen years," he writes, "I have encountered no few dangers to learn what here I write in these few leaves:... their fruits I am certain may bring both wealth and honor for a crown and a kingdom to his majesty's posterity." With 5,000, pounds he will undertake to establish a colony, and he asks of his Majesty a pinnace to lodge his men and defend the coast for a few months, until the colony gets settled. Notwithstanding his disappointments and losses, he is still patriotic, and offers his experience to his country: "Should I present it to the Biskayners, French and Hollanders, they have made me large offers. But nature doth bind me thus to beg at home, whom strangers have pleased to create a commander abroad.... Though I can promise no mines of gold, the Hollanders are an example of my project, whose endeavors by fishing cannot be suppressed by all the

King of Spain's golden powers. Worth is more than wealth, and industrious subjects are more to a kingdom than gold. And this is so certain a course to get both as I think was never propounded to any state for so small a charge, seeing I can prove it, both by example, reason and experience."

Smith's maxims were excellent, his notions of settling New England were sound and sensible, and if writing could have put him in command of New England, there would have been no room for the Puritans. He addressed letter after letter to the companies of Virginia and Plymouth, giving them distinctly to understand that they were losing time by not availing themselves of his services and his project. After the Virginia massacre, he offered to undertake to drive the savages out of their country with a hundred soldiers and thirty sailors. He heard that most of the company liked exceedingly well the notion, but no reply came to his overture.

He laments the imbecility in the conduct of the new plantations. At first, he says, it was feared the Spaniards would invade the plantations or the English Papists dissolve them: but neither the councils of Spain nor the Papists could have desired a better course to ruin the plantations than have been pursued; "It seems God is angry to see Virginia in hands so strange where nothing but murder and indiscretion contends for the victory."

In his letters to the company and to the King's commissions for the reformation of Virginia, Smith invariably reproduces his own exploits, until we can imagine every person in London, who could read, was sick of the story. He reminds them of his unrequited services: "in neither of those two countries have I one foot of land, nor the very house I builded, nor the ground I digged with my own hands, nor ever any content or satisfaction at all, and though I see ordinarily those two countries shared before me by them that neither have them nor knows them, but by my descriptions.... For the books and maps I have made, I will thank him that will show me so much for so little recompense, and bear with their errors till I have done better. For the materials in them I cannot deny, but am ready to affirm them both there and here, upon such ground as I have propounded, which is to have but fifteen hundred men to subdue again the Salvages, fortify the country, discover that yet unknown, and both defend and feed their colony."

There is no record that these various petitions and letters of advice were received by the companies, but Smith prints them in his History, and gives also seven questions propounded to him by the commissioners, with his replies; in which he clearly states the cause of the disasters in the colonies, and proposes wise and statesman-like remedies. He insists upon industry and good conduct: "to rectify a commonwealth with debauched people is impossible, and no wise man would throw himself into such society, that intends honestly, and knows what he understands, for there is no country to pillage, as the Romans found; all you expect from thence must be by labour."

Smith was no friend to tobacco, and although he favored the production to a certain limit as a means of profit, it is interesting to note his true prophecy that it would ultimately be a demoralizing product. He often proposes the restriction of its cultivation, and speaks with contempt of "our men rooting in the ground about tobacco like swine." The colony would have been much better off "had they not so much doated on their tobacco, on whose furnish foundation there is small stability."

So long as he lived, Smith kept himself informed of the progress of adventure and settlement in the New World, reading all relations and eagerly questioning all voyagers, and transferring their accounts to his own History, which became a confused patchwork of other men's exploits and his own reminiscences and reflections. He always regards the new plantations as somehow his own, and made in the light of his advice; and their mischances are usually due to the neglect of his counsel. He relates in this volume the story of the Pilgrims in 1620 and the years following, and of the settlement of the Somers Isles, making himself appear as a kind of Providence over the New World.

Out of his various and repetitious writings might be compiled quite a hand-book of maxims and wise saws. Yet all had in steady view one purpose—to excite interest in his favorite projects, to shame the laggards of England out of their idleness, and to give himself honorable employment and authority in the building up of a new empire. "Who can desire," he exclaims, "more content that hath small means, or but only his merit to advance his fortunes, than to tread and plant that ground he hath purchased by the hazard of his life; if he have but the taste of virtue and magnanimity, what to such a mind can be more pleasant than planting and building a foundation for his posterity, got from the rude earth by God's blessing and his own industry without prejudice to any; if he have any grace of faith or zeal in Religion, what can be more healthful to any or more agreeable to God than to convert those poor salvages to know Christ and humanity, whose labours and discretion will triply requite any charge and pain."

"Then who would live at home idly," he exhorts his countrymen, "or think in himself any worth to live, only to eat, drink and sleep, and so die; or by consuming that carelessly his friends got worthily, or by using that miserably that maintained virtue honestly, or for being descended nobly, or pine with the vain vaunt of great kindred in penury, or to maintain a silly show of bravery, toil out thy heart, soul and time basely; by shifts, tricks, cards and dice, or by relating news of other men's actions, sharke here and there for a dinner or supper, deceive thy friends by fair promises and dissimulations, in borrowing when thou never meanest to pay, offend the laws, surfeit with excess, burden thy country, abuse thyself, despair in want, and then cozen thy kindred, yea, even thy own brother, and wish thy parent's death (I will not say damnation), to have their estates, though thou seest what honors and rewards the world yet hath for them that will seek them and worthily deserve them."

"I would be sorry to offend, or that any should mistake my honest meaning: for I wish good to all, hurt to none; but rich men for the most part are grown to that dotage through their pride in their wealth, as though there were no accident could end it or their life."

"And what hellish care do such take to make it their own misery and their countrie's spoil, especially when there is such need of their employment, drawing by all manner of inventions from the Prince and his honest subjects, even the vital spirits of their powers and estates; as if their bags or brags were so powerful a defense, the malicious could not assault them, when they are the only bait to cause us not only to be assaulted, but betrayed and smothered in our own security ere we will prevent it."

And he adds this good advice to those who maintain their children in wantonness till they grow to be the masters: "Let this lamentable example [the ruin of Constantinople] remember you that are rich (seeing there are such great thieves in the world to rob you) not grudge to lend some proportion to breed them that have little, yet willing to learn how to defend you, for it is too late when the deed is done."

No motive of action did Smith omit in his importunity, for

"Religion above all things should move us, especially the clergy, if we are religious." "Honor might move the gentry, the valiant and industrious, and the hope and assurance of wealth all, if we were that we would seem and be accounted; or be we so far inferior to other nations, or our spirits so far dejected from our ancient predecessors, or our minds so upon spoil, piracy and such villainy, as to serve the Portugall, Spaniard, Dutch, French or Turke (as to the cost of Europe too many do), rather than our own God, our king, our country, and ourselves; excusing our idleness and our base complaints by want of employment, when here is such choice of all sorts, and for all degrees, in the planting and discovering these North parts of America."

It was all in vain so far as Smith's fortunes were concerned. The planting and subjection of New England went on, and Smith had no part in it except to describe it. The Brownists, the Anabaptists, the Papists, the Puritans, the Separatists, and "such factious Humorists," were taking possession of the land that Smith claimed to have "discovered," and in which he had no foothold. Failing to get employment anywhere, he petitioned the Virginia Company for a reward out of the treasury in London or the profits in Virginia.

At one of the hot discussions in 1623 preceding the dissolution of the Virginia Company by the revocation of their charter, Smith was present, and said that he hoped for his time spent in Virginia he should receive that year a good quantity of tobacco. The charter was revoked in 1624 after many violent scenes, and King James was glad to be rid of what he called "a seminary for a seditious parliament." The company had made use of lotteries to raise funds, and upon their disuse, in 1621, Smith proposed to the company to compile for its benefit a general history. This he did, but it does not appear that the company took any action on his proposal. At one time he had been named, with three others, as a fit person for secretary, on the removal of Mr. Pory, but as only three could be balloted for, his name was left out. He was, however, commended as entirely competent.

After the dissolution of the companies, and the granting of new letters-patent to a company of some twenty noblemen, there seems to have been a project for dividing up the country by lot. Smith says: "All this they divided in twenty parts, for which they cast lots, but no lot for me but Smith's Isles, which are a many of barren rocks, the most overgrown with shrubs, and sharp whins, you can hardly pass them; without either grass or wood, but three or four short shrubby old cedars."

The plan was not carried out, and Smith never became lord of even these barren rocks, the Isles of Shoals. That he visited them when he sailed along the coast is probable, though he never speaks of doing so. In the Virginia waters he had left a cluster of islands bearing his name also.

In the Captain's "True Travels," published in 1630, is a summary of the condition of colonization in New England from Smith's voyage thence till the settlement of Plymouth in 1620, which makes an appropriate close to our review of this period:

"When I first went to the North part of Virginia, where the Westerly Colony had been planted, it had dissolved itself within a year, and there was not one Christian in all the land. I was set forth at the sole charge of four merchants of London; the Country being then reputed by your westerlings a most rocky, barren, desolate desart; but the good return I brought from thence, with the maps and relations of the Country, which I made so manifest, some of them did believe me, and they were well embraced, both by the Londoners, and Westerlings, for whom I had promised to undertake it, thinking to have joyned them all together, but that might well have been a work for Hercules. Betwixt them long there was much contention: the Londoners indeed went bravely forward: but in three or four years I and my friends consumed many hundred pounds amongst the Plimothians, who only fed me but with delays, promises, and excuses, but no performance of anything to any purpose. In the interim, many particular ships went thither, and finding my relations true, and that I had not taken that I brought home from the French men, as had been reported: yet further for my pains to discredit me, and my calling it New England, they obscured it, and shadowed it, with the title of Canada, till at my humble suit, it pleased our most Royal King Charles, whom God long keep, bless and preserve, then Prince of Wales, to confirm it with my map and book, by the title of New England; the gain thence returning did make the fame thereof so increase that thirty, forty or fifty sail went yearly only to trade and fish; but nothing would be done for a plantation, till about some hundred of your Brownists of England, Amsterdam and Leyden went to New Plimouth, whose humorous ignorances, caused them for more than a year, to endure a wonderful deal of misery, with an infinite patience; saying my books and maps were much better cheap to teach them than myself: many others have used the like good husbandry that have payed soundly in trying their self-willed conclusions; but those in time doing well, diverse others have in small handfulls undertaken to go there, to be several Lords and Kings of themselves, but most vanished to nothing."

# XVII

## WRITINGS-LATER YEARS

If Smith had not been an author, his exploits would have occupied a small space in the literature of his times. But by his unwearied narrations he impressed his image in gigantic features on our plastic continent. If he had been silent, he would have had something less than justice; as it is, he has been permitted to greatly exaggerate his relations to the New World. It is only by noting the comparative silence of his contemporaries and by winnowing his own statements that we can appreciate his true position.

For twenty years he was a voluminous writer, working off his superfluous energy in setting forth his adventures in new forms. Most of his writings are repetitions and recastings of the old material, with such reflections as occur to him from time to time. He seldom writes a book, or a tract, without beginning it or working into it a resume of his life. The only exception to this is his "Sea Grammar." In 1626 he published "An Accidence or the Pathway to Experience, necessary to all Young Seamen," and in 1627 "A Sea Grammar, with the plain Exposition of Smith's Accidence for Young Seamen, enlarged." This is a technical work, and strictly confined to the building, rigging, and managing of a ship. He was also engaged at the time of his death upon a "History of the Sea," which never saw the light. He was evidently fond of the sea, and we may say the title of Admiral came naturally to him, since he used it in the title-page to his "Description of New England," published in 1616, although it was not till 1617 that the commissioners at Plymouth agreed to bestow upon him the title of "Admiral of that country."

In 1630 he published "The True Travels, Adventures and Observations of Captain John Smith, in Europe, Asia, Affrica and America, from 1593 to 1629. Together with a Continuation of his General History of Virginia, Summer Isles, New England, and their proceedings since 1624 to this present 1629: as also of the new Plantations of the great River of the Amazons, the Isles of St. Christopher, Mevis and Barbadoes in the West Indies." In the dedication to William, Earl of Pembroke, and Robert, Earl of Lindsay, he says it was written at the request of Sir Robert Cotton, the learned antiquarian, and he the more willingly satisfies this noble desire because, as he says, "they have acted my fatal tragedies on the stage, and racked my relations at their pleasure. To prevent, therefore, all future misprisions, I have compiled this true discourse. Envy hath taxed me to have writ too much, and done too little; but that such should know how little, I esteem them, I have writ this more for the satisfaction of my friends, and all generous and well-disposed readers: To speak only of myself were intolerable ingratitude: because, having had many co-partners with me, I cannot make a Monument for myself, and leave them unburied in the fields, whose lives begot me the title of Soldier, for as they were companions with me in my dangers, so shall they be partakers with me in this Tombe." In the same dedication he spoke of his "Sea Grammar" caused to be printed by his worthy friend Sir Samuel Saltonstall.

This volume, like all others Smith published, is accompanied by a great number of swollen panegyrics in verse, showing that the writers had been favored with the perusal of the volume before it was published. Valor, piety, virtue, learning, wit, are by them ascribed to the "great Smith," who is easily the wonder and paragon of his. age. All of them are stuffed with the affected conceits fashionable at the time. One of the most pedantic of these was addressed to him by Samuel Purchas when the "General Historie" was written.

The portrait of Smith which occupies a corner in the Map of Virginia has in the oval the date, "AEta 37, A. 1616," and round the rim the inscription: "Portraictuer of Captaine John Smith, Admirall of New England," and under it these lines engraved:

"These are the Lines that show thy face: but those
That show thy Grace and Glory brighter bee:
Thy Faire Discoveries and Fowle-Overthrowes
Of Salvages, much Civilized by thee
Best shew thy Spirit; and to it Glory Wyn;
So, thou art Brasse without, but Golde within,
If so, in Brasse (too soft smiths Acts to beare)
I fix thy Fame to make Brasse steele outweare.

"Thine as thou art Virtues

"JOHN DAVIES, Heref."

In this engraving Smith is clad in armor, with a high starched collar, and full beard and mustache formally cut. His right hand rests on his hip, and his left grasps the handle of his sword. The face is open and pleasing and full of decision.

This "true discourse" contains the wild romance with which this volume opens, and is pieced out with recapitulations of his former writings and exploits, compilations from others' relations, and general comments. We have given from it the story of his early life, because there is absolutely no other account of that part of his career. We may assume that up to his going to Virginia he did lead a life of reckless adventure and hardship, often in want of a decent suit of clothes and of "regular meals." That he took some part in the wars in Hungary is probable, notwithstanding his romancing narrative, and he may have been captured by the Turks. But his account of the wars there, and of the political complications, we suspect are cribbed from the old chronicles, probably from the Italian, while his vague descriptions of the lands and people in Turkey and "Tartaria" are evidently taken from the narratives of other travelers. It seems to me that the whole of his story of his oriental captivity lacks the note of personal experience. If it were not for the "patent" of Sigismund (which is only produced and certified twenty years after it is dated), the whole Transylvania legend would appear entirely apocryphal.

The "True Travels" close with a discourse upon the bad life, qualities, and conditions of pirates. The most ancient of these was one Collis, "who most refreshed himself upon the coast of Wales, and Clinton and Pursser, his companions, who grew famous till Queen Elizabeth of blessed memory hanged them at Wapping. The misery of a Pirate (although many are as sufficient seamen as any) yet in regard of his superfluity, you shall find it such, that any wise man would rather live amongst wild beasts, than them; therefore let all unadvised persons take heed how they entertain that quality; and I could wish merchants, gentlemen, and all setters-forth of ships not to be sparing of a competent pay, nor true payment; for neither soldiers nor seamen can live without means; but necessity will force them to steal, and when they are once entered into that trade they are hardly reclaimed."

Smith complains that the play-writers had appropriated his adventures, but does not say that his own character had been put upon the stage. In Ben Jonson's "Staple of News," played in 1625, there is a reference to Pocahontas in the dialogue that occurs between Pick-lock and Pennyboy Canter:

Pick.—A tavern's unfit too for a princess.

P. Cant.—No, I have known a Princess and a great one, Come forth of a tavern.

Pick.—Not go in Sir, though.

A Cant.—She must go in, if she came forth. The blessed Pocahontas, as the historian calls her, And great King's daughter of Virginia, Hath been in womb of tavern.

The last work of our author was published in 1631, the year of his death. Its full title very well describes the contents: "Advertisements for the Unexperienced Planters of New England, or anywhere. Or, the Pathway to Experience to erect a Plantation. With the yearly proceedings of this country in fishing and planting since the year 1614 to the year 1630, and their present estate. Also, how to prevent the greatest inconvenience by their proceedings in Virginia, and other plantations by approved examples. With the countries armes, a description of the coast, harbours, habitations, landmarks, latitude and longitude: with the map allowed by our Royall King Charles."

Smith had become a trifle cynical in regard to the news-mongers of the day, and quaintly remarks in his address to the reader: "Apelles by the proportion of a foot could make the whole proportion of a man: were he now living, he might go to school, for now thousands can by opinion proportion kingdoms, cities and lordships that never durst adventure to see them. Malignancy I expect from these, have lived 10 or 12 years in those actions, and return as wise as they went, claiming time and experience for their tutor that can neither shift Sun nor moon, nor say their compass, yet will tell you of more than all the world betwixt the Exchange, Paul's and Westminster.... and tell as well what all England is by seeing but Mitford Haven as what Apelles was by the picture of his great toe."

This is one of Smith's most characteristic productions. Its material is ill-arranged, and much of it is obscurely written; it runs backward and forward along his life, refers constantly to his former works and repeats them, complains of the want of appreciation of his services, and makes himself the centre of all the colonizing exploits of the age. Yet it is interspersed with strokes of humor and observations full of good sense.

It opens with the airy remark: "The wars in Europe, Asia and Africa, taught me how to subdue the wild savages in Virginia and New England." He never did subdue the wild savages in New England, and he never was in any war in Africa, nor in Asia, unless we call his piratical cruising in the Mediterranean "wars in Asia."

As a Church of England man, Smith is not well pleased with the occupation of New England by the Puritans, Brownists, and such "factious humorists" as settled at New Plymouth, although he acknowledges the wonderful patience with which, in their ignorance and willfulness, they have endured losses and extremities; but he hopes better things of the gentlemen who went in 1629 to supply Endicott at Salem, and were followed the next year by Winthrop. All these adventurers have, he says, made use of his "aged endeavors." It seems presumptuous in them to try to get on with his maps and descriptions and without him. They probably had never heard, except in the title-pages of his works, that he was "Admiral of New England."

Even as late as this time many supposed New England to be

an island, but Smith again asserts, what he had always maintained—that it was a part of the continent. The expedition of Winthrop was scattered by a storm, and reached Salem with the loss of threescore dead and many sick, to find as many of the colony dead, and all disconsolate. Of the discouraged among them who returned to England Smith says: "Some could not endure the name of a bishop, others not the sight of a cross or surplice, others by no means the book of common prayer. This absolute crew, only of the Elect, holding all (but such as themselves) reprobates and castaways, now made more haste to return to Babel, as they termed England, than stay to enjoy the land they called Canaan." Somewhat they must say to excuse themselves. Therefore, "some say they could see no timbers of ten foot diameter, some the country is all wood; others they drained all the springs and ponds dry, yet like to famish for want of fresh water; some of the danger of the ratell-snake." To compel all the Indians to furnish them corn without using them cruelly they say is impossible. Yet this "impossible," Smith says, he accomplished in Virginia, and offers to undertake in New England, with one hundred and fifty men, to get corn, fortify the country, and "discover them more land than they all yet know."

This homily ends—and it is the last published sentence of the "great Smith"—with this good advice to the New England colonists:

"Lastly, remember as faction, pride, and security produces nothing but confusion, misery and dissolution; so the contraries well practised will in short time make you happy, and the most admired people of all our plantations for your time in the world.

"John Smith writ this with his owne hand."

The extent to which Smith retouched his narrations, as they grew in his imagination, in his many reproductions of them, has been referred to, and illustrated by previous quotations. An amusing instance of his care and ingenuity is furnished by the interpolation of Pocahontas into his stories after 1623. In his "General Historie" of 1624 he adopts, for the account of his career in Virginia, the narratives in the Oxford tract of 1612, which he had supervised. We have seen how he interpolated the wonderful story of his rescue by the Indian child. Some of his other insertions of her name, to bring all the narrative up to that level, are curious. The following passages from the "Oxford Tract" contain in italics the words inserted when they were transferred to the "General Historie":

"So revived their dead spirits (*especially the love of Pocahuntas*) as all anxious fears were abandoned."

"Part always they brought him as presents from their king, *or Pocahuntas*."

In the account of the "masques" of girls to entertain Smith at Werowocomoco we read:

"But presently *Pocahuntas* came, wishing him to kill her if any hurt were intended, and the beholders, which were women and children, satisfied the Captain there was no such matter."

In the account of Wyffin's bringing the news of Scrivener's drowning, when Wyffin was lodged a night with Powhatan, we read:

"He did assure himself some mischief was intended. *Pocahontas* hid him for a time, and sent them who pursued him the clean contrary way to seek him; but by *her* means and extraordinary bribes and much trouble in three days' travel, at length he found us in the middest of these turmoyles."

The affecting story of the visit and warning from Pocahontas in the night, when she appeared with "tears running down her cheeks," is not in the first narration in the Oxford Tract, but is inserted in the narrative in the "General Historie." Indeed, the first account would by its terms exclude the later one. It is all contained in these few lines:

"But our barge being left by the ebb, caused us to staie till the midnight tide carried us safe aboord, having spent that half night with such mirth as though we never had suspected or intended anything, we left the Dutchmen to build, Brinton to kill foule for Powhatan (as by his messengers he importunately desired), and left directions with our men to give Powhatan all the content they could, that we might enjoy his company on our return from Pamaunke."

It should be added, however, that there is an allusion to some warning by Pocahontas in the last chapter of the "Oxford Tract." But the full story of the night visit and the streaming tears as we have given it seems without doubt to have been elaborated from very slight materials. And the subsequent insertion of the name of Pocahontas—of which we have given examples above—into old accounts that had no allusion to her, adds new and strong presumptions to the belief that Smith invented what is known as the Pocahontas legend.

As a mere literary criticism on Smith's writings, it would appear that he had a habit of transferring to his own career notable incidents and adventures of which he had read, and this is somewhat damaging to an estimate of his originality. His wonderful system of telegraphy by means of torches, which he says he put in practice at the siege of Olympack, and which he describes as if it were his own invention, he had doubtless read in Polybius, and it seemed a good thing to introduce into his narrative.

He was (it must also be noted) the second white man whose life was saved by an Indian princess in America, who subsequently warned her favorite of a plot to kill him. In 1528 Pamphilo de Narvaes landed at Tampa Bay, Florida, and made a disastrous expedition into the interior. Among the Spaniards who were missing as a result of this excursion was a soldier named Juan Ortiz. When De Soto marched into the same country in 1539 he encountered this soldier, who had been held in captivity by the Indians and had learned their language. The story that Ortiz told was this: He was taken prisoner by the chief Ucita, bound hand and foot, and stretched upon a scaffold to be roasted, when, just as the flames were seizing him, a daughter of the chief interposed in his behalf, and upon her prayers Ucita spared the life of the prisoner. Three years afterward, when there was danger that Ortiz would be sacrificed to appease the devil, the princess came to him, warned him of his danger, and led him secretly and alone in the night to the camp of a chieftain who protected him.

This narrative was in print before Smith wrote, and as he was fond of such adventures he may have read it. The incidents are curiously parallel. And all the comment needed upon it is that Smith seems to have been peculiarly subject to such coincidences.

Our author's selection of a coat of arms, the distinguishing feature of which was "three Turks' heads," showed little more originality. It was a common device before his day: on many coats of arms of the Middle Ages and later appear "three Saracens' heads," or "three Moors' heads"—probably most of them had their origin in the Crusades. Smith's patent to use this charge, which he produced from Sigismund, was dated 1603, but the certificate appended to it by the Garter King at Arms, certifying that it was recorded in the register and office of the heralds, is dated 1625. Whether Smith used it before this latter date we are not told. We do not know why he had not as good right to assume it as anybody.

[Burke's "Encyclopedia of Heraldry" gives it as granted to Capt. John Smith, of the Smiths of Cruffley, Co. Lancaster, in 1629, and describes it: "Vert, a chev. gu. betw. three Turks' heads couped ppr. turbaned or. Crest-an Ostrich or, holding in the mouth a horseshoe or."]

# XVIII

## DEATH AND CHARACTER

Hardship and disappointment made our hero prematurely old, but could not conquer his indomitable spirit. The disastrous voyage of June, 1615, when he fell into the hands of the French, is spoken of by the Council for New England in 1622 as "the ruin of that poor gentleman, Captain Smith, who was detained prisoner by them, and forced to suffer many extremities before he got free of his troubles;" but he did not know that he was ruined, and did not for a moment relax his efforts to promote colonization and obtain a command, nor relinquish his superintendence of the Western Continent.

His last days were evidently passed in a struggle for existence, which was not so bitter to him as it might have been to another man, for he was sustained by ever-elating "great expectations." That he was pinched for means of living, there is no doubt. In 1623 he issued a prospectus of his "General Historie," in which he said: "These observations are all I have for the expenses of a thousand pounds and the loss of eighteen years' time, besides all the travels, dangers, miseries and incumbrances for my countries good, I have endured gratis: ....this is composed in less than eighty sheets, besides the three maps, which will stand me near in a hundred pounds, which sum I cannot disburse: nor shall the stationers have the copy for nothing. I therefore, humbly entreat your Honour, either to adventure, or give me what you please towards the impression, and I will be both accountable and thankful."

He had come before he was fifty to regard himself as an old man, and to speak of his "aged endeavors." Where and how he lived in his later years, and with what surroundings and under what circumstances he died, there is no record. That he had no settled home, and was in mean lodgings at the last, may be reasonably inferred. There is a manuscript note on the fly-leaf of one of the original editions of "The Map of Virginia...." (Oxford, 1612), in ancient chirography, but which from its reference to Fuller could not have been written until more than thirty years after Smith's death. It says: "When he was old he lived in London poor but kept up his spirits with the commemoration of his former actions and bravery. He was buried in St. Sepulcher's Church, as Fuller tells us, who has given us a line of his Ranting Epitaph."

That seems to have been the tradition of the man, buoyantly supporting himself in the commemoration of his own achievements. To the end his industrious and hopeful spirit sustained him, and in the last year of his life he was toiling on another compilation, and promised his readers a variety of actions and memorable observations which they shall "find with admiration in my History of the Sea, if God be pleased I live to finish it."

He died on the 21 St of June, 1631, and the same day made his last will, to which he appended his mark, as he seems to have been too feeble to write his name. In this he describes himself as "Captain John Smith of the parish of St. Sepulcher's London Esquior." He commends his soul "into the hands of Almighty God, my maker, hoping through the merits of Christ Jesus my Redeemer to receive full remission of all my sins and to inherit a place in the everlasting kingdom"; his body he commits to the earth whence it came; and "of such worldly goods whereof it hath pleased God in his mercy to make me an unworthy receiver," he bequeathes: first, to Thomas Packer, Esq., one of his Majesty's clerks of the Privy Seal, "all my houses, lands, tenantements and hereditaments whatsoever, situate lying and being in the parishes of Louthe and Great Carleton, in the county of Lincoln together with my coat of armes"; and charges him to pay certain legacies not exceeding the sum of eighty pounds, out of which he reserves to himself twenty pounds to be disposed of as he chooses in his lifetime. The sum of twenty pounds is to be disbursed about the funeral. To his most worthy friend, Sir Samuel Saltonstall Knight, he gives five pounds; to Morris Treadway, five pounds; to his sister Smith, the widow of his brother, ten pounds; to his cousin Steven Smith, and his sister, six pounds thirteen shillings and fourpence between them; to Thomas Packer, Joane, his wife, and Eleanor, his daughter, ten pounds among them; to "Mr. Reynolds, the lay Mr of the Goldsmiths Hall, the sum of forty shillings"; to Thomas, the son of said Thomas Packer, "my trunk standing in my chamber at Sir Samuel Saltonstall's house in St. Sepulcher's parish, together with my best suit of apparel of a tawny color viz. hose, doublet jirkin and cloak," "also, my trunk bound with iron bars standing in the house of Richard Hinde in Lambeth, together—with half the books therein"; the other half of the books to Mr. John Tredeskin and Richard Hinde. His much honored friend, Sir Samuel Saltonstall, and Thomas Packer, were joint executors, and the will was acknowledged in the presence "of Willmu Keble Snr civitas, London, William Packer, Elizabeth Sewster, Marmaduke Walker, his mark, witness."

We have no idea that Thomas Packer got rich out of the houses, lands and tenements in the county of Lincoln. The will is that of a poor man, and reference to his trunks standing about in the houses of his friends, and to his chamber in the house of Sir Samuel Saltonstall, may be taken as proof that he had no independent and permanent abiding-place.

It is supposed that he was buried in St. Sepulcher's Church. The negative evidence of this is his residence in the parish at the time of his death, and the more positive, a record in Stow's "Survey of London," 1633, which we copy in full:

This Table is on the south side of the Quire in Saint Sepulchers, with this Inscription:

To the living Memory of his deceased Friend, Captaine John Smith, who departed this mortall life on the 21 day of June, 1631, with his Armes, and this Motto,

Accordamus, vincere est vivere.

Here lies one conquer'd that hath conquer'd Kings,
Subdu'd large Territories, and done things
Which to the World impossible would seeme,
But that the truth is held in more esteeme,
Shall I report His former service done In honour of his God and Christendome:
How that he did divide from Pagans three,
Their heads and Lives, types of his chivalry:
For which great service in that Climate done,
Brave Sigismundus (King of Hungarion)
Did give him as a Coat of Armes to weare,
Those conquer'd heads got by his Sword and Speare?
Or shall I tell of his adventures since,
Done in Firginia, that large Continence:
I-low that he subdu'd Kings unto his yoke,
And made those heathen flie, as wind doth smoke:

And made their Land, being of so large a Station,
A habitation for our Christian Nation:
Where God is glorifi'd, their wants suppli'd,
Which else for necessaries might have di'd?
But what avails his Conquest now he lyes
Inter'd in earth a prey for Wormes & Flies?

O may his soule in sweet Mizium sleepe,
Untill the Keeper that all soules doth keepe,
Returne to judgement and that after thence,
With Angels he may have his recompence.
Captaine John Smith, sometime Governour of Firginia,
and Admirall of New England.

This remarkable epitaph is such an autobiographical record as Smith might have written himself. That it was engraved upon a tablet and set up in this church rests entirely upon the authority of Stow. The present pilgrim to the old church will find no memorial that Smith was buried there, and will encounter besides incredulity of the tradition that he ever rested there.

The old church of St. Sepulcher's, formerly at the confluence of Snow Hill and the Old Bailey, now lifts its head far above the pompous viaduct which spans the valley along which the Fleet Ditch once flowed. All the registers of burial in the church were destroyed by the great fire of 1666, which burnt down the edifice from floor to roof, leaving only the walls and tower standing. Mr. Charles Deane, whose lively interest in Smith led him recently to pay a visit to St. Sepulcher's, speaks of it as the church "under the pavement of which the remains of our hero were buried; but he was not able to see the stone placed over those remains, as the floor of the church at that time was covered with a carpet.... The epitaph to his memory, however, it is understood, cannot now be deciphered upon the tablet,"—which he supposes to be the one in Stow.

The existing tablet is a slab of bluish-black marble, which formerly was in the chancel. That it in no way relates to Captain Smith a near examination of it shows. This slab has an escutcheon which indicates three heads, which a lively imagination may conceive to be those of Moors, on a line in the upper left corner on the husband's side of a shield, which is divided by a perpendicular line. As Smith had no wife, this could not have been his cognizance. Nor are these his arms, which were three Turks' heads borne over and beneath a chevron. The cognizance of "Moors' heads," as we have said, was not singular in the Middle Ages, and there existed recently in this very church another tomb which bore a Moor's head as a family badge. The inscription itself is in a style of lettering unlike that used in the time of James I., and the letters are believed not to belong to an earlier period than that of the Georges. This bluish-black stone has been recently gazed at by many pilgrims from this side of the ocean, with something of the feeling with which the Moslems regard the Kaaba at Mecca. This veneration is misplaced, for upon the stone are distinctly visible these words:

"Departed this life September....
....sixty-six ....years....
....months ...."

As John Smith died in June, 1631, in his fifty-second year, this stone is clearly not in his honor: and if his dust rests in this church, the fire of 1666 made it probably a labor of wasted love to look hereabouts for any monument of him.

A few years ago some American antiquarians desired to place some monument to the "Admiral of New England" in this church, and a memorial window, commemorating the "Baptism of Pocahontas," was suggested. We have been told, however, that a custom of St. Sepulcher's requires a handsome bonus to the rector for any memorial set up in the church which the kindly incumbent had no power to set aside (in his own case) for a foreign gift and act of international courtesy of this sort; and the project was abandoned.

Nearly every trace of this insatiable explorer of the earth has disappeared from it except in his own writings. The only monument to his memory existing is a shabby little marble shaft erected on the southerly summit of Star Island, one of the Isles of Shoals. By a kind of irony of fortune, which Smith would have grimly appreciated, the only stone to perpetuate his fame stands upon a little heap of rocks in the sea; upon which it is only an inference that he ever set foot, and we can almost hear him say again, looking round upon this roomy earth, so much of which he possessed in his mind, "No lot for me but Smith's Isles, which are an array of barren rocks, the most overgrowne with shrubs and sharpe whins you can hardly passe them: without either grasse or wood but three or foure short shrubby old cedars."

Nearly all of Smith's biographers and the historians of Virginia have, with great respect, woven his romances about his career into their narratives, imparting to their paraphrases of his story such an elevation as his own opinion of himself seemed to demand. Of contemporary estimate of him there is little to quote except the panegyrics in verse he has preserved for us, and the inference from his own writings that he was the object of calumny and detraction. Enemies he had in plenty, but there are no records left of their opinion of his character. The nearest biographical notice of him in point of time is found in the "History of the Worthies of England," by Thomas Fuller, D.D., London, 1662.

Old Fuller's schoolmaster was Master Arthur Smith, a kinsman of John, who told him that John was born in

Lincolnshire, and it is probable that Fuller received from his teacher some impression about the adventurer.

Of his "strange performances" in Hungary, Fuller says: "The scene whereof is laid at such a distance that they are cheaper credited than confuted."

"From the Turks in Europe he passed to the pagans in America, where towards the latter end of the reign of Queen Elizabeth [it was in the reign of James] such his perils, preservations, dangers, deliverances, they seem to most men above belief, to some beyond truth. Yet have we two witnesses to attest them, the prose and the pictures, both in his own book; and it soundeth much to the diminution of his deeds that he alone is the herald to publish and proclaim them."

"Surely such reports from strangers carry the greater reputation. However, moderate men must allow Captain Smith to have been very instrumental in settling the plantation in Virginia, whereof he was governor, as also Admiral of New England."

"He led his old age in London, where his having a prince's mind imprisoned in a poor man's purse, rendered him to the contempt of such as were not ingenuous. Yet he efforted his spirits with the remembrance and relation of what formerly he had been, and what he had done."

Of the "ranting epitaph," quoted above, Fuller says: "The orthography, poetry, history and divinity in this epitaph are much alike."

Without taking Captain John Smith at his own estimate of himself, he was a peculiar character even for the times in which he lived. He shared with his contemporaries the restless spirit of roving and adventure which resulted from the invention of the mariner's compass and the discovery of the New World; but he was neither so sordid nor so rapacious as many of them, for his boyhood reading of romances had evidently fired him with the conceits of the past chivalric period. This imported into his conduct something inflated and something elevated. And, besides, with all his enormous conceit, he had a stratum of practical good sense, a shrewd wit, and the salt of humor.

If Shakespeare had known him, as he might have done, he would have had a character ready to his hand that would have added one of the most amusing and interesting portraits to his gallery. He faintly suggests a moral Falstaff, if we can imagine a Falstaff without vices. As a narrator he has the swagger of a Captain Dalghetty, but his actions are marked by honesty and sincerity. He appears to have had none of the small vices of the gallants of his time. His chivalric attitude toward certain ladies who appear in his adventures, must have been sufficiently amusing to his associates. There is about his virtue a certain antique flavor which must have seemed strange to the adventurers and court hangers-on in London. Not improbably his assumptions were offensive to the ungodly, and his ingenuous boastings made him the object of amusement to the skeptics. Their ridicule would naturally appear to him to arise from envy. We read between the lines of his own eulogies of himself, that there was a widespread skepticism about his greatness and his achievements, which he attributed to jealousy. Perhaps his obtrusive virtues made him enemies, and his rectitude was a standing offense to his associates.

It is certain he got on well with scarcely anybody with whom he was thrown in his enterprises. He was of common origin, and always carried with him the need of assertion in an insecure position. He appears to us always self-conscious and ill at ease with gentlemen born. The captains of his own station resented his assumptions of superiority, and while he did not try to win them by an affectation of comradeship, he probably repelled those of better breeding by a swaggering manner. No doubt his want of advancement was partly due to want of influence, which better birth would have given him; but the plain truth is that he had a talent for making himself disagreeable to his associates. Unfortunately he never engaged in any enterprise with any one on earth who was so capable of conducting it as himself, and this fact he always made plain to his comrades. Skill he had in managing savages, but with his equals among whites he lacked tact, and knew not the secret of having his own way without seeming to have it. He was insubordinate, impatient of any authority over him, and unwilling to submit to discipline he did not himself impose.

Yet it must be said that he was less self-seeking than those who were with him in Virginia, making glory his aim rather than gain always; that he had a superior conception of what a colony should be, and how it should establish itself, and that his judgment of what was best was nearly always vindicated by the event. He was not the founder of the Virginia colony, its final success was not due to him, but it was owing almost entirely to his pluck and energy that it held on and maintained an existence during the two years and a half that he was with it at Jamestown. And to effect this mere holding on, with the vagabond crew that composed most of the colony, and with the extravagant and unintelligent expectations of the London Company, was a feat showing decided ability. He had the qualities fitting him to be an explorer and the leader of an expedition. He does not appear to have had the character necessary to impress his authority on a community. He was quarrelsome, irascible, and quick to fancy that his full value was not admitted. He shines most upon such small expeditions as the exploration of the

Chesapeake; then his energy, self-confidence, shrewdness, inventiveness, had free play, and his pluck and perseverance are recognized as of the true heroic substance.

Smith, as we have seen, estimated at their full insignificance such flummeries as the coronation of Powhatan, and the foolishness of taxing the energies of the colony to explore the country for gold and chase the phantom of the South Sea. In his discernment and in his conceptions of what is now called "political economy" he was in advance of his age. He was an advocate of "free trade" before the term was invented. In his advice given to the New England plantation in his "Advertisements" he says:

"Now as his Majesty has made you custome-free for seven yeares, have a care that all your countrymen shall come to trade with you, be not troubled with pilotage, boyage, ancorage, wharfage, custome, or any such tricks as hath been lately used in most of our plantations, where they would be Kings before their folly; to the discouragement of many, and a scorne to them of understanding, for Dutch, French, Biskin, or any will as yet use freely the Coast without controule, and why not English as well as they? Therefore use all commers with that respect, courtesie, and liberty is fitting, which will in a short time much increase your trade and shipping to fetch it from you, for as yet it were not good to adventure any more abroad with factors till you bee better provided; now there is nothing more enricheth a Common-wealth than much trade, nor no meanes better to increase than small custome, as Holland, Genua, Ligorne, as divers other places can well tell you, and doth most beggar those places where they take most custome, as Turkie, the Archipelegan Iles, Cicilia, the Spanish ports, but that their officers will connive to enrich themselves, though undo the state."

It may perhaps be admitted that he knew better than the

London or the Plymouth company what ought to be done in the New World, but it is absurd to suppose that his success or his ability forfeited him the confidence of both companies, and shut him out of employment. The simple truth seems to be that his arrogance and conceit and importunity made him unpopular, and that his proverbial ill luck was set off against his ability.

Although he was fully charged with the piety of his age, and kept in mind his humble dependence on divine grace when he was plundering Venetian argosies or lying to the Indians, or fighting anywhere simply for excitement or booty, and was always as devout as a modern Sicilian or Greek robber; he had a humorous appreciation of the value of the religions current in his day. He saw through the hypocrisy of the London Company, "making religion their color, when all their aim was nothing but present profit." There was great talk about Christianizing the Indians; but the colonists in Virginia taught them chiefly the corruptions of civilized life, and those who were despatched to England soon became debauched by London vices. "Much they blamed us [he writes] for not converting the Salvages, when those they sent us were little better, if not worse, nor did they all convert any of those we sent them to England for that purpose."

Captain John Smith died unmarried, nor is there any record that he ever had wife or children. This disposes of the claim of subsequent John Smiths to be descended from him. He was the last of that race; the others are imitations. He was wedded to glory. That he was not insensible to the charms of female beauty, and to the heavenly pity in their hearts, which is their chief grace, his writings abundantly evince; but to taste the pleasures of dangerous adventure, to learn war and to pick up his living with his sword, and to fight wherever piety showed recompense would follow, was the passion of his youth, while his manhood was given to the arduous ambition of enlarging the domains of England and enrolling his name among those heroes who make an ineffaceable impression upon their age. There was no time in his life when he had leisure to marry, or when it would have been consistent with his schemes to have tied himself to a home.

As a writer he was wholly untrained, but with all his intro-versions and obscurities he is the most readable chronicler of his time, the most amusing and as untrustworthy as any. He is influenced by his prejudices, though not so much by them as by his imagination and vanity. He had a habit of accurate observation, as his maps show, and this trait gives to his statements and descriptions, when his own reputation is not concerned, a value beyond that of those of most contempo-rary travelers. And there is another thing to be said about his writings. They are uncommonly clean for his day. Only here and there is coarseness encountered. In an age when nastiness was written as well as spoken, and when most travelers felt called upon to satisfy a curiosity for prurient observations, Smith preserved a tone quite remarkable for general purity.

Captain Smith is in some respects a very good type of the restless adventurers of his age; but he had a little more pseudo-chivalry at one end of his life, and a little more piety at the other, than the rest. There is a decidedly heroic element in his courage, hardihood, and enthusiasm, softened to the modern observer's comprehension by the humorous contrast between his achievements and his estimate of them. Between his actual deeds as he relates them, and his noble sentiments, there is also sometimes a contrast pleasing to the worldly mind. He is just one of those characters who would be more agreeable on the stage than in private life. His extraordinary conceit would be entertaining if one did not see too much of him. Although he was such a romancer that we can accept few of his unsupported statements about himself, there was, nevertheless, a certain verity in his character which showed something more than loyalty to his own fortune; he could be faithful to an ambition for the public good. Those who knew him best must have found in him very likable qualities, and acknowledged the generosities of his nature, while they were amused at his humorous spleen and his serious contemplation of his own greatness. There is a kind of simplicity in his self-appreciation that wins one, and it is impossible for the candid student of his career not to feel kindly towards the "sometime Governor of Virginia and Admiral of New England."

# Choose from Thousands of 1stWorldLibrary Classics By

A. M. Barnard
Ada Leverson
Adolphus William Ward
Aesop
Agatha Christie
Alexander Aaronsohn
Alexander Kielland
Alexandre Dumas
Alfred Gatty
Alfred Ollivant
Alice Duer Miller
Alice Turner Curtis
Alice Dunbar
Allen Chapman
Alleyne Ireland
Ambrose Bierce
Amelia E. Barr
Amory H. Bradford
Andrew Lang
Andrew McFarland Davis
Andy Adams
Angela Brazil
Anna Alice Chapin
Anna Sewell
Annie Besant
Annie Hamilton Donnell
Annie Payson Call
Annie Roe Carr
Annonaymous
Anton Chekhov
Archibald Lee Fletcher
Arnold Bennett
Arthur C. Benson
Arthur Conan Doyle
Arthur M. Winfield
Arthur Ransome
Arthur Schnitzler
Arthur Train
Atticus
B.H. Baden-Powell
B. M. Bower
B. C. Chatterjee
Baroness Emmuska Orczy
Baroness Orczy
Basil King
Bayard Taylor
Ben Macomber
Bertha Muzzy Bower
Bjornstjerne Bjornson

Booth Tarkington
Boyd Cable
Bram Stoker
C. Collodi
C. E. Orr
C. M. Ingleby
Carolyn Wells
Catherine Parr Traill
Charles A. Eastman
Charles Amory Beach
Charles Dickens
Charles Dudley Warner
Charles Farrar Browne
Charles Ives
Charles Kingsley
Charles Klein
Charles Hanson Towne
Charles Lathrop Pack
Charles Romyn Dake
Charles Whibley
Charles Willing Beale
Charlotte M. Braeme
Charlotte M. Yonge
Charlotte Perkins Stetson
Clair W. Hayes
Clarence Day Jr.
Clarence E. Mulford
Clemence Housman
Confucius
Coningsby Dawson
Cornelis DeWitt Wilcox
Cyril Burleigh
D. H. Lawrence
Daniel Defoe
David Garnett
Dinah Craik
Don Carlos Janes
Donald Keyhoe
Dorothy Kilner
Dougan Clark
Douglas Fairbanks
E. Nesbit
E. P. Roe
E. Phillips Oppenheim
E. S. Brooks
Earl Barnes
Edgar Rice Burroughs
Edith Van Dyne
Edith Wharton

Edward Everett Hale
Edward J. O'Biren
Edward S. Ellis
Edwin L. Arnold
Eleanor Atkins
Eleanor Hallowell Abbott
Eliot Gregory
Elizabeth Gaskell
Elizabeth McCracken
Elizabeth Von Arnim
Ellem Key
Emerson Hough
Emilie F. Carlen
Emily Bronte
Emily Dickinson
Enid Bagnold
Enilor Macartney Lane
Erasmus W. Jones
Ernie Howard Pie
Ethel May Dell
Ethel Turner
Ethel Watts Mumford
Eugene Sue
Eugenie Foa
Eugene Wood
Eustace Hale Ball
Evelyn Everett-green
Everard Cotes
F. H. Cheley
F. J. Cross
F. Marion Crawford
Fannie E. Newberry
Federick Austin Ogg
Ferdinand Ossendowski
Fergus Hume
Florence A. Kilpatrick
Fremont B. Deering
Francis Bacon
Francis Darwin
Frances Hodgson Burnett
Frances Parkinson Keyes
Frank Gee Patchin
Frank Harris
Frank Jewett Mather
Frank L. Packard
Frank V. Webster
Frederic Stewart Isham
Frederick Trevor Hill
Frederick Winslow Taylor

Friedrich Kerst
Friedrich Nietzsche
Fyodor Dostoyevsky
G.A. Henty
G.K. Chesterton
Gabrielle E. Jackson
Garrett P. Serviss
Gaston Leroux
George A. Warren
George Ade
Geroge Bernard Shaw
George Cary Eggleston
George Durston
George Ebers
George Eliot
George Gissing
George MacDonald
George Meredith
George Orwell
George Sylvester Viereck
George Tucker
George W. Cable
George Wharton James
Gertrude Atherton
Gordon Casserly
Grace E. King
Grace Gallatin
Grace Greenwood
Grant Allen
Guillermo A. Sherwell
Gulielma Zollinger
Gustav Flaubert
H. A. Cody
H. B. Irving
H.C. Bailey
H. G. Wells
H. H. Munro
H. Irving Hancock
H. R. Naylor
H. Rider Haggard
H. W. C. Davis
Haldeman Julius
Hall Caine
Hamilton Wright Mabie
Hans Christian Andersen
Harold Avery
Harold McGrath
Harriet Beecher Stowe
Harry Castlemon
Harry Coghill
Harry Houidini

Hayden Carruth
Helent Hunt Jackson
Helen Nicolay
Hendrik Conscience
Hendy David Thoreau
Henri Barbusse
Henrik Ibsen
Henry Adams
Henry Ford
Henry Frost
Henry James
Henry Jones Ford
Henry Seton Merriman
Henry W Longfellow
Herbert A. Giles
Herbert Carter
Herbert N. Casson
Herman Hesse
Hildegard G. Frey
Homer
Honore De Balzac
Horace B. Day
Horace Walpole
Horatio Alger Jr.
Howard Pyle
Howard R. Garis
Hugh Lofting
Hugh Walpole
Humphry Ward
Ian Maclaren
Inez Haynes Gillmore
Irving Bacheller
Isabel Cecilia Williams
Isabel Hornibrook
Israel Abrahams
Ivan Turgenev
J.G.Austin
J. Henri Fabre
J. M. Barrie
J. M. Walsh
J. Macdonald Oxley
J. R. Miller
J. S. Fletcher
J. S. Knowles
J. Storer Clouston
J. W. Duffield
Jack London
Jacob Abbott
James Allen
James Andrews
James Baldwin

James Branch Cabell
James DeMille
James Joyce
James Lane Allen
James Lane Allen
James Oliver Curwood
James Oppenheim
James Otis
James R. Driscoll
Jane Abbott
Jane Austen
Jane L. Stewart
Janet Aldridge
Jens Peter Jacobsen
Jerome K. Jerome
Jessie Graham Flower
John Buchan
John Burroughs
John Cournos
John F. Kennedy
John Gay
John Glasworthy
John Habberton
John Joy Bell
John Kendrick Bangs
John Milton
John Philip Sousa
John Taintor Foote
Jonas Lauritz Idemil Lie
Jonathan Swift
Joseph A. Altsheler
Joseph Carey
Joseph Conrad
Joseph E. Badger Jr
Joseph Hergesheimer
Joseph Jacobs
Jules Vernes
Julian Hawthrone
Julie A Lippmann
Justin Huntly McCarthy
Kakuzo Okakura
Karle Wilson Baker
Kate Chopin
Kenneth Grahame
Kenneth McGaffey
Kate Langley Bosher
Kate Langley Bosher
Katherine Cecil Thurston
Katherine Stokes
L. A. Abbot
L. T. Meade

L. Frank Baum
Latta Griswold
Laura Dent Crane
Laura Lee Hope
Laurence Housman
Lawrence Beasley
Leo Tolstoy
Leonid Andreyev
Lewis Carroll
Lewis Sperry Chafer
Lilian Bell
Lloyd Osbourne
Louis Hughes
Louis Joseph Vance
Louis Tracy
Louisa May Alcott
Lucy Fitch Perkins
Lucy Maud Montgomery
Luther Benson
Lydia Miller Middleton
Lyndon Orr
M. Corvus
M. H. Adams
Margaret E. Sangster
Margret Howth
Margaret Vandercook
Margaret W. Hungerford
Margret Penrose
Maria Edgeworth
Maria Thompson Daviess
Mariano Azuela
Marion Polk Angellotti
Mark Overton
Mark Twain
Mary Austin
Mary Catherine Crowley
Mary Cole
Mary Hastings Bradley
Mary Roberts Rinehart
Mary Rowlandson
M. Wollstonecraft Shelley
Maud Lindsay
Max Beerbohm
Myra Kelly
Nathaniel Hawthrone
Nicolo Machiavelli
O. F. Walton
Oscar Wilde

Owen Johnson
P.G. Wodehouse
Paul and Mabel Thorne
Paul G. Tomlinson
Paul Severing
Percy Brebner
Percy Keese Fitzhugh
Peter B. Kyne
Plato
Quincy Allen
R. Derby Holmes
R. L. Stevenson
R. S. Ball
Rabindranath Tagore
Rahul Alvares
Ralph Bonehill
Ralph Henry Barbour
Ralph Victor
Ralph Waldo Emmerson
Rene Descartes
Ray Cummings
Rex Beach
Rex E. Beach
Richard Harding Davis
Richard Jefferies
Richard Le Gallienne
Robert Barr
Robert Frost
Robert Gordon Anderson
Robert L. Drake
Robert Lansing
Robert Lynd
Robert Michael Ballantyne
Robert W. Chambers
Rosa Nouchette Carey
Rudyard Kipling
Saint Augustine
Samuel B. Allison
Samuel Hopkins Adams
Sarah Bernhardt
Sarah C. Hallowell
Selma Lagerlof
Sherwood Anderson
Sigmund Freud
Standish O'Grady
Stanley Weyman
Stella Benson
Stella M. Francis

Stephen Crane
Stewart Edward White
Stijn Streuvels
Swami Abhedananda
Swami Parmananda
T. S. Ackland
T. S. Arthur
The Princess Der Ling
Thomas A. Janvier
Thomas A Kempis
Thomas Anderton
Thomas Bailey Aldrich
Thomas Bulfinch
Thomas De Quincey
Thomas Dixon
Thomas H. Huxley
Thomas Hardy
Thomas More
Thornton W. Burgess
U. S. Grant
Upton Sinclair
Valentine Williams
Various Authors
Vaughan Kester
Victor Appleton
Victor G. Durham
Victoria Cross
Virginia Woolf
Wadsworth Camp
Walter Camp
Walter Scott
Washington Irving
Wilbur Lawton
Wilkie Collins
Willa Cather
Willard F. Baker
William Dean Howells
William le Queux
W. Makepeace Thackeray
William W. Walter
William Shakespeare
Winston Churchill
Yei Theodora Ozaki
Yogi Ramacharaka
Young E. Allison
Zane Grey

www.ingramcontent.com/pod-product-compliance
Lightning Source LLC
Chambersburg PA
CBHW030133180626
46812CB00002B/673